MW00696399

African Arguments

Written by experts with an unrivalled knowledge of the continent, *African Arguments* is a series of concise, engaging books that address the key issues currently facing Africa. Topical and thought-provoking, accessible but in-depth, they provide essential reading for anyone interested in getting to the heart of both why contemporary Africa is the way it is and how it is changing.

African Arguments Online

African Arguments Online is a website managed by the Royal African Society, which hosts debates on the African Arguments series and other topical issues that affect Africa: http://africanarguments.org

Titles already published

Alex de Waal, *AIDS and Power: Why There is No Political Crisis – Yet*

Tim Allen, *Trial Justice: The Lord's Resistance Army, Sudan and the International Criminal Court*

Raymond W. Copson, *The United States in Africa: Bush Policy and Beyond*

Chris Alden, *China in Africa*

Tom Porteous, *Britain in Africa*

Julie Flint and Alex de Waal, *Darfur: A New History of a Long War*, revised and updated edition

Jonathan Glennie, *The Trouble with Aid: Why Less Could Mean More for Africa*

Peter Uvin, *Life after Violence: A People's Story of Burundi*

Bronwen Manby, *Struggles for Citizenship in Africa*

Camilla Toulmin, *Climate Change in Africa*

Orla Ryan, *Chocolate Nations: Living and Dying for Cocoa in West Africa*

Theodore Trefon, *Congo Masquerade: The Political Culture of Aid Inefficiency and Reform Failure*

Léonce Ndikumana and James Boyce, *Africa's Odious Debts: How Foreign Loans and Capital Flight Bled a Continent*

Mary Harper, *Getting Somalia Wrong? Faith, War and Hope in a Shattered State*

Gernot Klantschnig and Neil Carrier, *Africa and the War on Drugs: Narcotics in Sub-Saharan Africa*

Alcinda Honwana, *Youth and Revolution in Tunisia*

Lorenzo Cotula, *The Great African Land Grab? Agricultural Investments and the Global Food System*

Forthcoming

Michael Deibert, *The Democratic Republic of Congo: Between Hope and Despair*

Gerard McCann, *India and Africa – Old Friends, New Game*

Adam Branch and Zachariah Mampilly, *Popular Protest in Africa*

Published by Zed Books with the support of the following organizations:

International African Institute promotes scholarly understanding of Africa, notably its changing societies, cultures and languages. Founded in 1926 and based in London, it supports a range of seminars and publications including the journal *Africa*.

www.internationalafricaninstitute.org

Royal African Society is Britain's prime Africa organization. Now more than a hundred years old, its in-depth, long-term knowledge of the continent and its peoples makes the Society the first stop for anyone wishing to know more about the continent. RAS fosters a better understanding of Africa in the UK and throughout the world – its history, politics, culture, problems and potential. RAS disseminates this knowledge and insight and celebrates the diversity and depth of African culture.

www.royalafricansociety.org

World Peace Foundation, founded in 1910, is located at the Fletcher School, Tufts University. The Foundation's mission is to promote innovative research and teaching, believing that these are critical to the challenges of making peace around the world, and should go hand in hand with advocacy and practical engagement with the toughest issues. Its central theme is 'reinventing peace' for the twenty-first century.

www.worldpeacefoundation.org

About the author

Marc Epprecht is a professor in the Department of Global Development Studies at Queen's University, Canada. He has consulted and published extensively on the history of gender and sexuality in Africa. Marc holds his PhD in History from Dalhousie University, and has also taught at the University of Zimbabwe.

MARC EPPRECHT

Sexuality and social justice in Africa

Rethinking homophobia and forging resistance

Zed Books
LONDON | NEW YORK

in association with

International African Institute
Royal African Society
World Peace Foundation

Sexuality and social justice in Africa: rethinking homophobia and forging resistance was first published in association with the International African Institute, the Royal African Society and the World Peace Foundation in 2013 by Zed Books Ltd, 7 Cynthia Street, London N1 9JF, UK and Room 400, 175 Fifth Avenue, New York, NY 10010, USA

www.zedbooks.co.uk
www.internationalafricaninstitute.org
www.royalafricansociety.org
www.worldpeacefoundation.org

Set in OurType Arnhem and Futura Bold by Ewan Smith, London
Index: <ed.emery@thefreeuniversity.net>
Cover design by www.roguefour.co.uk

A catalogue record for this book is available from the British Library
US CIP data are available from the Library of Congress

ISBN 978 1 78032 382 4 hb
ISBN 978 1 78032 381 7 pb

Contents

Acknowledgements

The list of people and funders who have helped me to understand the issues and connections I discuss here is a substantial one indeed, especially considering the many editors and anonymous reviewers of early efforts to articulate my ideas. Thank you to all for your generosity and critical insights, and may I be able to reciprocate if you ever need my help in turn.

To confine myself to the specific people and institutions that facilitated this specific piece of work, I should begin with the main direct funder, the Social Science and Humanities Research Council (Canada). My employer, Queen's University, enabled the time and space for me to complete this book. Unoma Azuah and E. Egba Sule made my first visit to Nigeria a much richer experience than it would have been had I not known them. Thank you to Kåre Moen and the University of Oslo for inviting me to participate in the Muhimbili University workshop on MARPs, plus of course all the individual participants who taught me so much about the issues as they are unfolding in Tanzania, Uganda, Madagascar, Kenya and Ethiopia. Jochen Lucksheiter and other staff at the Heinrich Böll Foundation, Cape Town office, enabled my participation in a very exciting colloquium there in November 2010. Many of the people involved in the International Resource Network from its inception in Senegal in 2007 have kept in touch and shared their work in progress. S. N. Nyeck, above all, has shown a lot of wisdom and grace under fire, working with me to pull together essays by IRN contributors in another project. Thanks to Patricia McFadden, Tendai Huchu and Cary Alan Johnson for being supportive and encouraging when I fretted about the wisdom of this project.

I am a professional historian by training and inclination, and this book is thus a somewhat unexpected foray for me into contemporary debates. It arises from two invitations – first, from Rita Abrahamson, who requested an article for *African Affairs*, and then from Stephanie Kitchen of the International Africa Institute, who thought the issues deserved expansion into an 'African Argument'. It has been a great pleasure to work with you, Ken Barlow, and all the other people at the IAI and Zed Books. Richard Dowden, Alex de Waal, Amelia Hight and Oliver Phillips also read the manuscript closely and pressed me to clarify my assumptions and choices of words, for which I am grateful. Of course I am responsible for any and all missteps that remain.

During the months of writing this book, I had the great pleasure to engage in some very insightful conversations with – and to listen to some moving poetry by – Gabeba Baderoon and Shailja Patel. My student, Sonny Dhool, challenged me to catch up with the latest in queer theory, while friends at GALZ pressed me to defend my guarded optimism. Thanks especially to Chesterfield Samba for organizing that visit. Mohammed Abdou offered me some welcome inputs on the Islam section, and generously shared parts of his own soon-to-be published manuscript.

On a personal note, let this book allow me to honour Keith Goddard, whose honesty, integrity, humility, brilliance as a musician and courage in his commitment to human rights in Zimbabwe deeply moved me. I believe he inspired many others in the sexual rights movement in southern Africa as well. It was my great good fortune to have been able to work with him.

Lastly, but by no means least, I thank Allison, Jennifer, Adriane and Gabriel, my immediate loving family who have grown with me throughout this journey.

to Keith

1 | Introduction

Remarkable progress has been made towards the recognition of sexual minority rights in Africa in recent years. At the state level, South Africa is already well known as a leader in the world, not just in Africa, for protecting the right to freedom from discrimination on the basis of sexual orientation in its constitution. South Africa, with Brazil, also led the way in June 2011 to have the United Nations Human Rights Council explicitly commit to that principle. Mauritius was the sole African member of the Council to support this successful resolution, but altogether ten African nations have now signed a separate joint statement in the General Assembly condemning violence and criminalization based on sexual orientation and gender identity. Cape Verde became the second African country to decriminalize sodomy in 2004 and several other countries are moving towards that goal. The former presidents of Botswana and Zambia, meanwhile, openly criticized the then president of Malawi for his homophobic rhetoric, a rare breaking of ranks among African nationalist patriarchs.

At the level of civil society, sexual rights associations allied with other civil society groups can now be found in most African countries. They are working with well-heeled donors, faith associations, global solidarity groups and health professionals to promote HIV prevention and honest sexuality education even in countries where the official line is hostile. African lesbian, gay, bisexual, trans and intersex people (lgbti) and their allies have also taken the struggle to the courts and won. The courts in Uganda, for example, in 2009 affirmed the right to privacy for lgbti by issuing an injunction to stop a newspaper from publishing names and addresses of alleged 'top homosexuals'. In the sphere of arts and letters, a rich, growing trove of research and representations of non-normative sexualities and gender identities is debunking hurtful stereotypes. New social media enable activists and scholars to share this trove, along with breaking news and views within expanding transnational networks. There is an archive with a professional staff that actively documents the history of homosexualities (Gay and Lesbian Memory in Action, on the campus of the University of Witwatersrand). I could go on.

These developments have largely escaped due attention in both the popular media and, I would argue, critical scholarship on the topic. The persecution of people in Africa on the basis of homosexual orientation or practices – whether admitted, assumed or simply alleged – has by contrast received disproportionate coverage. Uganda's proposed Anti-Homosexuality Bill has been a particularly powerful magnet for newshounds and sexual rights activists, and understandably so. Its threat to create a range of new crimes and to impose a death penalty for 'aggravated homosexuality' was shocking on several levels. Its further threat to criminalize advocates for sexual minority rights ('aiding and abating' [sic] and 'promoting homosexuality'); its targeting of those who fail to report suspected homosexual activity (which could of course include family members, heterosexual friends, reporters, health professionals, lawyers and even police); its requirement that Uganda withdraw from international bodies and treaty obligations that promote rights for sexual minorities (such as now the United Nations); and its empowerment of the state to seek the extradition of Ugandans who commit any of the new crimes while outside of the country gave fresh meaning to the words extreme, self-destructive and delusional.

The Anti-Homosexuality Bill contributed to an escalation of rhetoric and significant policy shifts at the highest levels of global governance. Close to a million people worldwide signed a petition to protest against the bill, which also drew unusually frank condemnations from political and religious leaders in the West. In the case of Steven Monjeza and Tiwonge Chimbalanga, two anatomically male people in Malawi who were jailed for 'indecent practices' after symbolically marrying in 2009, no less a figure than the secretary-general of the United Nations intervened to appeal for the protection of sexual minorities. Large donors in the struggle against HIV/AIDS have meanwhile begun to throw their considerable resources and influence into research and policy formulation concerning men who have sex with men, at times positioning themselves at direct odds with elected African leaders. UK prime minister David Cameron raised the bar in the latter respect in October 2011 by threatening to withdraw Britain's development assistance from countries that violate sexual minority rights. The same threat is also implicit in US president Barack Obama's pledge to 'use foreign aid as a tool to improve Lesbian, Gay, Bisexual, and Transgender rights abroad', which he described as a 'central' objective of US human rights policy. In the same year the World Bank threw its prodigious weight into the ring by calculating the economic burdens of stigmatization of same-sex practices, and by praising countries like Kenya whose governments have quietly intervened to protect the health and dignity of men who have sex with men (Beyrer et al. 2011).

On the surface, these events appear to be a clash between liberal Western and conservative African values, and indeed both sides often present themselves in those terms. Yet the situation is clearly much more complex. To begin with, 'the West' was not particularly liberal on this issue historically until quite recently, and some of the most outspoken advocates of hatred against homosexuals in Africa today are in fact directly linked to Western Christian missionary activity, so-called ex-gay or sexual reorientation ministries from the USA in particular. Meanwhile, a growing number of proudly nationalist African leaders have come out in favour of the decriminalization of homosexual acts. These include Prime Minister Morgan Tsvangirai of the country where political homophobia first got started in a big way (Zimbabwe). Appearances of extreme homophobia in Africa can also be deceiving. Mauritania, to give one example, has one of the most draconian laws against homosexual acts in the world, with punishment up to the death sentence. Yet in 2009 the US State Department found 'no evidence of either societal violence or systematic government

3

One

discrimination based on sexual orientation, and there were no criminal prosecutions during the year' (USA 2010).

There is, in short, a form of 'don't ask, don't tell' tolerance that appears to make places like Mauritania safer to discreetly take same-sex lovers than countries where full legal rights cannot compensate for high levels of public revulsion, vigilantism, extortion and blackmail. South Africa is the main case in point of the latter. Indeed, the 2010 controversy around anatomically ambiguous runner Caster Semenya exposed the big discrepancy in that country between the high level of rights that sexual minorities theoretically enjoy and lingering hostility or negative stereotypes about 'hermaphrodites' in popular culture. During the controversy, South African politicians and media promoted national pride over the gay-friendly constitution even as they remained largely silent about a spate of hate crimes against black lesbians. They embraced Semenya as part of the South African family, but only to the extent that her femaleness and femininity were publicly confirmed. They vigorously denounced as racist those who questioned her credentials as a woman, as if gender ambiguity was an affront to the very idea of blackness and, hence, an insult to all Africans.

All this and more makes for a rich stew of international, domestic and media politics, on top of the private passions and anguish that sexuality has always, everywhere, entailed. Still, many people do not understand why there is all the fuss now about the private lives and sex organs of a presumably small number of certain individuals. Beyerer et al. (2011), for example, assume that only 3 per cent of males in the African countries that they study engage in sex with males, admittedly based on virtually no data but nevertheless a significant revision *upwards* from the previously assumed negligible. Shouldn't we be concentrating on bigger things like climate change, famine, civil wars, violence against women, recession, new and old diseases, US troops and drone attacks, and economic development, among so many other issues that directly affect the well-being of hundreds of millions of people? As Tsvangirai put it in his lukewarm call for constitutional

4

protections for sexual orientation, 'This is an elitist debate when people have no food, when people have no jobs, when people have so many problems. It is a diversionary attitude, to try and put this issue at the focus of the nation is a real diversionary. There are more important issues to deal with.'

No doubt. My view, however, is that development studies as a field of academic enquiry, and development work as a practice, actually tend to understate the importance of sexuality to broad questions of political and economic change. Same-sex sexuality in particular remains marginal to most of the scholarship and development practice, notwithstanding the flurry of headline stories in the last few years. Yet once one lifts the lid of scandal and secrecy around same-sex sexuality in Africa, many striking stories emerge that shed light upon a wide range of related non-elitist issues. There are stories of individual personal courage or tragedy, but also of quite radical political engagement by sexual rights advocates with the big questions of the day. Beyond the obvious homophobic rhetoric and laws, the conflicts over sexual diversity and gender variance lead us to debates about gender-based violence and women's rights, communicable disease, commercial sex, racist and tribalist stereotyping, xenophobia, street kids, witchcraft beliefs and practices, elite hypocrisy and abuse of power, police corruption, sham elections, the meaning of culture and cultural appropriation, Christian fundamentalist and Islamist movements to promote intolerance, non-Africans' involvement and funding for such movements, foreign policy, and much more. They reveal hints of a profound cynicism on the part of African elites and their foreign backers to keep the pot on the boil as a strategy to distract public attention from deeply unpopular policies in other spheres (the rich getting richer, land grabs for biofuel exports, etc.). They also conveniently divert discussion of pervasive *hetero*sexual 'secrets' arising from patriarchal privilege, not least of all the sugar daddy phenomenon whereby rich men exploit young girls and women. Even if one accepts the 3 per cent assumption, these issues all affect the lives of the other 97 per cent.

The purveyors of homophobia in Africa today certainly seem to agree, and intuitively grasp the connections. Indeed, attacks on sexual minorities in the name of national or African or traditional values are often also only thinly veiled attacks on feminism, gender equality and religious and other civil freedoms generally. This was evident in the undercurrent of misogyny – hatred of and violence against women – that has been reported in the case of Egypt's street protests, and in political rhetoric from around the continent that equates homosexuality with miniskirts, prostitution and other supposed signs of Western decadence. It is evident as well in a particular form of violence widely reported against suspected lesbians: 'corrective rape', which perpetrators commonly rationalize as a patriotic act. It is evident in the fact that anti-homosexual politics often coincides with (and is often articulated by the very same people) anti-condom, anti-sex work, anti-abortion campaigns and (in Nigeria) even a proposed anti-'nudity' bill directed primarily at women. It is a far-reaching agenda that calls itself conservative, moral and patriotic yet, ironically, broadly attacks long-standing aspects of many African cultures.

The headlines are admittedly often quite discouraging for those who want to see Africa emerge as a healthy, democratic, prosperous and culturally vibrant place. In this book I look past those headlines. This is not to understate the very real pain and other costs that the many strands of homophobia are causing. Rather, it is to make the argument that African initiatives to foster new cultures of gender and sexuality that embrace human rights and promote sexual health among sexual minorities are not only happening alongside that pain but are seeing some real successes. They represent a quite positive turn that has the potential to bring significant improvements to quality of life for society as a whole. I want to show as well that some of the dichotomies that are upheld through the debates are less rigid than commonly assumed or asserted: modern versus traditional, African communitarian values versus Western individualism, African 'folk' knowledge versus the canon of Western academic theory, rights versus health strategies, religious faith versus secular reason,

Islam versus Christianity, 'failed states' versus democracy, luxury (elitism, decadence) versus need (populism, authenticity), and so forth. The lines between these assumed incompatibles are in fact significantly blurred in the lived experience of people, and that blurring in itself offers a source of hope for positive change.

I will also argue that people in the West (and elsewhere) who want to support these initiatives need to pay closer attention to the ways in which they show their solidarity. The desire to speak out against homophobic discrimination is an admirable one, and the temptation to be angry or mocking against people who promote hateful stereotypes is understandable. I find it hard to refrain from as much myself. Activism and media attention to the topic can, however, create new problems in the short run that may undermine the long-term objectives. Heaping money and awards on select gay rights activists, for example, can cause resentment and division among other rights activists (the right to clean water, right to vote, and so on), and is a tried and true recipe for petty corruption that can tear movements apart. When Westerners ridicule African leaders or threaten broad sanctions without first taking the time to understand the context or to consult African activists, they may also provoke a nationalist defensiveness among African people. A backlash against perceived beneficiaries of Western support could then inadvertently make life worse for the very group that the critics claim to be supporting (African lgbti). African lgbti can also be patriotic and may be deeply alienated by Western expectations of 'real' activism and 'real gayness' which do not translate very well to African contexts and which implicitly demean African culture.

The potential for backlash against 'gay imperialism' from the West is all the greater when Western media accounts and well-meaning activists/donors focus solely on frustrations and setbacks, always assume the worst, and fail to praise or appear to even notice success stories. In those ways they may be unwittingly promoting stereotypes of 'Darkest Africa' – homophobic, violent, irrational, childlike in their vulnerability to manipulation by foreigners, fundamentalists and evil-doers in general. YouTube and other

7

Internet platforms make it very easy for those who like to sneer at or patronize Africans in such terms to find a mass, global audience. Where perhaps hundreds of scholars and policy-makers read reasoned, respectful, well-researched studies on the issues, literally millions of ill-informed consumers can now simply click on their mouses to watch select African homophobes held up to contempt and ridicule, and thrill to the sight of bold Western media heroes coming to Africans' rescue!

Let me put it this way. Is it fair to make generalizations about homophobia as a kind of stand-alone project uniformly affecting the whole of Africa based on the extremist statements of select fundamentalist Christians or demagogic politicians? Is it fair to say that the situation in the whole of Africa is 'going from bad to worse', and that 'chaos' is 'universal' in the struggle for sexual minority rights, as does the International Lesbian and Gay Association in its 2011 annual report (Bruce-Jones and Itaborahy 2011)? Is it fair to focus condemnation on today's homophobes without reflecting on the complex history of colonial violence, racial capitalism, liberal paternalism and neoliberal diktat that sometimes inform their anger at apparent (to them) cultural proxies of the West? Is it helpful to cite the case of Monjeza and Chimbalanga in Malawi as a proof of the persecution of 'gay men' in Africa when Monjeza and Chimbalanga never considered themselves to be gay men? (Monjeza claimed he was really heterosexual while Chimbalanga identified as a transwoman).

The fact is that coverage of homophobia and related stories in Africa often is neither fair nor sensitive to the many factors that are contributing to the apparent upsurge in homophobic speech and violence. Some of those factors are specific to distinct African cultures and local political economies. But others are directly linked to decisions made in the West. Notably, decisions about trade and aid that were imagined to be gender- and sexuality-blind when taken in Washington in the 1980s have had profound unforeseen impacts on gender and sexuality from Mali to Mozambique. Structural adjustment is the classic example. Many authors have argued that the economic recessions that typically followed the imposition of neoliberal programmes pushed many African women into 'survival sex', undermined the aspirations of a generation of African men and youth to achieve masculine status through employment, marriage and other cultural norms, and hence contributed to rapid changes in fertility rates and family configurations. Western interventions with cash and 'confessional technologies' intended to promote knowledge and reduce HIV/ AIDS stigma have meanwhile, by numerous accounts and with varying degrees of self-awareness, played a subtle role in engendering new identities which are in turn profoundly changing notions of self, citizenship and community throughout Africa (Nguyen 2010). AIDS service organizations and African lgbti groups are alike often highly dependent upon Western donors for both funding and ideological orientation. Reflective of the latter, they commonly use language that closely approximates 'recruitment' or 'teaching'. In Graeme Reid's remarkable study of one small South African city, for example, he found men who talk of 'workshopped gays' and 'how to be a real gay' – hardly the kind of natural or virtuously indigenous evolution of identity that some activists claim (Reid 2013). It is *not* paranoia when Africans express their anxiety about such rapid changes.

Understanding that history makes it more difficult to place African ignorance and prejudice at the centre of the analysis, and in that way it takes ammunition away from the patriotic reaction against critics of 'African homophobia'. Understanding the rich, historical context of the debates can also undercut one of the arguments that opponents of sexual minority rights often make: African lgbti voices are new (1990s or later), which 'proves' they are not really African. In fact, many of today's debates have been around for decades or even longer in quieter form. The argument that compulsory heterosexuality is necessary to preserve the national population and morals, for example, was eloquently destroyed in a fictional story by an Africanized character who mocked bourgeois European values of sexual repression and hypocrisy, published *over two hundred years ago*. To be sure, almost no one has read or even heard of that story, but it exists and, for all its whimsy, it is based in part upon the early writings of European explorers in Africa (the Marquis de Sade's *Aline et Valcour*, 1788).

Conversely, inattention to history plays into the hands of those who would have us believe that nothing in Africa happens unless inspired by the West. US ex-gay minister Scott Lively, for example, casually expressed that arrogance, in the first instance by blaming American and European homosexuals for recruiting Ugandan youth into homosexuality. He then went on to claim that Ugandans needed him to teach them about family. Even the slightest knowledge of history would offset some of that arrogance, reminding us, for starters, that the concepts of family and marriage were well known in Africa long before Dr Lively felt obliged to offer his lessons. History also reminds us that Europeans were once at the forefront of the battle not to promote but to suppress homosexual practices, along with many other expressions of sexual and family diversity that they encountered in their supposed mission to civilize Africans during the colonial period. And it reminds us that the idea 'homosexuality is un-African' owes a great deal to European and North American authors and propagandists who had their own interests in promoting that sweeping generalization, regardless of what Africans themselves had to say.

Much of the scholarship that makes these points is clear and convincing, and I am proud to have been able to contribute to it. Yet some of it adds to the 'two solitudes' phenomenon – that is, mostly Western scholars speaking largely to each other while African audiences listen to those who promote less complicated narratives of intolerance. Western intellectuals with many years of study on the complicated intellectual and cultural history of sexualities, and with cool mastery of highly specialized academic language, sometimes write in a way that alienates newcomers to the field. I do not exempt myself from that criticism. They also sometimes forget that the concept that homosexual orientation is not a sin or against nature takes many people by surprise when they first hear it, and they can sound bossy along the way. Incomprehension, impatience and testiness may result. Is it possible, I wonder, to interpret the specialized language of sexuality studies developed in the West for a wider audience in Africa without being patronizing or over-simplistic? Is it possible to bridge the gap between the two solitudes?

This book is going to try, with an eye to the framework of what social ethicist Marvin M. Ellison has called 'erotic justice', a concept also used in a rousing manifesto on lgbti rights out of Kenya (republished in Tamale 2011). As I explain below, the concept of erotic justice strikes me as having excellent potential to bring reasonable people of goodwill from diverse positions together in 'an inclusive conversation', which is how Indian legal scholar Ratna Kapur describes the term's major objective (Kapur 2005: 11). The point of such a conversation would be to challenge both cultural and national stereotypes about sexuality (such as 'homosexuality is un-African'). It would also address lingering colonial or patronizing discourses in global sexuality debates (such as 'Africans are ignorant homophobes'). Tying these debates to broader questions of the maldistribution of wealth globally, conversations about erotic justice might help us to imagine ways to build societies with mutuality, respect, community well-being, human dignity and fairness as core values, enacted and constantly re-created at the level of day-by-day intimacy and relationship-building.

The book is not intended to debate the homophobes and fundamentalists who are inflaming the rhetoric against lgbti, let alone queer theorists in the West. Rather, it is addressed to people who are directly concerned by the health and rights implications of the homophobic turn in the rhetoric and of gender-based violence in general. These are people who are also concerned with the polarizing and stereotyping tendencies in some of the media and activist language. They want to know how to navigate between these polarizing tendencies in order to build alliances and to develop more effective ways of delivering the goods (democracy, sexual rights, sexual health, empowerment of women, sustainable economic development, and so on). I am thinking of healthcare professionals, lawyers, journalists, feminists, trade unionists, family members, educators, police officers, aid workers and non-literalist imams and ministers, among many others. These are people who are working to improve people's lives in their diverse communities, recognizing that the status quo is not working well. They are doing so in spite of the hostility, mockery or apathy they commonly face from both political leaders and the grassroots populations with whom they deal in their day-to-day work. These are people in Africa, in the West and perhaps in other countries like China or India who are increasingly active in supporting African development initiatives. Indeed, China and India are especially interesting in terms of these debates. With their ancient civilizations, proud histories of resistance to Western imperialism, and complex cultural stigmas against (yet recognized spaces for) same-sex sexualities, both countries have recently adopted policies and legal reforms that recognize lgbti as citizens with specific social and sexual health needs that the state is obliged to address. Brazil is another country of interest in these debates. With hundreds of years of Catholic indoctrination and now a majority of its population identifying as having African descent with proudly African cultural traditions, Brazil was South Africa's co-sponsor of the UN resolution on sexual minorities mentioned above.

This book is also addressed to people in the West who worry that a) homophobia is not yet as dead and buried in the West as many people believe and b) that the fight against homophobia globally is being co-opted to promote other forms of intolerance or colonialism in and by the West. In the first instance, as in Africa, the 'recession' in the West since 2008 has clearly broadened the political market for simple-sounding solutions and moral certainties such as homophobic 'family values'. The boldness of the anti-homosexuality discourse in Africa today to a certain extent gives confidence to those in the West who want to promote homophobia on their own home fronts. We can see this in North Americans who have broken away from their gay-tolerant or gay-friendly churches to join with African bishops and evangelicals in defending anti-homosexual, anti-feminist and anti-science theology. We can see it as well in the sanctimony of the good Dr Lively, who unabashedly uses Uganda's extremists to paint himself as a moderate in his own campaign to purge the United States of supposed moral corruption. Persistent internalized stigma meanwhile leads to high-risk and sometimes outright self-destructive behaviours among many same-sex-practising people in the West. It is a deeply disturbing fact that, notwithstanding so many successes in the fight against HIV/AIDS in the 1990s, and despite almost universal access to medicines and high levels of education, the incidence of HIV/AIDS among men who have sex with men is once again increasing in many Western countries. Can activists in the West learn anything from African struggles that might help their own ability to address such concerns?

Homophobia's flip side, or homonationalism, in Jasbir Puar's striking term (2007), is another worrisome development that has become apparent in some heated, even bitter, debates in recent years. Homonationalism means taking excessive pride in the achievements of gay rights activism in the West and showing chauvinistic regard for the Western model of outness. It has in some cases been used to justify racism against people of colour and anti-immigration policies, as politicians like Pim Fortuyn or Geert Wilders in the Netherlands exemplified. Puar links homonationalism specifically to Islamophobia, and the Israeli occupation of Palestinian lands. The 'pinkwashing' of Israel has indeed been a particular sore point in Canada lately, as Israel's supporters contrast its gay-friendly constitution to 'queer apartheid' under Islamist regimes in the region. That contrast then provides them with a moral justification for Israel's refusal to negotiate the end of Jewish settlements in the occupied territories.

The fight against homophobias and other forms of intolerance is, in short, a global one tied to other complex conflicts, and it is not possible to definitively win on one front when losing on another. Hence, while my title focuses attention on Africa, I hope to show how developments in Africa and the West in this sphere are closely linked, and how we might build on that knowledge to strengthen sexual rights, sexual health and the erotic justice movement, globally.

§

Let me emphasize that the situation for lgbti and allies in places like Malawi, Nigeria and Senegal is without question bad and in real danger of becoming worse. The context is one where young people feel a great deal of frustration with an economy that marginalizes the majority while enriching a tiny, often corrupt elite. It is a context where sexuality is directly linked to a devastating yet seemingly cruelly haphazard disease. In such a context, simplistic fundamentalist ideologies and scapegoating minorities have a powerful appeal. The rise of political and religious homophobia is just one aspect of such scapegoating, often dovetailing closely with anti-feminism, blame-the-West-for-everything and other xenophobic rhetoric. Such homophobia can then have rippling negative impacts upon health, democratic culture and economic development. How is Cameroon going to escape from its malaise if it loses part of a generation of bright young professionals seeking asylum in the West, or who escape from homophobic stigma and persecution through alcohol and narcotics? How can donors or investors in Uganda turn a blind eye when the recipients of their aid money or investments increasingly and brazenly flout decades-old principles of public health and international human rights conventions? How best to promote sexual health in contexts where terms like 'national emergency', 'catastrophe' and 'urgent' are belied by many leaders' inability to pronounce, let alone deal with, a significant public health problem of secretive homosexualities?

Compounding the problem is that lgbti in Africa are not automatically in agreement with, and prepared to fight for, sexual rights as generally understood by Western activists and multilateral donors. On the contrary, for many the status quo is just fine. As long as they appear to conform to public expectations of heterosexuality and gender norms they can express their same-sex desires in private. To take a public stance, and to demand recognition and rights independent of gender and sexuality norms, puts this don't ask, don't tell situation in danger. Others, having been socialized in patriarchal cultures that emphasize heterosexuality, deeply share the values of those cultures. Self-doubt, self-stigma and self-destructive behaviours ('internalized homophobia') are common. Also extremely problematic from a rights perspective is that many lgbti in Africa today embrace the dominant culture's ideals and stereotypes of gender identity. Whether this is inherently bad is a subject for debate – many feminists would say it is, while others find harmless or erotic charm in the exaggeration of gender differences between the sexes. It ceases to be debatable, however, when the performance of gender identity among lgbti mimics the worst (most unequal, dehumanizing) aspects of heterosexual gender roles. This happens in butch lesbian masculinity that valorizes the accumulation of multiple sexual conquests and violence against girlfriends, and among gay male 'queens' whose femininities eroticize passivity, deception and tactical incompetence.

The task at hand, in short, is much bigger than protesting a continent-wide, singular plague of homophobia, and it is easy to get discouraged when people call you racist or elitist for even trying. Yet in acknowledging the dangers and dispiriting turns, we should not lose sight of the many signs of hope. As noted above, change is now unfolding at the state level in some surprising and encouraging ways. At the individual level, when we listen closely, we can also hear more and more stories of enduring love, of personal courage and of sophisticated understandings of family, community, political activism and faith from people who in the past tended to keep a very low profile. Not all is bad news.

Some readers may be aware from my previous publications that I lean towards a cautiously hopeful view of things. In this, however, I am far from alone. The gist of my research so far has in fact been closely in line with a growing body of other implicitly optimistic scholarship, art, fiction and film on the topic. It supports four main basic arguments: a) that same-sex sexuality is not 'un-African', and that African cultures in fact often had sophisticated and humane ways of explaining and enabling a certain amount of sexual difference within extended family networks; b) that sexual secrets can be revealed and traditions modified without causing the downfall of African civilization; c) that human rights for sexual minorities would be beneficial for the whole population, not just the minorities themselves; and d) that excessive focus on the negative (abuses, defeats, weaknesses) undermines the potential to achieve those rights. On the last point, I find the words of Ugandan lesbian activist Val Kalende are astute and compelling:

> ... our struggle must move away from the victimization narrative and begin to focus on positive stories. It doesn't help us when foreign journalists, bloggers, and allies present our struggle as 'desperate' and come to Uganda simply to write about what is wrong with our country while ignoring our success stories. While the 'desperate' narrative puts us in the international spotlight and does hold our leaders accountable, it also pits us against our fellow nationals. A balance of both narratives will bring the change we all need. I have been involved with LGBT community organizing in Uganda long enough to observe how far we have come and what we have managed to achieve amidst very difficult circumstances. (Kalende 2012)

A corollary of all this research is that the status quo, let alone a return to romanticized traditions, is not a feasible option. Whether 'don't ask, don't tell' traditions or cultures of discretion really worked so well in the past is up for debate. But whether they can be sustained in the future is not. Like it or not, this is the age of iPhones, of mind-boggling surveillance technologies, of HIV and aggressive new forms of homophobia, of rapid urbanization, and of populations where the average age is fifty, sixty or even seventy years less than that of the political leadership. Going back to a village life where a certain amount of sexual diversity could happen under cover of a fictively universal heterosexual culture is not a realistic strategy.

Most of my research so far has appeared in academic journals and books by university presses. The idea was that these media provided a certification of intellectual respectability, and that the research would eventually trickle down into less elite circles such as the donor world and civil society groups. The hope was that those groups might be able to use the evidence I had found to support their efforts to press for policy changes. To help speed that trickle-down effect along, I have also always made it a priority to present the research to general audiences in person whenever possible. It may be that practice which gives me a bit more optimism as compared to some of my colleagues. It is definitely that practice which gave me the inspiration to organize this book around questions that have been put to me on those occasions either in Africa or with non-academic audiences elsewhere. The questions are exactly as asked or very slightly paraphrased, grouped in chapters according to common themes.

Chapter 2 aims to address some of the underlying concerns about the value or reliability of the research. In the first instance, there is a widespread perception that the research is being driven by non-Africans, using concepts and language that are not just clumsy at capturing African evidence but alienating, even colonizing over Africa's own research priorities. Another common response to the research is to worry that time spent talking about homosexuality means time lost to act upon climate change (etc.). I want to tackle these anxieties up front, before getting to the meat of the evidence, analysis and argument. Fundamentally, this means challenging misleading dichotomies such as elite versus masses, or African ways of knowing versus the Western academic canon. My goal is to demystify commonplace assumptions that imply a need for Africans to resist the research. I am not interested in promoting the Western canon, but I do want to show how tools originally developed through gender and sexuality studies in the West can be (and are being) very helpfully adapted to facilitate sensitive investigation of sexualities in Africa by Africans.

The chapters that follow from there are grouped around the big themes of the day, beginning with the risks and potential of religious faith. Can Africans' strong sense of spirituality be harnessed to the cause of erotic justice? Can the widely acknowledged

17

benefits of spiritual faith, including its ability to help people fight the harms of HIV/AIDS (Haddad 2011, for example), be enhanced by understanding the ways in which faith has changed over time? Part of this chapter involves querying what traditional beliefs, the Bible and the Qur'an *really* say about the topic. However, I am not interested in theology per se. Rather, most of the chapter focuses on how Africa's major faiths are more complicated, and have historically allowed more room to accommodate sexual diversity than is commonly believed or claimed. I hope to demonstrate that the current observed rise of various fundamentalisms has less to do with theology than with other factors such as – discussed in the chapter that follows – the politics of nationalism and the restructuring of economies in line with globalization orthodoxies.

Chapter 4 explores the latter point by considering the roles of the state, and changes in the political economy that underpin the homophobias – plural – that are in play today. The main points here are that, however bad African states may seem today from a sexual minorities perspective, a) they cannot be understood in isolation from a long history of pressures upon them by non-African forces and b) the state is essential to the struggle to achieve erotic justice. African states will somehow have to be brought on side, and we can identify some key areas where civil society and donor pressures might help in that task.

Finally, I look at the history of activism: what worked, what did not, what might work better and so forth. The focus is the debate between sexual rights and sexual health as rival (?) or complementary (?) strategies for change. In what ways are African activists trying to resolve tensions between interim strategies such as emphasizing the health risks of homophobia, and long-term goals both of addressing underlying social stigmas against same-sex-practising people and achieving other developmental and social justice goals?

For queer intellectuals and theorists of sexuality in the West the questions posed (and indeed, my answers) may seem too accommodating to the logic of oppression. I sympathize with those who feel that 'debating' the Bible or Qur'an is not just a waste of effort but actually cedes time, energy and intellectual ground to those who would justify homophobia. I concede as well that skipping over centuries and borders may be taken to imply that Africa is a country, itself a harmful stereotype. But the fact is that these questions come up time and time again almost everywhere I travel, and not just from opponents of sexual rights. Much more commonly in my experience, questions come from sceptics who sincerely want to understand the issues and to use that knowledge to effect change. They wish to contribute to finding solutions to the problems that they observe or come to hear about, often quite unexpectedly. One of the first big studies of men who have sex with men in Africa, for example, started as a research project focused on how to help female sex workers in Senegal protect themselves against HIV/AIDS from their male clients (Niang et al. 2003). The women cooperated but then asked the researchers why they weren't asking the same questions to the male and transgender sex workers right there on the next corner? Why indeed, but how to do it?

Responding to people's questions in such a way that the answers will be heard and respected is a big, sometimes discouraging challenge. But a shared belief has tended to help both me and audiences along the way – that is, that the ability to speak from a position of wide-ranging scientific, historical and transnational knowledge is more empowering than selectively remembered local opinion, anecdotes and inherited stereotypes or 'common sense'. On a purely personal level, it is always gratifying to me to encounter this shared belief, so let me try it again in a published format that hopefully reaches beyond my usual academic and professional audiences.

In addressing these questions to a wide audience, I have opted not to encumber the narrative with footnotes or to establish a definitive summation of all pertinent works on the topic. For those who are interested, my own original research, discussions of methodology and references to the primary sources upon which I base key claims can be found in my earlier publications on the topic (Epprecht 2006, 2008 and 2012b). Here I should probably just mention the basics: combing through as many historical documents as I could get my hands on, including criminal court cases involving men who had sex with men, memoirs and old ethnographies; conducting interviews with traditional healers and contemporary lgbti activists; and reading a lot of fiction and watching films that touched upon same-sex issues. In addition to those sources, for this book I consulted ancient sacred texts and the tide of new reports by the secular giants of the development industry. Many of my arguments here also draw upon personal observation and informal discussions with colleagues, students, journalists, lawyers and activists over the years. I have learned a great deal from peer review of unpolished anonymous manuscripts, raw data that students have shared with me, and affidavits by African lgbti making asylum claims in the West, for which footnotes are obviously not possible. In the Notes, therefore, rather than specific references to the vast, sprawling and often highly specialized bodies of knowledge that colleagues and I have relied upon over the years, I simply steer readers towards a select list of the major published sources that substantiate or elaborate upon the claims I will be making. I also steer readers towards some of the most engaging artistic and filmic perspectives that have been coming out of Africa over the last couple of decades, with a focus on African creators.

Now, eager as I am to get to the substance of the book, let me take time to clarify some of the terms and concepts that I have chosen to use, starting with 'sexual minorities'. How best to express the wide range of people who fall within that category and still capture a sense of common aspirations?

§

Words almost always have hidden meanings and contested uses. Sharp philosophical and cultural conflicts may be embedded in them without speakers even being aware. Words that on the face of it look merely descriptive or scientifically objective can, again often unintentionally, cast a hint of blame or stigma. As such they have the power to hurt and to alienate our friends and allies, or to suggest false analogies across cultures. Moreover, that power can change drastically over time – an insult can become a marker of pride, subtle coded language or sly puns can become crude mockery, and vice versa.

These truisms are especially pronounced when we begin to talk of generally disapproved forms of sexuality and gender identity, and choice of terminology thus acquires added meaning. Indigenous African terms for people whose behaviour does not conform to heterosexual expectations, for example, often have their roots firmly in local, traditional, patriarchal cultures. Such terms abound, and there is some agitation to 'modernize' them for contemporary struggles so as not to be dependent on Western vocabularies. Yet indigenous terms commonly imply an age/power hierarchy, oppressive or restrictive gender roles, a specific ethnic identity, and/or the occult, none of which fits very well with today's transnational human rights and sexual health agendas. The words can be almost as controversial as the sexual acts or identities they connote.

Given the sensitivity of the topic, I want to carefully explain the assumptions and motives that underlie my own choices and meanings when it comes to language. To begin with sexual minorities and sexual orientation, my task is fairly simple. I go with the overwhelming consensus reached through over a century of scientific and historical scholarship and on the whole expressed by African lgbti themselves. This scholarship finds that a certain percentage of the population does not share the majority feeling of heterosexual desire, for complex reasons that are still not fully understood. Sexual orientation, or general feelings of erotic attraction, is towards people of the same sex. Try though they might, a certain percentage of people cannot happily conform to the practice of exclusive heterosexual sexuality, although many will unhappily conform when there are no realistic alternatives or to avoid conflict.

Some people claim that this sexual minority is 'unnatural' compared to the assumed naturalness of the majority, and that sexual orientation is not an innate quality but a 'lifestyle choice'.

No doubt choice, or sexual opportunism, comes into play in some situations. Yet humans hold diversity of sexual behaviour in common with many other species of animal, from primates that are genetically close to us to simple organisms like insects and worms. With a keen eye to their domestic animals, Africans certainly must have realized this from time immemorial. One of the oldest and most common domesticated animals in Africa is actually quite close to humans in this respect. The sheep is a species with a rate of exclusive male–male sexuality of about one in twelve. Will anyone seriously tell me that in over six thousand years of herding sheep, Africans never noticed that 8 per cent of rams only mounted other rams? Is it coincidence that one of the words in isiZulu for 'homosexual' is *inkhonkhoni*, or blue wildebeest, an animal observed to sometimes make that same lifestyle choice?

Among humans the size of the minorities who are willing and able to express their same-sex desire varies from place to place and over time depending on a wide range of factors including culture and availability of private spaces. The number of people who publicly identify themselves on the basis of sexual orientation has also changed over time, and indeed, this issue of identity, rather than changes in sexual practices, is the nub of the controversy in much of Africa today. How sexual desire and practices relate to gender roles, and how a society determines what exactly about sex and gender is considered erotic, are similarly variable – think of the changing history of female nudity in Africa, for an obvious example. But the existence of sexual minorities, whether they identify themselves as such or not, seems to be a relative constant across cultures and throughout history.

Africa, as I will be showing, is no exception. This is a fact that will not go away no matter how strongly one wishes it to go, no matter how many times one quotes the Bible or the Qur'an, and no matter how fiercely one tries to suppress sexual minorities through the law or violence or so-called sexual reorientation/ conversion therapy. People can, of course, hold back from express- ing their sexual desire and can suppress it by all kinds of means, but they cannot be 'cured' of it. As the World Bank study put it in its inimitable way,

> An overwhelming body of evidence supported by the inter-national community of professional organizations who have reviewed the extant literature on the efficacy of conversion therapy has rejected it as ineffective, unnecessary, potentially harmful, and ethically controversial. On the basis of expert con-sensus in combination with a lack of biologic plausibility and efficacy data, reparative or corrective therapy is given a Grade 4, or inappropriate recommendation. (Beyrer et al. 2011: xxxiii)

In other words, attempts to engineer 100 per cent conformity to heterosexual ideals are bound to fail.

Many terms have been coined to capture the many forms of human sexual desire and expression that differ from major-ity·norms (in academic language, the blanket word for all that diversity would be 'non-normative sexuality'). Many are overtly stigmatizing or hateful, and are often based on demonstrably false beliefs. The most common insult for gays and lesbians in southern Africa, for example, is *istabane*, literally meaning 'hermaphrodite' (intersexed, possessing both male and female genitals). Yet even scientific, ostensibly descriptive terms can suggest a pathology and misleading timelessness or essence. When does bicurious become bisexual and does that differ from msm or wsw (see below) in precisely knowable ways? When, exactly, does a transgender person become transsexual? Can we be certain if homosexuality is congenital or situational? If not, are these terms really helping us?

For all the diversity and uncertainty around non-normative sexuality, some scholars have preferred to use the word 'homo-sexualities', in the plural form. The term 'queer' has also gained some popularity both for the way it fudges the misleading preci-sion of the scientific language, and for inviting people of all persuasions into the common political project. The undeniable successes of queer liberation in the West, and the insightful-ness of much queer theory, suggest a lot of potential here. I am partial to 'queer' myself to the extent that it is used as a verb rather than as a noun ('to queer', meaning to be meticulously critical of received wisdom about gender and sexuality identity claims, including 'queer'). Yet for many in Africa and the global South more broadly, queer remains a somewhat offensive term, specific to a certain kind of activism or academic self-labelling in the West. Some critics see it as a subtle assertion of white privilege, if nothing else through the power of naming. I cannot say I have noticed a groundswell of enthusiasm on the part of African scholars to take ownership of the concept, although some have found it useful and liberating when qualified by 'African'.

My preference is to steer close to the preferred vocabularies of the people under discussion. A consensus has emerged in that regard around lgbti, which captures a sense of the diversity and changeability of identities in a broadly shared alliance, as well as linking Africa to global struggles, where the acronym is also widely used. Readers will have probably noticed my quibble with the dominant usage in that I prefer the lower-case form. My reading of proper nouns in the English language is that capitalization implies a certainty, stability or essential nature that contradicts the main intention of this particular acronym. The individual components (lesbian, gay, etc.) for that reason are almost always rendered in lower case, which seems fittingly respectful and non-essentializing. In pursuit of that same goal of respectful inclusiveness, some people now refer to lgbtia or lgbtiq, the 'a' standing in for 'ally', and 'q' as above. The term that Amharic-speaking msm prefer to use to identify themselves is even simpler and intriguing for the same reasons: *zega*, meaning citizen (Tadele 2012: 182).

Of course, a common front is not always easy to maintain between allies and citizens, and in fact there are significant tensions between people who identify as bisexual, trans and intersexed (bti), on the one hand, and 'pure' lesbians or gays (lg) on the other. That becomes even more difficult when msm are added. These are males who have sex with males but do not necessarily think of themselves as gay, homosexual or even bisexual. They just happen to have sex with males sometimes, no reasons asked for or provided. The same applies to wsw, meaning women who have sex with women but do not necessarily consider themselves to be lesbian or bisexual – indeed, may firmly reject such labels.

These acronyms have increasingly gained popularity on the grounds that they are simply descriptive. For the same reason, some people prefer 'same-sex-practising' or 'attracted' – which describe a fact without suggesting any kind of firm identity, orientation or larger political agenda. 'People', rather than males and females, avoids the suggestion that these two physiological conditions can be known with definitive confidence. Indeed, the tenuousness of the relationship between physical body and gender identity has led one African scholar to coin yet new terms: anamale and anafemale (that is, anatomically male or female without specifying what sociological meaning or sexual orientation attaches to those physical attributes – Oyéwùmí 1997). That formulation has not caught on, for which I have to admit I am thankful.

In this book I use most of these terms depending on the context I am describing, on how much vagueness or uncertainty is most appropriate to the specific situation being discussed, and on what the individuals being described themselves have used. I also like the term sexual minorities, notwithstanding the worry that it can be taken to suggest, erroneously, that a uniform and knowable majority exists in clear distinction to the pesky few. An advantage with this term is that it does not pin people down with scientific-sounding certainty, or imply that Africa is directly following in the footsteps of the pioneering West – 'gay identity migration', as Roberts (1995) put it. The second advantage is a political one. Few dispute that in a democracy minority groups need protection from tyranny or abuse by the majority. The term sexual minorities thus makes a crucial point with people who believe that sexual orientation is a lifestyle choice or an inherently immoral decision. It places lgbti people, msm and wsw on the same linguistic plane as ethnic or religious minority groups that face discrimination and require legal instruments to protect them.

What, however, of those who believe that the concept of 'sexual rights' is itself 'un-African,' deriving from the modern West and now imposed on Africa as a new articulation of a long-standing colonizing project? How can we bring them fruitfully into the discussion?

§

The concept of sexual rights starts by recognizing the futility or harm that can arise from attempting to suppress a natural aspect of human sexuality, its diversity. The concept at its most fundamental level simply says that every adult person should have the right to choose their sexual partners and practices free from coercion. They should not suffer harm or discrimination on the basis of their actual or assumed sexuality or gender identity. Children should have the right to learn about the diversity of human sexuality and their own developing identity similarly free from coercion, including the coercion of deliberate misinformation. This does not mean, as enemies of sexual rights often argue, a licence for perversion or debauchery ('freedom to fuck in the streets', as I once heard a Zimbabwean politician claim with reference to South Africa's post-apartheid constitution). On the contrary, sexual rights implies an obligation by individuals not to trespass on the rights of others, and calls upon the state to mediate a balance between conflicting claims through transparent enquiry, legal processes, blind peer review and parliamentary debate, as appropriate to the many different areas in which conflicts can arise.

Sexual rights in this basic sense derives from numerous internationally sanctioned treaties and is now incorporated in the mandate of powerful multilateral institutions, including the United Nations Human Rights Commission, the International Covenant on Civil and Political Rights (ICCPR), the Convention for the Elimination of Discrimination against Women (CEDAW), UNAIDS, the World Health Organization and the World Bank. At the time these instruments and statements were originally drafted, sexual orientation was not considered an inherent quality requiring explicit protection, and the concept of sexual minorities did not exist. The drafters, however, left the door open to the eventual inclusion of unforeseen qualities by the term 'any other status', and on that basis sexual orientation is gradually wending its way into revised documents. The ICCPR, meanwhile, also prohibits states from introducing new laws aimed at the destruction or limitation of existing rights and precluding attempts to define sexual orientation as falling outside 'any other status'. Article 20 further declares that 'Any advocacy of national, racial or religious hatred that constitutes incitement to discrimination, hostility or violence shall be prohibited by law.'

The African Union's Charter on Human and Peoples' Rights (ACHPR) for its part does not name sexual orientation and gender identity as being included within its definition of human rights. Moreover, a strong view maintains that any human (individual) rights to sexual orientation that may be conceded to exist in theory are necessarily subordinate to people's (collective) rights to the preservation of cultural integrity. Yet the ACHPR leaves the door wide open to challenge by unambiguously declaring that 'every citizen', 'every human being' and 'every individual' has the right to 'freedom, equality, justice and dignity', not to mention 'life and integrity' and 'the best attainable state of physical and mental health'. These rights cannot be taken away for any reason arising from that person's intrinsic qualities, such as race or sex, but also including 'other status', 'other grounds' or by 'all forms of discrimination [presumably including those not yet explicitly identified, understood, or named]'. The African Commission on Human and Peoples' Rights has so far been unwilling to consider making sexual orientation explicit as an 'other status', and in fact has actively discriminated against homosexuals by blocking the Coalition of African Lesbians from observer status. But unless it rules that lgbti are not human beings and that homophobia does not fall under 'all forms of discrimination', then by its own terms of reference and by its respectful acknowledgement of international frameworks, its current intransigence will be difficult to sustain. One can see the attraction of the term *zega.*

I will elaborate on some specific potential challenges to the rights status quo in Chapter 5. For now, I will simply acknowledge that few jurisdictions in the world have achieved all of the rights laid out in these international treaties, and indeed, even in much of the West, many of them are still considered to be quite radical. In Africa, where public opinion polls have shown that 90 per cent and more of people claim to disapprove of homosexuality under any circumstances, even a fraction of the potential rights probably sounds like madness. Equal rights for sexual minorities clearly pose fundamental challenges to many aspects of traditional patriarchal cultures, to deeply entrenched religious beliefs, to existing laws, to strapped government budgets, and to the personal feelings of authoritarian leaders. No wonder that some states have already taken pre-emptive action with constitutional amendments seeking to block those who would slip rights for sexual minorities through the court system 'under cover' of some general principle.

Many brave and articulate people are trying to do exactly that and, I will be reiterating, they have scored some impressive victories. One useful move in that direction is to anticipate reaction by clarifying what sexual rights does *not* mean. It notably does not mean 'gay rights' in the sense of giving special rights unique to non-heterosexuals. All should be entitled to the same rights, with allowances made for a period of transition as needed for social attitudes to change to accept the concept. The term 'gay rights' also does not really account for the fact that heterosexuals may also fall victim to homophobic discrimination and violence if they do not conform to gender norms. Transvestites, for example – that is, men who dress like women and vice versa – or men and women who take on gender roles of the opposite sex may be perceived as homosexual when in fact they are not. Likewise, heterosexuals who refuse to marry or who choose lifelong celibacy may be exposed to violence and shaming to enforce conformity with family expectations. To acknowledge that, 'gender identity' or 'gender variance' (from the heteronorm) is now also often added to sexual orientation as a closely related but distinct category that can lead to victimization, and hence falls within a concern of sexual rights. In the usual pattern of donor language, this package has become the acronym SOGI.

Here it is important to clarify the distinction between SOGI and sexual preference. To be fair, opponents of sexual rights have some grounds for their belief that an expansive definition of rights could open the door to all kinds of evil behaviours. There are in fact people who claim to suffer discrimination or infringement of their rights on the basis of their preference for specific types of sexual acts or sex objects. Many of these are harmless enough when they involve private consenting acts between adults (top or bottom, bondage, group sex, polyamory or 'ethical non-monogamy', fetishes and so on). Some preferences, however, are not just offensive to the dominant culture but manifestly harmful to at least one of the people involved in both health and rights terms. In North America, where they are probably most organized and vocal, such preference activists include heterosexual paedophiles (men who prey on underage girls), self-described 'men who love boys' and 'bug-chasers' or 'bare-backers' (people who deliberately seek HIV infection through unprotected anal intercourse). But sexual preference is not a quality intrinsic to any individual comparable to sexual orientation. Preference is a learned desire, a religious belief, an erotic choice, or in some cases a progressive psychological disorder. As such there is no more right to a specific sexual preference than there is a right to go shopping at all times or to leave tuberculosis untreated. Such preferences may cause harms to others and therefore legitimately need to be regulated up to and including criminalization as indicated by the best available scientific and sociological knowledge. Indeed, if we go back to the definition of rights that includes adulthood, consent, equality, bodily integrity, mutual obligation and well-being, then the claims of discrimination by paedophiles and others on the basis of sexual preference quickly fall away. The claim that sexual rights takes away the power of the state to regulate or criminalize certain sexual preferences similarly falls away.

The same thinking would apply to the concepts of men's 'right to sex' or 'conjugal rights', irrespective of their partners' wishes.

Many men assume they have such rights by virtue of marriage or gifts or just because they are male. Rights in these cases, however, when seen through a sexual rights or erotic justice lens, are downgraded to preference or cultural expectation and hence still require consent each and every time.

The desire for rights should not be mistaken for a call for tolerance. Tolerance is obviously a big improvement over intolerance, and establishing basic legal rights is a critical step towards educating people away from overt discrimination. Realistically, that may be the best we can hope to achieve in the medium term under present-day circumstances in Africa. But tolerance still implies a hierarchy that betrays the justice principle. The presumed good, moral and normal majority assumes the power to define what and who is bad, immoral and abnormal. Then, to further consolidate its goodness, that majority agrees (for now) to tolerate the bad – that is, to patronize rather than persecute. Tolerance also sets the bar rather low: grudging acceptance, apathy or consent not to ask. Justice as a long-term project would require moving beyond that frame of mind to one that respects and values difference as a vital element of a healthy society.

Finally, sexual rights does not imply the United States as a model. On the contrary, while the United States has some of the oldest and clearest articulations of human rights in the world, while Americans have historically, sometimes aggressively, promoted the concept when it suited their interests as now seems to be the case with lgbti rights, and while American popular culture often appears to celebrate sexual freedom and diversity, sexual and reproductive rights are *not* very well entrenched in that country. Where they have been won, they are constantly contested by political and religious conservatives who would roll back those rights to an idealized, yet strictly enforced, conformity to heterosexual marital norms. The judicial system in the USA is heavily politicized, while even secular political discourse is profoundly shaped by Protestant cultural assumptions. The liberatory potential of information technology is meanwhile deeply compromised by the proliferation of commodified relationships and Internet pornography. Indeed, new information technologies and the process of production (and subversion) of scientific knowledge are vulnerable to the corrosive influence of highly concentrated and unevenly distributed wealth. Where individual rights have been won in the United States (such as the right to same-sex marriage in nine out of fifty states), or threatened assaults on progressive legislation have been turned back (notably by the 2012 re-election of Barack Obama as president), collective and structural injustices around gender, class, race and other inequalities preclude large swathes of the population from exercising their individual rights.

Many of the strongest critiques of erotic injustice that inform my own thinking are primarily attentive to widespread practices and frustrations arising from the struggle for sexual and reproductive rights in the United States. I want to stress this point not just for those who fear sexual freedom and dehumanizing pornography as the ugly side of US cultural imperialism, but also for African lgbti who, sometimes, idealize the attractive aspects of American-style freedom. My point is that we can actually do much better; in fact, we need to.

The general concept of sexual rights leaves a great deal of room for debate over specific interpretations. Within the notion that individuals should not trespass on the rights of others, for example, is the question of who is an 'other' – would that include fertilized eggs, embryos or 'pre-born people' as anti-abortionists claim in order to negate a woman's claim to rights over her own body? Do sex workers have the right to market their bodies as commodities, to freely negotiate the conditions of their work, and to enjoy freedom from state harassment similar to other forms of labour? Do women have the right to choose certain forms of dress, for example the niqab or the micro-miniskirt, or can they choose to 'mutilate' their genitals when such individual choices conflict with the collective goal of women's equality? Can polygyny (one man, multiple wives) stand as a right if the wives are consenting, without balancing that right by an equal right to polyandry (one woman, multiple husbands)? How can a collective right to cultural integrity be preserved when the culture includes inherited forms of discrimination or violence against specific others? How can we respect the principle of freedom of religion, and recognize the great benefits religious faith can bring, when religions are so often used to justify the negation of sexual and reproductive rights?

Notwithstanding the many unresolved specific questions, most African countries have accepted some form of sexual rights as a general principle, including recognition that long-standing aspects of culture will need to change. In most cases, they have the vulnerable majority population (heterosexual women and children) front and centre if not exclusively in mind. To give an example of one of many documents committing to achieving this goal, the Protocol to the ACHPR on the Rights of Women in Africa in 2003 required all member states to: 'modify the social and cultural patterns of conduct of women and men through public education, information, education and communication strategies, with a view to achieving the elimination of harmful cultural and traditional practices and all other practices which are based on the idea of the inferiority or the superiority of either of the sexes, or on stereotyped roles for women and men'. Why? Because African leaders have come to realize that the lack of sexual/social and reproductive rights for women is a major impediment to economic development, democratic governance and health for all. The collective right to defend inherited patriarchal culture is offset by the collective right to health in vulnerable populations which, under patriarchal culture, represent the majority.

Some African states have gone so far as to enshrine the concept of sexual rights in their constitutions (as in South Africa in the very broadest terms) or committed to enacting it (eventually) in national policy and law. In practice, however, even when talk of sexual rights is narrowly focused on heterosexual women, most governments have been slow to change specific policies and laws, to challenge long-standing cultural practices, or to intervene against the spread of new forms of discrimination, exploitation and violence related to sexuality and gender. Even where sexual rights are enshrined in the constitution or where public servants are educated and legally obligated to defend them, states typically lack the capacity to follow through in meaningful ways. Compounding the problem is that people do not know their rights and do not have the financial or other personal resources needed to stand up for them. Who can afford a lawyer? Who wants to bring outsiders into family disputes? Who wants to publicly admit that their dignity has been violated, especially when, as is often the case, an admission of rape or of one's sexual orientation can bring ostracism, unemployment and a high risk of further indignities and violence? Who wants to take a chance that the police or press or family will treat the victim with compassion? The plain observed fact is that they often do not. Victims of sexual violence are often revictimized by the police, in the courts, in the media, and in the most intimate relationships.

In short, sexual rights for women and children may exist on paper but are daily violated on a massive and, many would argue, growing scale as the underlying economic malaise exposes people to sexual violence, exploitation and trafficking. This contradiction between rights on paper and rights in practice becomes sharper when sexual rights are extended to sexual minorities. Some of the most horrific reported acts of homophobic violence happen in the country with the most rights, South Africa. Democratic government is meanwhile no guarantee that the contradiction will be easily resolved. Festus Mogae, former president of Botswana and now an advocate for sexual minority rights, frankly conceded that he could not have taken this position publicly when he was in power and still hoped to have won re-election. He claims to have taken a pro-rights position only in private by giving secret instructions to the police not to harass lgbti (BBC 2011).

Moving the discussion away from the language of rights to the language of justice can help to address such complications. Where talk of rights sounds Western and carries a significant amount of colonial and donor cultural baggage, everyone understands justice as a universal desire. The word justice clarifies that sexual rights advocates are not seeking to extend selfish or criminal freedoms and preferences, as opponents often allege, but rather are seeking something that is fair and ethical for everyone. The word justice also introduces an awareness that class and other historically entrenched inequalities are at play that can frustrate the achievement of fairness even when fine-sounding laws and constitutions are put in place. Justice may therefore mean temporarily suspending or qualifying the historical privileges of some groups and individuals in order that the rights playing field can be levelled. Rather than an either/or struggle of rights versus culture, the concept of justice opens the door to a step-by-step or layered approach that pragmatically grounds the long-term rights aspirations in traditional idioms and institutions. Where rights suggest litigation and protest, justice proposes quieter forms of negotiation, translation, education and mobilization as circumstances require. Where rights suggests the state and the political economy, justice encourages us to think more expansively about the often subtle role of culture in validating or eroticizing inequality. That is, historical privileges by class, race and gender have not only been built into the capitalist political economy over hundreds of years of unequal globalization, they are now very densely built into cultural notions about what is and is not sexy. As Ellison put it (1996: 114), the struggle for erotic justice will therefore need to unfold on several stages if we are to achieve what he called a 'liberating ethic of sexuality'. 'We must make clear our commitment to reverse sexism, racism, heterosexism, and economic exploitation, and to redress these injustices that have distorted human sexuality.' Without doing all these things, a narrow focus on rights will surely fail.

Why erotic rather than sexual justice? That is simple. Many people understand sexual as 'genital', and 'sex' even more narrowly as the penis ejaculating in the vagina. Other acts and other body parts fall outside the definition, leaving wide scope for a great deal of injustice and deception to play out. If putting the penis in the mouth is not regarded as sex (and I recall no less an authority than former US president Bill Clinton making this point to defend himself against accusations of having had sex while at work), a person might not consider it necessary to practise safer sex when doing such a thing. They might not take no for an answer if refused certain sex acts that are not regarded as 'real' sex. Likewise, if sex is admitted to be dangerous but sex means penis-in-vagina only, then penis-in-anus is logically safe. Studies reveal that this exact thinking is commonplace, and may be a significant factor in increasing the risk of men's and women's exposure to HIV.

By contrast, erotic extends the analysis to the whole body, to innumerable combinations of those body parts, and to the imagination. It does not fetishize genitals and ejaculation but may include all kinds of sensual touching, physical activity including solitary dancing, singing and even just talking. Erotic justice means freedom to experience, fantasize, explore, advocate and represent all these diverse aspects of sexuality without fear, provided of course that such freedom does not impose injustice on others. Where 'sexual' sounds focused on the physical and medical, erotic encompasses politics, family, spirituality and much more. Indeed, to feel erotic one needs to be well nourished and healthy, something that is simply not possible for many millions of people in the world today, however they understand their sexuality. Erotic justice requires us to think big and to ask, for example, why are so many people still hungry in this world of plenty, and what can the well fed do in their own countries to begin to address global inequalities?

The erotic is in fact so enmeshed with other inherited inequalities that I worry that the word, as commonly understood, might actually detract from the scale of the project. It is not to titillate. It is not to depoliticize. Bearing that in mind, let us settle therefore on linking sexuality with *social* justice, broadly conceived, the erotic being subsumed within and essential to the social, and vice versa.

In that spirit, join me in wondering, first, are there not more important things to do in Africa today than to worry about sexual minorities?

2 | Demystifying sexuality studies in Africa

Not so long ago, sexuality was not generally considered to be a development issue at all. Sexuality belonged to the category of nature or perhaps culture, whereas development was economics, infrastructure and good governance. For the state or donors to meddle in matters of the bedroom was to raise suspicions of the days when European policies to control African populations or to 'civilize' African sexual mores were a major source of Africans' anger at the modernization project.

Feminism and HIV changed all that, and by now most African leaders and the biggest donors to Africa accept that fostering healthy sexuality is a legitimate and important development priority for the state. They understand that unhealthy sexuality leaves a big, insidiously destructive footprint upon a society. They recognize that you can build all the wells and roads and dams that you like, and even have free and fair elections. But if women and female children have no rights or means to achieve sexual autonomy and fulfilment, and if their disempowerment relative to men is portrayed as sexually desirable in popular culture, then gender-based violence and sexually transmitted infections including HIV/AIDS are going to continue to impose significant costs on the economy and body politic. If women's and girls' right to sexuality education is not promoted, fertility rates will remain dangerously high and the continent can expect a doubling or even tripling of the population in the next few decades, with all that that implies for fragile environments and resources conflict.

A common response to such arguments is to bemoan that women's empowerment with sexual rights requires men's relative disempowerment. People say that women and girls can be more effectively protected from the ills noted above by returning to idealized traditional practices such as virginity testing or seclusion. On the contrary, however, women's lack of rights weighs heavily on men. When men and boys are socialized to conceive that their sexuality, and their identity as Africans, hinges upon their ability to command, protect, provide for and impregnate women, then there is a very powerful recipe for stress, frustration and psychological alienation. Not all boys and men can live up to this expectation of masculinity and African-ness, and all the more so as traditional means for men to exercise a dominant or provider role within the family have declined (not just in Africa; this is a common trend globally). Alienation in turn can lead to violence that undermines or negates the normal measurements of developmental progress.

This is not just a liberal intuition, nor is it a particularly radical or 'Western feminist' insight. Hard-nosed economists have begun to put sobering dollar figures on the high cost of gender-based violence to economic growth. The burden of sexual and reproductive ill-health upon women and girls, and of stress upon men, can also be measured through the concept of Disability Adjusted Life Years or DALYs. The World Bank consequently now describes gender equality as quite simply 'smart economics' (World Bank 2012: xx). At the level of official policy commitments, almost all African governments have signed the African Union protocol calling for the elimination of cultural practices that require or abet women's inequality – as of the time of writing thirty had ratified that protocol, that is, agreed to reform their national laws and policies in order to achieve its goals.

From this point of view, healthy sexuality among heterosexuals is a public good. It would mean, for example, fewer teenage pregnancies since girls would not need to get pregnant to prove their womanhood, or boys to impregnate to prove their worth as men. Girls would have the ability, knowledge and confidence to resist pressures for unprotected vaginal intercourse, and perhaps explore other, safer means to achieve sexual satisfaction and sense of personhood. Healthy sexuality would mean fewer septic

37

abortions – the cause of death of tens of thousands of Africans every year – since there would be fewer unwanted pregnancies and safe options for their termination. It would mean lower infant and maternal mortality, less sexual exploitation and trafficking, less child abuse, including of boys by men, less rape (ditto), and reduced sexually transmitted infections. It would mean less of the kinds of psychological, health and criminal problems that arise from chronic alienation and substance abuse among males who cannot fulfil their social and sexual roles as fathers and family providers. In today's structurally adjusted capitalist environment, with land and housing shortages and looming environmental pressures, healthy sexuality would also include the ability for women to control their fertility with the eventual result of smaller, more economically secure and sustainable families.

This is not to suggest that Africans don't love big families and gain profoundly through motherhood and fatherhood. It is simply to say that when sexual and reproductive choices derive from mutual erotic desire and knowledge rather than duty, fear, ignorance or a skewed sense of public performance of gender identity, then fewer pregnancies will be needed to ensure a family survives to adulthood. The consequent need for women to give birth to eight or ten children each will be reduced. One can see this happening already in sometimes very dramatic drops in the number of births per woman as reproductive health and rights improve, nowhere in Africa more so than Morocco (from over seven with a high mortality rate in 1960 to just over two, with two surviving, in 2011). Motherhood rights would actually be strengthened in this scenario as well by empowering women to resist coercion to abort or have tubal ligations to prevent pregnancy, as is reported to be a fairly common unethical practice with HIV-positive women.

If, and it is of course a very big if, other factors like good jobs and trust in government are in place, then healthy sexuality should make people less stressed, happier and able to act as better and more productive citizens – a virtuous circle, as economists might say.

Anyone who lived in Africa through the structural adjustment years will be understandably sceptical of World Bank recommendations, and we should be wary of an economistic frame of mind that comes with other conceptual baggages like intellectual property rights for live-saving pharmaceutical products. The same appraising view of healthy sexuality, however, is shared by most people who research the topic, backed by their thousands of footnotes, formulas and scientific fandangos. Crucially, that view is also widespread in traditional cultures throughout Africa. One of the most striking features of African traditional cultures in the eyes of many European observers during the age of colonialism was that African views on sexuality were in fact healthier, more 'natural', more respectful of desire and *less* repressive than in Europe at that time. Anthropological studies and much fiction set in pre-colonial or rural settings in Africa, for example, shows that women traditionally practised child spacing by various methods which they controlled. Under the umbrellas of family obligations and respect, women also had moral claims to sexual satisfaction. What constituted 'satisfaction' would have varied from place to place, of course, but people would know when it was not there. Importantly, they had recourses if they unjustly did not get it. Some Muslim scholars have also suggested that Islam as traditionally practised in Africa was 'sex positive' for women, again within the framework of marriage and family honour. Others have gone so far as to claim that gender inequality did not exist in Africa until introduced by the colonialists. Moreover, children also had a right to know about, and in many cultures to explore, their sexuality in preparation for adulthood. They could do so safely and without guilt or shame as long as it was done in the approved way. A practice widely known throughout eastern and southern Africa, for example, allowed adolescents to have sex before marriage in a private space on the absolute condition that no penetration took place. Such sexual 'outercourse' was a way to learn about sexuality and to let off all that young adult energy without the health risks and social complications that pregnancy can entail.

This practice, and many other customs around sexuality including initiation or circumcision schools, labial stretching by girls, and traditional forms of same-sex marriage, were typically dismissed as barbarism by European Christian missionaries when they began coming to Africa. African sexual mores were then subject to intense campaigns of repression and mockery during the colonial era. The aim was to remake savages into civilized people on the presumption that middle-class western Europeans represented the pinnacle of the latter. Erotic injustice was meanwhile at the heart of the colonial political economy by coercively separating husbands and wives, even to the extent of criminalizing women who moved to town to be with their men. In Islamic parts of the continent, the colonialists systematically favoured more conservative, male-controlling interpretations of the faith which undermined African women's autonomies. In that sense, working towards healthy sexuality and erotic justice could be considered an African nationalist project insofar as it aims to rescue some aspects of traditional ideas and practices from the long onslaught of colonial racism, abuse and injustice.

That, then, is my first response to the misplaced priorities or the elitist and diversionary claim: sexuality in general is a core development issue, and sexual rights in general are inseparable from gender equality. Both are justifiable in scientific, economic, traditional cultural and African nationalist political terms. Indeed, some of Africa's most famous revolutionary heroes made precisely that point decades ago, however unevenly they applied it in their personal lives. It is official policy as articulated by democratically elected governments right across the continent.

How to convey the idea that sexual and reproductive rights include, indeed demand, sexual minority rights is a bigger challenge, and several common misperceptions make it hard for people of good will to make that mental jump. Perhaps easiest to clear up is the notion that the research which supports calls for sexual minority rights comes primarily from outside of Africa rather than being driven by Africans themselves. Homosexuality, in crude terms, is an obsession of white folks rather than an indigenous or organically felt agenda. Sex positivity in African cultures did not extend to sexual minorities, they will say, and they will point to the relative silence of African scholars compared to Europeans and Americans making claims about Africans as a proof.

This misperception is understandable if one looks only at scholarship and donor activism since the 1990s. Taking a longer view, we can see that research on same-sex sexuality has in fact *never* been a priority let alone an obsession for non-African Africanists. A four-page appendix to an ethnography first published in 1916. A couple of sentences of speculation about woman–woman marriages among the Akan from the 1950s. A chapter in a semi-pornographic book from 1964 which basically says primitive people like Africans do not do complicated things like homosexuality. One two-page article on the topic among the Azande people of southern Sudan was published in 1971, another two-page article explaining the infrequency of homosexuality among the Shona people in 1979. Other than these and a sprinkling of other studies, one has to look very carefully to find even passing references or footnotes that acknowledge the existence of same-sex sexuality in Africa, even as something to be condemned. Either complete silence or a single sentence in a book of hundreds of pages is typical of the ethnography and other scholarship written by European and American researchers prior to the 1980s.

When HIV/AIDS appeared in the middle of the 1980s, one might have expected a change, given that the disease was so closely associated with gay men in the West (and among whites in South Africa). Yet in Africa virtually no research was done on the possibility of male–male transmission of the virus. Huge, multi-country surveys asking Africans intimate questions about their sex lives simply did not bother to ask about same-sex relations. Everyone either just accepted the claim that they did not need to be asked since homosexuality, by common knowledge, did not exist in Africa, or they asked in such culturally and context-insensitive ways that they invited the answer 'no'. Those who knew differently – that is, that African men did sometimes have sex with men in certain contexts – censored themselves out of respect for the sensitivities of African leaders and fear of backlash against the research. Two decades passed, and countless thousands of preventable HIV infections happened, before proper scientific studies of male–male sex in Africa began to be conducted.

In short, whether as colonial officials, missionaries, industrial leaders, journalists or scholars, Europeans mostly colluded in keeping secrets about same-sex sexuality, and in some cases they actively promoted the idea that Africa was a place with no room for people who did not conform to heterosexual norms. Why would non-Africans invest so much in creating such a stereotype about 'African sexuality'? It is a complicated story which I discuss elsewhere (Epprecht 2008), but the title of that ethno-pornographic book mentioned above gives a hint of one of the main factors: 'Voodoo-Eros' (Bryk 1964 [1925]). The word voodoo was synonymous in European culture of the day with primitive and more than just a bit scary. In this case it was also used as a synonym for 'black African'. But the stereotype of close-to-nature Africans just didn't fit with the popular stereotype of homosexuality as a manifestation of decadence or over-civilization. Since the idea of Africa's primitivity was so important to the justification of colonial rule, it had to be defended, even if subconsciously, by ruling out investigations that might complicate the picture.

Since the late 1990s, there has been a big shift, an awakening to the fact that the claim of no same-sex sexuality in Africa was misleading. Yet the topic of homosexualities still remains quite marginal to the mainstream of Africanist scholarship. As an example, the European Conference on African Studies in 2011 featured over 1,100 scholarly papers. Six discussed same-sex issues. At smaller conferences it is not unusual for me to be the only presenter on the topic to audiences I can count on one hand. Looking over donor documents and debates in the United Nations, meanwhile, one gets the impression of considerable caution on the part of Western governments and aid partners. The World Bank report on gender equality for its part does not name homosexuality or sexual minority rights anywhere in its 400-plus pages. I will come back to this later but for now suffice to say that, if there is such a thing as obsession with same-sex sexuality or 'pink imperialism' coming from the West, it pales in comparison to other obsessions and imperialisms at work on the continent today. To the extent that it exists in books like this one, it could be seen as making up for the much longer period of time when the dominant thrust of cultural imperialism out of Europe was *against* African sexual and gender diversity.

A look at the longer history of writing about sexuality in Africa also dispels the misperception that African scholars historically were unaware of or uninterested in sexual orientation and gender variance. In the first place, some were, and in the second, Africans' relative silence on the topic can be explained by factors other than lack of awareness or interest. It takes a bit of searching, but one can find references to non-normative sexuality and gender identity as told by Africans to European explorers and traders going back to the earliest written accounts of African societies. One can also find African authors writing about homosexual or bisexual characters in their fiction and memoirs going back to the 1950s. In some cases African artists drew rather sympathetic portrayals of the (usually) men involved. Authors like Yambo Ouologuem, Yulisa Amadu Maddy, Wole Soyinka and Ayi Kwei Armah in the 1970s created African or African-American characters who engaged in same-sex relations in Africa. They provided a foil to condemn European and Arab racism as well as abusive *hetero*sexual relationships or patriarchal arrogance in African society.

Beginning in the early 1990s, African lgbti activists in South Africa began to express themselves directly to public audiences. In the case of Zackie Achmat, this was in the form of both a memoir and as a hard-hitting critique of Western scholars who wrote about African msm in functionalist language (they had to do it because ...), but who did not listen carefully to what African men themselves were saying about erotic desire in those relationships.

Artists elsewhere on the continent joined in as well, not to romanticize lgbti characters as heroic or mod, but to place them in context and to enable them to reflect on the broad social problems of the day. Senegalese film-maker Mohammed Camara, for example, treated a male–male love affair sensitively in his 1998 feature film *Dakan* (including the first-ever on-screen erotic kiss between two African men). The movie is about much more than sex, however, as it also provided a vehicle to question gender, class, race and other inequalities in Guinean society. Nigerian author Jude Dibia, in his novel *Walking with Shadows*, created a gay African character who is sharply critical of the promiscuity and thoughtlessness of European gays. South African Sello Duiker's gay black sex worker comes to reflect upon the poverty and injustices faced by illegal African migrants in Johannesburg. Calixthe Beyala (Cameroon) and Monica Arac de Nyeko (Uganda) in their stories portray young African women whose love of other women provides a means for the authors to critique abusive mothers and cruelly gossipy neighbours. The black homosexual character in Tendai Huchu's *The Hairdresser of Harare* shines a powerful critical light on the hypocrisy and greed of the black nouveau riche in the post-land-grab era of Zimbabwe. It is difficult to keep up with the burgeoning literature.

That said, it is true that Africans have to this point mostly left the field of scientific research open to domination by non-Africans. But this is not entirely due to lack of interest or a blanket homophobia among African scientists. Rather, it is because open-minded individuals in African research institutions face very significant structural barriers to the research. To put it bluntly, focusing on same-sex issues has not been a wise career move for young scholars in most African countries, nor even possible given resource constraints. Even in South Africa, the prevailing intellectual and political environment has long been and remains for the most part openly sceptical of or hostile to homosexuality as a 'frivolous' (or worse) research topic, the kiss of death to the career aspirations. In such an environment those bold enough to take on the topic also face difficulties in gaining access to the international scholarship needed to frame the research questions without appearing hopelessly naive. This may not always be the result of institutional homophobia, per se, but rather choices made in the face of very tight library budgets.

Subscribe to the *Journal of African History* or to the *Journal of Homosexuality*? Purchase an expensive imported volume by Judith Butler or several copies of locally published Frantz Fanon? Employ faculty to elucidate queer theory and French cultural criticism or find people to teach remedial maths and the basic history of your own country? Young African researchers in such circumstances can be forgiven if they have been relatively slow to realize that links exist, needing careful exploration, between same-sex sexuality and the many other questions relating to the distribution and exercise of power in society.

Yet that situation too is changing rapidly, powered not only by a growing appreciation of the strengths of the arguments in favour of more research, but also by Google. 'Google is our friend' could be the motto of African sexuality researchers and lgbti individuals alike. Much of their research is still in the form of unpublished dissertations and conference papers, or appears in specialized journals and reports. But it is getting hard to ignore, unfolding as it is in tandem with African lgbti activists, artists, memoirists and bloggers whose voices are getting into the public domain as never before (Ekine and Abbas 2013, Tamale 2011, Awondo 2011, Semugoma et al. 2012, among many examples). As I will discuss in Chapter 5, the prominent role of Africans in authoring key documents addressed to the international community is especially noteworthy (UN 2011b and Global Commission on HIV and the Law 2012, for example). Their main points – that sexual rights are human rights and that Africans are human – are fully consistent with theorization of human rights and African belief systems by African philosophers like Kwame Appiah and Fabien Eboussi Boulaga, and indeed with the writings on gender and women's emancipation by African revolutionaries like Samora Machel, Thomas Sankara and Desmond Tutu. The argument that the sexual rights agenda is being driven by whites only, without legs to stand on in African political philosophy, does not hold much water.

To be sure, the number of African lgbti and allies stepping out explicitly to claim rights for sexual minorities sometimes makes this a difficult point to argue. Gays and Lesbians of Zimbabwe (GALZ) used to debate this question itself. At the time I joined in the late 1990s, GALZ had about three hundred members out of a national population of 12 million. Did they want to tell people how few they actually were? Would that not only make it easier for GALZ's enemies to dismiss it as irrelevant? Rather than weight of numbers to make their case, therefore, GALZ opted to stress the weight of political principle. In a democracy, injustice against even one person is as wrong in principle and as poisonous to the body politic as injustice against a thousand or a million. If the rights of that one person can be protected, therefore, however much the majority population may disapprove of his or her political beliefs (or faith, or colour of skin, or choice of sexual partners), then the rights of the majority population will also be strengthened against all potential abuses of power.

This may sound a bit like Western political theory and idealistic concepts of liberal democracy. However, it is quite consistent with *Ubuntu*, or African humanism. Harm or injustice done against one community member is an affront to the ancestors, through whom the harm may be passed on to the community of the living and even generations to come. Unless one believes that lgbti are inherently and irrevocably outside of the community, then the whole community gains strength and dignity by respecting their humanity, a topic to which I will return in the next chapter with reference to witches, avenging spirits and djinns.

It is also the case that discrimination against lgbti people is linked to, and reinforces, other historical forms of intolerance, as the African authors I noted above quite pointedly show. Perhaps most commonly, homophobia intensifies the contempt and discrimination that underpin sexism and xenophobia. Who has not heard foreigners being accused of spreading homosexuality in order to inflame public opinion against them for other reasons (stealing our jobs, for example)? Who has not heard of straight women being accused of lesbianism simply because they spoke out against male chauvinism, or straight men called faggots, wussies and wives when they did not exercise decisive power over women? Homophobia in this sense shores up a repressive heteropatriarchal masculinity that constitutes a far more direct threat to the well-being of straight African boys than any putative foreign homosexual recruitment drives. This is especially evident when traditional, relatively complex expectations of masculine honour are abandoned in favour of a stripped-down version of modern (hip, cool, fly-ass, bad, etc.) masculinity that is primarily defined by obligation to penetrate, irrespective of consent or even the identity of the one penetrated (infant, granny, boy). Indeed, some men will preserve their self-image as 'real men' by raping young boys cast in an effeminate role.

Homophobic insults and rape in these cases act as amplifiers for other hatreds whose violence tears through the majority population in tragic ways. To take a stand against homophobia is thus to take a stand for all people who suffer from discrimination or violence on other grounds, including by gender, ethnicity and nationality, *but also by class and poverty*. The decision of the South African Constitutional Court in 1998 to decriminalize sodomy remains one of the clearest articulations of this view. The homophobic perspective that underlay the old law against sodomy, it concluded, 'gives rise to a wide variety of other discriminations, which collectively unfairly prevent a fair distribution of social goods and services'.

An intriguing expression of this sophisticated view has recently come from a somewhat unexpected source, the government of Rwanda. In the late 2000s, Rwanda seemed to be moving in the direction of its most homophobic neighbours by proposing harsh new laws to criminalize homosexuality. Yet in 2010, it suddenly switched course – a PhD project awaits for someone to unravel the influences that were at play here: the memory of genocide, the very high number of women in Rwanda's parliament, the influence of public health officials, a cynical move by an authoritarian regime to deflect criticism from former allies in the West? We do not yet understand quite why, but it began during the United Nations General Assembly debate on whether to include sexual orientation as an explicit category deserving protection from human rights violations. That category had been included in Human Rights Commission documents since 1994, but it was removed by a narrow majority vote in 2009 in a vote spearheaded by Egypt and supported by most of the voting African countries, including Rwanda. During the debate on restoration of the clause, the Rwandan delegate first acknowledged that sexual orientation was a sensitive and 'personal' topic. But he then urged the General Assembly to recognize that sexual orientation was indeed a factor in torture and extrajudicial killing in some parts of the world. As such it should be explicitly named and condemned. It was necessary to deal with the urgency of those matters whether their lifestyles were approved of or not, said the delegate. Recognizing that was not a call for special rights – the right to life should not be refused for legal, ideological or political reasons. Doing so was 'hiding our heads in the sand', he said.

In 2011, Rwanda even spoke against South Africa's initiative to broker a compromise on the topic in the UN Human Rights Commission. South Africa had suggested that a definition of sexual orientation be developed that everyone could safely agree upon (that is, to be honest, couched in such banal language that it would be easy to ignore). Rwanda came out against such a diplomatic dodge. It maintained that the experience of genocide had taught Rwandans that any attempt to define minorities legal-istically is a slippery slope to disaster. This then seemed to give the South African government the courage of its convictions. It dropped its attempted compromise position and co-sponsored the ultimately successful resolution to restore the sexual orientation clause without any cluttering definitions or convenient loopholes.

Admittedly, principled argument remains a risky strategy to advance sexual minority rights. The UN resolution (A/HRC/17/L.9/Rev.1) was an important symbolic achievement but is almost certain to be offset by language elsewhere that uses deliberately vague terms and is open to wildly different interpretations. The African Charter statement on ending gender discrimination is a prime example. It uses the word 'normal' to qualify what kind of family the member states are obliged to protect. Who gets to define 'normal'? Similarly, the Charter almost seems to invite states to ignore its own recommendations on ending discrimination against women and children: 'The State shall have the duty to assist the family which is the custodian of morals and traditional values recognized by the community' (Article 19/2). In a place like Nigeria, with hundreds of ethnic groups, languages, religions and discrete traditional values, who gets to define 'the community'? And what exactly do 'positive' and 'moral' mean in Article 29/7 when it says that every individual should 'preserve and strengthen positive African cultural values in his [sic] relations with other members of the society, in the spirit of tolerance, dialogue and consultation and, in general, to contribute to the promotion of the moral well-being of society'?

When principled argument stumbles over definitions, it can help to return to numbers to convince people that sexual minorities do indeed fall within a reasonable understanding of 'normal', 'traditional' and 'community', and that rights for sexual minorities can benefit the majority population. This can be done by shifting focus from the small groups of out lgbti to the much larger population of hidden msm, wsw and trans people who 'pass' for the opposite sex, and others who use traditional idioms to stay out of the limelight. Early studies suggest that this hidden population is having a much bigger impact on the HIV/AIDS pandemic than previously ever imagined. The government of Kenya, for example, recently estimated that as many as 15 per cent of all new HIV infections can be traced to msm, while the World Bank puts that number as high as 20 per cent in the case of Senegal's co-epidemics (HIV-1 and 2). One in five is no longer a diversionary issue. Moreover, these new infections are not concentrated among the elites, as many people assume based on a common stereotype of gays. Rather, the people most at risk from male–male transmission of HIV are those who have no access to education about the risks, and who are most vulnerable to rape, transactional sex and pressure not to request condom use. Obviously that includes males taking the bottom or 'wife' role in a sexual relationship. But it also includes street children and prisoners who may be incarcerated for any number of unjust reasons in countries where police prey on the weak. It includes as well the female wives and loving girlfriends of men who have unprotected sex with men without disclosing those relationships.

Presenting the issue this way is highly problematic from an erotic justice perspective. It could easily backfire to create a witch-hunt effect and drive msm even deeper into secrecy. But it does pack a punch. Instead of a few dozen or hundred people in a country of millions, we are now talking hundreds of thousands. We are also talking about 'innocent victims' of infection – men and boys falsely accused of crimes or arrested for failing to pay a bribe and then thrown into hellish jail cells tend to be more sympathetically regarded than out gays. Even more so are the wives, girlfriends and even children (indirectly through birth or breastfeeding from their infected mothers). Homophobes may not have a problem interpreting the human rights principles to exclude lgbti. It takes a remarkably callous person, however, to dismiss high numbers of women and children unwittingly infected by their husbands, boyfriends and fathers who pick up HIV or other sexually transmitted infections through unprotected homosexual intercourse.

Sexual rights for sexual minorities would reduce the fears that drive msm underground and prevent or inhibit effective (honest) sexuality education. They would enable prevention and treatment interventions that would protect both the men themselves and their female partners. As has been the case in China, the public health or harm reduction argument has been increasingly successful in recent years in the task of bringing pragmatists on board. We can also see it in the quiet adoption of programmes directed at msm in countries where homosexual acts remain illegal. Unfortunately, bringing these kinds of numbers into play also raises new worries. Who are all these men infecting men *and* women, why are there so many of them? How can we catch them and stop them from endangering the worthy majority? This anxiety is often expressed as 'These people were not there before so where exactly are they coming from?'

As with doubts about the relevance of sexuality research to Africa's developmental needs, this question too needs to be addressed before the anxiety can be exploited to justify intensified surveillance and repression. Theories developed in the West can help in this goal, not by suggesting a path that African researchers and activists must follow in order to catch up, but by providing us with concepts that help us to know where to look, what to look for, and how to interpret what we find (or do not find!). The following section provides a short cut into that often very dense theory, highlighting important commonalities between the Western scholarly canon and African ways of knowing. It asks, how might aspects of that canon be useful for researching and writing about the history of sexualities in Africa that can be applied to the broad justice project?

§

For sexual rights activists in Africa, the question 'Where does homosexuality in Africa really come from?' can be maddening. Same-sex sexuality and the problems that accompany it are now clear and present in Africa no matter when or where they came from. So deal with them. Find the msm and educate them on how to protect themselves and their partners. Provide condoms, water-based gel and counselling services. Protest against the homophobic laws that drive lgbti underground and into self-harming behaviours. Fix the curriculum so that people will know that anal sex is riskier than vaginal sex. Lobby to have sexual orientation included in the bill of rights or national constitutions. Do the research needed to find out about specific local practices, secret languages and other knowledge that is needed to design culturally sensitive public health and other policy interventions that will bring down the rates of disease, gender-based violence, extortion and other associated ills and injustices. And so on, all the while recalling that policies based on denial, repression and heterosexist definitions of 'traditional values', 'positive', 'moral', 'normal' and 'community' tend to fuel the very problems which they claim to eliminate.

The question where does homosexuality in Africa really come from is in fact often posed precisely as a way to avoid these choices. It says, if we only knew the exact origins of homosexuality in Africa, then we could design responses that will effectively contain or eliminate it. If it comes from an absence of faith (or presence of the Devil), then prayer and religious discipline and fellowship are called for. Maybe it's an addiction and, if so, twelve-step recovery programmes should help. If it comes from either poverty (necessitating prostitution) or wealth (giving some people excessive leisure time) then a healthy dash of socialism should probably fix it. If it comes from bad parenting (absent or abusive fathers, over-indulgent mothers, for example) then perhaps the state can design and mandate good parenting courses. If it stems from people's disappointment in the opposite sex then maybe the opposite sex needs a lesson in how to behave (for example, raping lesbians to make them appreciate the penis). If it comes from simple ignorance about the dangers of deviation from the heterosexual ideal, then scaring young people with lurid stories of gay diseases, self-loathing and eating excrement should convince them to keep straight. Unfortunately, I am not exaggerating positions that have been expressed to me personally by opponents of sexual minority rights.

In my experience, people who ask this question almost invariably expect a certain general answer – 'from away'. Something that is socially and morally disapproved *must* come from away to contaminate the nation, tribe, family, faith or continent. In this Africans are hardly different to people anywhere else. In ancient times the Romans blamed the Greeks. Later, Christians blamed Muslims, Protestants blamed Catholics, the British blamed the Portuguese, the Japanese blamed the Chinese, the Arabs blamed the Persians, and so on and on. Africans tend to tell me that Europeans or Arabs are the main source of the problem in Africa, perhaps specifying 'the North' or 'the coast' in reference to Muslim-dominated parts of Nigeria, Sudan and Kenya. One highly respected Senegalese historian was even more specific. Cheikh anta Diop not only named where 'sodomy' in black Africa came from (Morocco). He even placed a precise date on this momentous event – 13 March 1591, the day the Moroccans invaded and destroyed the Songhai empire in what is now Mali.

My reply to this question, therefore, tends to spark a heartily incredulous laugh. Homosexuality comes from Africa.

If we understand homosexuality without reference to cultural stereotypes from some away place but rather simply as erotic desire and practices between people of the same sex, then it is obviously part of human nature. Indeed, same-sex behaviour is abundantly evident in many other species of animal, so clearly nature has no problem with it. Since human nature originated in Africa, we can logically conclude that modern humans from Africa introduced homosexuality (in the above sense) wherever they migrated all those tens of thousands of years ago – to Europe, Asia, the Americas, the Pacific Islands and, of course, back to and throughout Africa as humans peopled the continent. Some of the oldest known depictions of or references to same-sex sexuality in the world come from Africa, including from cave paintings of at least two thousand years old in Zimbabwe, and in Egyptian myths and written histories. There is a reference to a love affair between Pharaoh Pepi II and his top general from over four thousand years ago, notably, while the *Book of the Dead* (a collection of prayers, spells and priestly confessions written down over three millennia ago) contains clear references to man–boy sex, something shameful, it implies, but something known to happen.

That homosexuality comes from Africa may be a good ice-breaker but it does not really get me too far with sceptics. People will often accept the human nature argument, and allow for the fact that not all Africans in the past conformed to heterosexual ideals, all the time. However, they will also correctly observe that Africans in the past did not identify themselves as homosexuals on the basis of their individual sexual orientation and that they do now. Hence homosexuals in the above sense must have come from somewhere or be copying people from somewhere else. People will also correctly observe that there are more such people with a high public visibility in the West, and that the language and demeanour of many Africans who today identify as homosexual appears to conform to Western models, ergo ... A further common misconception in this line of thinking is that the public visibility and social tolerance towards lgbti that we see in the West today have always been there, rather than being (as they are) a relatively recent phenomenon.

Another way to answer the question of where homosexuality comes from therefore is to focus not on same-sex desire and practice but on the word now so widely used to describe these. The answer in that case is 'Germany', and the scholar most responsible for reconstructing its history is Michel Foucault. The outlines of that history – and the questions it raises – can be useful for the search for answers in Africa. As a starter, it is critical to recall that the West was not always 'gay friendly'. Foucault noted that the word *Homosexualität* did not exist prior to its invention in 1869 by a German/Hungarian translator, Karl Maria Kertbeny. Kertbeny was lobbying the then government to drop its law criminalizing sex between men. Such men had hitherto be known as sodomites, nancy boys, Millies and any number of other derogatory terms reflecting the terrible stigma attached to them by Church and society. Kertbeny hoped to take some of that stigma away with a word that shifted the emphasis from sinful choice or criminal act to a natural condition for which individuals could not be blamed. The word homosexuality was later picked up by Richard von Krafft-Ebing, the author of an influential encyclopaedia who has been called the 'father' of sexology. It then migrated into French and English as a scientific term around 1907, in competition for acceptance with other scientific-sounding terms like Urning, Uranist and invert.

Sexology itself was a new academic discipline in the late nineteenth century whereby scholars like Krafft-Ebing devoted themselves to the study of sex following more or less scientific principles. This had never happened before. Of course, there had been lots of observation, philosophical debate and legal opinion about sex, but until the late nineteenth century sex remained deeply mysterious and difficult to talk about without creating scandal. That sexology appeared as a discipline at the same time as the great age of European imperialism is no coincidence. Europeans at that time were discovering new peoples with sexual relationships and customs that differed sometimes quite radically from their own. Things that were once taken for granted as natural, normal and universal were suddenly seen to vary according to race or culture or climate ... who knew exactly what combination determined these matters? It begged for disciplined research to find out.

Sexology, and subsequently anthropology and ethnopsychiatry, also offered a means to apply knowledge about non-European peoples back home in Europe. That goal for some researchers was quite clear. They were not so much interested in non-Europeans per se but rather wondered how the new knowledge of other cultures could be used to fix problems related to sexual and related forms of repression in Europe. For example, in the 1920s German scholars found evidence among so-called primitive people in Namibia and Angola which they used to argue against the then widespread belief in Germany that homosexuality was caused by cultural decadence or 'over-civilization', especially among Jews hiding in the body politic. The belief that such decadence weakened the German nation was exploited by fascist politicians to promote their cult of militarism and racism – that is, to re-discipline German men so they could become the vanguard of a virile world master race. For opponents of fascism like Kurt Falk, Bushmen who masturbated each other offered a proof, of sorts, that Hitler and company were wrong.

To give another example, Marie Bonaparte was an influential French psychiatrist in the 1930s who believed that African women were sexually more satisfied and hence emotionally more stable than European women. Why? Because they practised clitoridectomy – the ritual cutting or even complete removal of the clitoris. This operation supposedly reduced the destabilizing effect of uncontrolled female desire emanating from the clitoris, hence allowing mature African women to be sexually satisfied through penetration and impregnation by their husbands (no other stimulation necessary). So strongly did Bonaparte believe and advocate for this that she had the operation herself. The political implications were to relieve some public pressure on colonial states to repress clitoridectomy in Africa, a delicate matter, and to undermine feminists in Europe who wanted more not less sexual rights and pleasure.

Over the decades, many other scholars and clinicians put forward their own pet theories on what causes people to desire as they do. Big arguments took place between those who saw desire for same-sex partners as innate or inborn, and those who believed it was largely socially determined or dependent upon circumstances. The work of Sigmund Freud was particularly influential in promoting a non-stigmatizing meaning of homosexuality. His enduring psychiatric approach held that every human was born with the capacity to be sexually and emotionally responsive to touch by any other human, male or female, father or mother, sister or brother. This 'polymorphous perversity' lingered through infancy but in most people withered away with maturity. The important point was that every human has the potential to feel adult sexual attraction to the same sex. Whatever specific factors led them to fulfil that desire, the main issue from a psychiatric point of view was how to help homosexuals live a life of self-esteem in a society that for the most part judged them harshly and often led them to self-hating or self-destructive behaviour.

The real bombshell in changing attitudes in the West, however, was the research of Alfred Kinsey and team in the late 1940s. Kinsey was a bug scientist by training, and looked neither to complicated psychological explanations nor to dubious anthropological research from faraway places to make his points. Rather, to be blunt, he applied his bug-counting methods to the study of humans. In so doing he and his team created the first ever detailed, methodical study of human sexual practices. The results came as a big surprise to almost everyone. Indeed, Americans were shocked to learn what other Americans were actually doing in bed, as opposed to what they were supposed to be doing by the standards of respectable morality. Kinsey's report showed that homosexual experiences were much more common than previously assumed. It popularized the word homosexuality in the United States as a generation of novelists like Gore Vidal began to identify themselves and characters in their work using the term.

Kinsey in that way laid the basis for a radical change in American attitudes and, eventually (and unevenly), to changes in the policies and laws governing sexual relationships. It's a classic case of research opening the doors to new ways of thinking about ourselves and our fellow citizens, which in turn makes it possible for politicians to advocate for changes in public morality.

This is not to suggest a straightforward progression from knowledge or naming to rights. On the contrary, every step forward was met by resistance. In Kertbeny's time, some intellectuals and state officials seized upon the notion of homosexuality as a condition that posed a greater danger to society than could be contained by the Church or public shaming of discrete sins. Effeminate men ('fops'), notably, who may have been fine as aristocratic horsemen in the past, were reconstituted as a weak link in national defence, poor leaders and soldiers for mass industrial-scale warfare. Lesbians were presumed to betray the population-building ethic needed to sustain the nation against its enemies. Those errant individuals therefore had to be understood and controlled more effectively, nowhere more violently than in Germany under the Nazi regime.

Violence, of course, was only one path to resisting the liberal intentions of thinkers like Kertbeny and Freud. They were also contested in the realm of scientific debate, and over time homophobic interpretations of science set the terms of reference that came to be understood as 'common sense'. As Marxist intellectual Antonio Gramsci described, and as Foucault elaborated with his concept of governmentality, common sense in fact conditions us to accept being bossed around and exploited as part of an inevitable, desirable or natural state of affairs. In this case, the science convinced us that nature abhorred homosexuality and it was labelled a mental disorder. The Cold War era was particularly harsh in overdetermining homophobia (meaning multiple layers of mutually supportive confirmation or discipline – Freud, *encore*). Tellingly, the word to describe fear and hatred of homosexuals comes from that period of confrontation between the United States and allies and the Soviet Union and allies. 'Homophobia' was coined by an American psychotherapist in 1971, just about a century after the object of its fear and hatred had been invented.

That context of pervasive homophobia – overdetermined by science, by law, by art, by social attitudes, by faith, by fear of communism – is critical to understanding what came next. Gay liberation in the 1970s required not just some tinkering with the law or staid academic studies. For a minority of committed activists, it demanded the revolutionary overthrow of homophobic bourgeois notions of sexual propriety, including such notions as internalized by lgbti themselves. The feminist insight that the personal is political then gave rise to the often ribald and raucous 'gay lifestyle' and 'gay ghettoes' that now so appal anti-homosexuality campaigners in Africa.

The main lesson we can take from this history is that language and imagery (or discourse, in Foucault's famous term) comprise a subtle form or partially hidden archaeology of power by which people shape the unfolding of events. Unlike a bullet, discourse can be subverted and negotiated by the people at whom it is aimed. In that process new expressions of power are generated over time, albeit in often unseen and unpredictable ways. Indeed, the ultimate results of a certain discourse may not match the original intentions at all. Among the big ironies in this case are that a term invented with a liberating ethic in mind became part of the language of control and repression, but, in turn, 'the homosexual' went on to became a source of self-awareness and eventually of political mobilization to achieve gay rights. That mobilization was remarkably successful in many ways. It also, as many gay liberation activists quickly recognized in the early 1980s, fuelled the spread of a terrible new disease.

Let me mention just two more Western theorists whose work is potentially useful for the task of unravelling secrets in African history. Eve Kosofsky Sedgwick's major contribution was to distinguish between homosexuality and homo*sociality*. She showed how a culture (English in her case) governs the need for men to be together in very close and emotionally intimate contact without becoming involved sexually. Sexual relations in the military would have been especially destabilizing to the mission, or so it was assumed. The term homo*erotic* also establishes an important nuance in meaning by describing something that represents or evokes same-sex desire without implying physical consummation of that desire. A key point here is that a set of social rules was developed that allowed men to be together, to touch each other, to admire each other's bodies or sexual exploits with women, and to share the most intimate feelings *without* becoming sexual with each other. Yet those same rules also enable some men secretly to be sexual with each other without anyone suspecting. When those rules break down, and when secretive homosexuality becomes known, intensified homophobia is required to enforce homosocial institutions.

Homosociality is an extremely important concept for Africa given how much men's and boys' lives take place in separate spheres from women's and girls'. The tension it generates between the sexes is perhaps one of the most common tropes in African literature. It may also explain some of the intensity of anger often expressed against African lgbti who come out, who rock the homosocial boat, as it were. Indeed, non-Africans are often surprised to observe a degree of physical intimacy between boys or men which would raise eyebrows in England or Japan: hugging, holding hands, even kissing. The short stories of Tatamkhulu Afrika allude to as much quite strongly. In 'The Quarry', for example, two men develop a close friendship, work out together, shower together and even share a bed with female prostitutes, all the while thinking of themselves as heterosexual. But when one reveals that he had a homosexual relationship in prison, the other becomes extremely violent towards him – in fact, rapes him. Is the rape repressed homoerotic desire or is it homophobic hatred by a man whose trust in a homosocial space/relationship has been shaken? Or are these two sides of the same coin?

Finally, American philosopher Judith Butler has been enormously influential in terms of our understanding of the complicated relationship between gender, sexuality and sexual orientation. Basically she argued that we cannot assume a direct and natural relationship between these distinct aspects of human character. We cannot, for example, assume that a male body leads naturally to a masculine or manly gender identity and a heterosexual orientation. Similarly, there is no direct and natural relationship between possessing a female body, identifying and behaving as feminine or womanly, and feeling sexual desire for men. Those discrete relationships have to be learned, and constantly relearned through repetitive performance and public ritual. Without such performance and ritual, human nature would presumably re-assert itself with a dizzying diversity of combinations of physical bodies, gender roles and sexual desire. Since the performance of 'heteronormativity' supports a status quo that is patriarchal – that is, oppressive to women and sexual minorities – to subvert the categories of normal is to perform a revolutionary act.

Why are these Western theorists pertinent to current debates in Africa? Certainly not to establish our credentials as in-the-know. Rather, pioneering studies done in the West on same-sex sexuality can help us to frame the questions, to suggest potentially fruitful places to look for answers, and to be able to read between the lines of strategic silences and blind spots in public discourse. Freud, Kinsey, Foucault, Butler, Sedgwick and other Western theorists of sexuality can also help us, as critics of homophobias in Africa, to understand and perhaps be a bit sympathetic to those Africans who worry that increasing knowledge about sexual minorities will result in an increase of people who come out as lgbti, with a rise as well in the kinds of conflict that accompany greater visibility of a controversial issue. When a silence is broken, even to denounce the hitherto unspoken, it creates a space for curious people to find out more, and to demand more. As fear of ostracism, public shaming, loss of employment, extortion and violence is diminished, the number of people who choose to live openly as lgbti will almost certainly rise. When education and emotional support are provided to youth who feel confused about their sexuality, some will come to realize that they feel like, and wish to be known as, lgbti rather than simply bowing to societal and family expectations. Greater visibility of homosexuality, however, will also place pressure on homosocial spaces, potentially to fuel homophobic rhetoric to police those spaces, with all the hatred of foreigners and feminists that commonly accompanies such rhetoric. Historical experience in the West shows that these are legitimate anxieties.

If we acknowledge the risk, Western scholarship on same-sex sexuality can also reassure on at least two grounds. First, not-withstanding Butler or others on the fluidity of human desire, increased numbers of out lgbti are unlikely ever to be very big, especially when seen against the numbers of same-sex-practising people who currently live out their desires secretively and at heightened risk. Perhaps a few more heterosexual people will experiment with homosexual relationships, bicuriously, as they say. However, abundant evidence from places in the world where sexual minority rights are more or less established shows quite clearly that sexual minorities will always be minorities. Exhaustive studies on sexuality in the USA in the 1990s and 2000s actually put the numbers of exclusively or predominantly homosexual males down in comparison to Kinsey's 1940s and 1950s estimates (from 10 to 6 per cent of the total population; in these studies exclusively or predominantly lesbian females also dropped as a percentage of the total population from 9 to 5). Such a small minority poses no danger to population growth, and indeed, North America has a higher birth rate than Russia, Italy or Poland. Israel, with more or less fully realized legal equality for sexual minorities, has a higher fertility rate than Iran, which has none. The history of 'the gay lifestyle' and 'gay ghettoes' that brought HIV/AIDS into the public eye might also be reassuring at a certain level. It reveals that lifestyle to be a minority phenomenon among same-sex-practising people in a very specific period of time. It grew out of a social and political context characterized by pervasive homophobia. In a different context – for example, where monogamous same-sex relationships are legal and can be publicly celebrated or where extended family continues to be honoured as a social good – lifestyles (and political activism) will follow different paths.

Western theorists of sexuality do tend to use a highly special-ized language to make their points, and can be off-putting for it. Yet when you listen carefully, what they are saying is not so different from what most Africans probably know and value in-tuitively. Take Butler, for example: we are who we are by relating to, being seen by and being judged by other people. Our sense of personhood is intimately tied to and constantly renewed through the ways we ritually mark it through performance before other people. Sounds a lot like *Ubuntu* to me. Indeed, when we listen to what indigenous African theories say about where homosexuality in Africa comes from, we find that the language may be different but the meaning is surprisingly close to what the scientists and queer theorists in the West have to say. Let me conclude this chapter with three brief points to illustrate.

First, African lgbti people themselves are virtually unanimous in testifying that their sexual orientation and gender identities are inherent. Memories of feeling different from other boys and girls, and of unhappiness with how they were supposed to behave as normal children, often go back to long before puberty and independently of any social or sexual experience. Such feelings also go back to before they knew any words that explained the difference. A strikingly common theme in writing by African lgbti is that they fell in love or had sexual infatuations with people of the same sex first, and only second, sometimes many years later, did they learn that there were words to explain such desires. Learning those words brought peace of mind, self-esteem and self-confidence in standing up in public, but it did not bring the desire to begin with.

Secondly, African grandparents of lgbti also often say the very same thing and even express relief when grandchildren (especially) finally come out (that is, realize the obvious). Nor is this a new thing. I have written before about the story of Maggie and her father in 1920s Zimbabwe ('I have never noticed anything peculiar about [him], I have always thought him sound in his mind ... My son has been wearing dresses ever since he was a baby'), but let me also recall *After Nines!*, a remarkable play performed in Johannesburg in 1998. Yes, I know it's just a play, it's not 'real'. But the script was based on a serious oral history project conducted in the city's townships. One of the central findings of the research and a strong theme of the play was that the grandparents of today's young black gays and lesbians were more understanding of their predicament than parents and siblings, for whom homophobia had become the norm.

Where do such feelings and behaviours come from? Many of the published coming-out stories describe scenarios and use language that sound 'Western' or modern and individualized – boarding school infatuations, initiation by older relatives or mentors, urban settings, or simply, as Kenyan 'Kamau' put it in an interview with Stephen O. Murray, 'a feeling within me' (Murray 1998). Traditional African religions also provide several explanations. I am going to look at these in the next chapter, but here I want to highlight one of the most common. Once again it sounds intriguingly familiar in terms of the science discussed above, although instead of genes and hormones, it says spirits and, in particular, the spirits of ancestors of the opposite sex. When people die they don't go to heaven or hell or simply turn to dust. Rather, like genes and hormones, they may be invisible but they remain active in the world of the living. They watch us, play with us, reward us, get angry with us, and even exploit us for their own needs. Like genes and hormones, they also direct us to seek sexual satisfaction. Yet since they have no physical bodies of their own they must enjoy that satisfaction vicariously through the living. If a male ancestor happens to occupy the body of a woman, would he enjoy her having sex with a man? If he is an ancestor that means by definition he had children, and perhaps many female wives. He is surely not going to be pleased if the body he inhabits in this world has sex with a man. He will influence her to have sex with a woman of his desire, befitting his nature as a heterosexually virile spirit.

Traditional African religion contains much that is worrisome from a scientific and human rights perspective. On this issue, however, when one looks past the language of spirits and possession or embodiment, there is strong compatability between them. No one has yet expressed that as clearly as Nkunzi Nkabinde in her remarkable memoir of 'my life as a lesbian sangoma [traditional healer among the Zulu people of South Africa]'. My final point, then, is to quickly recount her story.

Nkabinde first realized she was attracted to girls without being able to name that desire. She came to understand herself as a lesbian through an experience of seduction by an older professional woman, through exposure to gay pornography and literature from the West, and through growing involvement in gay rights activism. In other words, she seemed to have followed the supposedly Western road of recruitment and gay identity migration. Only later did she come to relate her sexual orientation to the will of her powerful male ancestor, Nkunzi or 'Black Bull'. His unpredictable presence required discipline and training to control, including in his choice of lovers. But in learning to control him Nkabinde gained self-confidence and insight into both her own and other people's characters. That made her a better *sangoma*, able to provide healing and comfort to the people of her community. Learning to understand her ancestor also made her a proud citizen of her nation and an astute witness to the complexity of the human spirit. In her own words:

> Each of my different roles, as a Zulu woman, as a lesbian and as a sangoma, comes with its own challenges. Working at Constitution Hill gives me a high view. I can stand with my back to our apartheid history which is still alive in the Old Fort and the Women's Prison and see the Constitutional Court and be reminded of all that is good in our country; and I can stand on top of the hill outside the Constitutional Court and get an overview of Johannesburg. I can see the good and bad of the city. This is what I try to do when I think about my own life. I try to take a look from a high place and see the good and the bad

... And sometimes I become emotional or even cry and people don't expect me to be emotional. I have a serious side and a side that smiles. I have a male side and a female side. I have a traditional side and a modern side ... My life is not only for me, it is also for my ancestor, Nkunzi. (Nkabinde 2008: 150, 156)

Can modern and traditional be reconciled in other contexts and by less self-assured individuals than Nkabinde? That is the question I would like to take up in the next chapter, with a focus on religion.

3 | Faiths

Africa has three main groups of faiths: traditional or ancestral, Christianity and Islam. I put it this way because the diversity within these broad groups is so great that the word religion (singular) can be misleading. There may be more in shared practice between Roman Catholics and ancestral religions than between the Catholics and their fellow Christians, the evangelicals. Similarly, some forms of Islam in Africa are quite comfortable with many traditional practices and beliefs, to the extent that African Muslims have been frequent targets of war on doctrinal grounds on the part of fellow Muslims. Traditional, meanwhile, is often mistakenly thought to mean unchanging and simple. In fact traditions are in constant flux. Some are forgotten or renegotiated and new ones get invented as people move around, as the political and material conditions of society change, and as younger generations interpret old customs to be meaningful in their differing circumstances.

Many scholars have commented on the fluidity of belief systems in Africa, and have used the word 'syncretic' to describe some of the unusual combinations of faiths or religious imagery and practice that one can find throughout the continent (syncretic meaning dynamically mixing, non-dogmatic, adaptive, augmentative, improvisational). Such syncretism is made possible in part because of a common philosophical thread that wends its way through the huge variety of local beliefs. That common thread goes by several terms but *Ubuntu* and African humanism are among the most widely used. Their meaning is best captured in the aphorism 'I am who I am as a consequence of my relationships with other people'. I will be considering what exactly that might mean for the struggle for lgbti rights. For now let me just say that many African lgbti, just as has often been said of Africans as a whole, are proudly, happily and deeply religious within the spirit of *Ubuntu*. This religiosity often strikes secular activists and scholars from the West as surprising, not least given how religious leaders are commonly at the forefront of whipping up homophobic hatred: homosexuality is 'against African traditions', is 'unIslamic' and 'unbiblical', in the milder language. How to explain that apparent contradiction, and how to harness Africans' religiosity to the project of combating homophobia (and other repressive ideas on gender and sexuality, stigma against people living with HIV, or opposition to condoms and sexuality education)?

In this chapter, I want to examine how the different groups of faiths have explained and dealt with sexual difference in the past. My reading of key texts and the historical record suggests that they do not provide anywhere near the kind of clear and consistent condemnations of homosexuality that are so often made by some of today's religious leaders. On the contrary, all three groups of faiths in Africa have historically been and remain more amenable to accepting sexual difference than is generally understood. Religious literalists or fundamentalists will never be convinced of that, I quite realize. But I do believe that it can be empowering to sexual rights activists in Africa to know precisely how opponents of sexual minority rights select their arguments and ignore or deny 'gay-friendly' elements of key texts. Those elements could potentially be harnessed as a source of emotional strength, community- or network-building, and even physical health in the face of the demoralizing impacts of HIV.

A second point I want to underscore here is that overemphasizing the homophobia (and sexism) in African religions, and constructing faith unambiguously as an enemy of progress, creates a further danger. It contributes to the impasse between people on the extremes of the debate, and closes down some of the community-building, humanistic potential of those faiths. Such an overemphasis can feed into a 'homonationalist' or 'homopatriotic' narrative of Western superiority over African backwardness, an unwarranted and unhelpful arrogance. A better understanding of African faiths and culture is thus crucial for activists in the

West who wish to show solidarity with African lgbti who draw strength from faith and culture, and to counter that strand of homonationalism in Western writing and activism.

Let me begin in this chapter with a focus on the foundations of *Ubuntu* upon which traditional religions stand, and consideration of some of the ways that Africans explained, contained and in some cases honoured sexual difference within the rubric of custom and family.

Traditional religions

Religions give people a way to understand their place in the universe. They provide a guide to achieving harmonious relations between people, and a moral framework to manage or cope with the material world, including the natural environment and individuals' own physical health. Traditional religions among the dominant agriculturalist and pastoralist peoples in Africa were an expression of these complex needs. They developed over many centuries as those peoples migrated to settle in and adapt to new, often very challenging environments. Indeed, the bottom line in Africa is that nature does not make life easy for farmers and herders of domestic animals. As a result, until very recently the continent remained sparsely populated with dangers and disaster for humans apparent at any time. Even in a land with one of the most predictable climates and the most fertile soil in the world, Egypt, the fragility of human habitation and civilization was there for a child to see. Without the annual flooding of the Nile, the starkest desert and death threatened settled life. Africa's oldest documented religion had at its heart the pragmatic goal of ensuring that flooding and the fertility of the land continued without interruption, and hence assured the survival of the people who lived there.

Throughout Africa, myths, symbols, gods, spirits, fetishes, monuments, potions, spells, zombies, witches, priests, healers, diviners, cutters, rituals, prayers, incantations, masks, drummers, sacrifices, ghosts, feasts, fasts, shrines, 'divine kings', mysteries, mermaids, the evil eye, dancers, and more, all emerged over time in often remarkably accommodating combinations with each other as people struggled to gain a sense that they could exert some control over the forces that threatened their survival. Despite the proliferation of spirits and otherworldly forces, in short, traditional religions are at root highly focused on managing the present world with an often astutely empirical or pragmatic bent.

Sexuality is obviously one of those very powerful forces that affects people's ability to survive, and in Africa the need to channel sexuality towards reproduction was very strong. Small populations colonizing forest, desert and mountain frontiers typically faced labour shortages at key points in the agricultural and pastoral cycles. In times of bad weather, locust invasions or wild animal movements, such shortages posed an ever-present danger of famine. That danger created a powerful incentive to maximize fertility, and it rewarded societies which successfully ensured population growth and cooperation through broad social networks. Throughout most of African history, this meant that the most successful cultures were those that constructed gender roles and identities, moral codes, religious beliefs, concepts of health, honour and respect, and state structures that wove together in a seamless fabric of social obligations. That fabric celebrated marriages that produced many children connected through a host of rituals to large extended families, clans and other kinship or lineage ties.

Kinship and lineage brought economic (labour), political (marital alliances, patron–client relationships) and spiritual benefits. Indeed, social obligations to marry and have children extended well beyond the grave. Ancestors required abundant offspring to maintain their memory and power as benevolent spirits who could ensure rain, bountiful harvests and harmonious relationships among the living down through the generations. Marriage and reproduction were thus far too important to leave to the young to negotiate on their own, and people's sexuality was not an individual choice or orientation but in a very powerful sense belonged to the wider community. Children were socialized from the earliest age to understand this and to respect their central obligations to the family, whether living, dead or yet to be born.

Semen and blood in this context were not just bodily fluids but came to be invested with rich symbolic value. In the right place at the right time, they contributed to the well-being and health of all. In the wrong place or in the wrong combination, they could bring disaster. Traces of these beliefs appear throughout the vast ethnographic literature on African cultures compiled over a century of professional research, and many of them still crop up in contemporary accounts of how people explain their own sexual choices. Anthropologist Isak Niehaus's informants, for example (industrial workers in a very modern South African setting), explained to him why it was so important for a man's health to ejaculate in a woman's vagina when she was not menstruating. During ejaculation, they asserted, the penis draws in from its surroundings (Niehaus 2002). To masturbate was thus to draw air into the bloodstream; anal and oral sex presumably posed even greater dangers of pollution to the blood, as would intercourse at the wrong time of the menstrual cycle. By contrast, the vagina provided the man with the fluids needed for continued good health. Health benefits to the woman were also believed to accompany vaginal intercourse, over and above the social and emotional benefits of pregnancy.

For an individual in such an environment to choose not to conform to community norms and obligations regarding sexuality would have been almost impossible to conceive as an option, let alone to act upon. To put one's penis in the wrong place would be to risk ill health, maybe insanity. To choose not to marry according to proper rituals and in due time to have children would be to choose poverty, shame, isolation, intense family pressure and possible violence, and lack of spiritual and social meaning. To marry but then misbehave with sexual partners outside of marriage would also be courting potential disaster. Sneaking around at night did not necessarily provide much cover since the community was well known to be watched by the unseen eyes of the ancestors and other spirits.

Nonetheless, people being people, there were inevitably cases where individuals did transgress norms. By so doing they potentially endangered the reputation and well-being of their families, the stability of the wider community, and the goodwill of the ancestors. How to explain such a threat and contain the danger? Religion, law, morality and politics came together to provide answers in, I would argue, the fundamentally humane and pragmatic way that is *Ubuntu*. Let me outline some general points that can be made drawing upon the rich ethnography on African cultures and religions but with specific reference to the people I know best from my own direct research in southern Africa (Shona, Ndebele/Zulu and Basotho).

To begin with, *Ubuntu* says that the extended family, neighbours, friends and elders all shared in the responsibility of watching over, advising and chastising if necessary young people on the path to adulthood. But it also understood that mistakes happen. Given human nature, publicly naming and blaming those mistakes might compound the evil. Important traditions thus developed to enable communities to avert their collective eyes when people strayed from the ideal of heterosexual marriage and reproduction, even as they worked behind the scenes to restore stability. We might call such practised blindness face-saving, for it allowed public dignity to be maintained despite private lapses. A widespread practice, for example, has been termed 'fictive marriage', by which rituals were performed to recognize and reinforce the claims of the lineage while disregarding the precise biological origins of offspring. The 'real' father could be a woman or even be dead, provided that the marriage was performed with due regard to inter-family payments and appropriate celebrations; the actual biological father was nobody's business, and had no claims over the offspring or the mother.

Another widespread custom related to this has been called 'the raising of seed' after a similar practice described among the ancient Jews in the Old Testament of the Bible. This allowed families to avoid the shame of a young husband's inability to make his wife pregnant by secretly inviting a trusted male relative to step in to discreetly fulfil the task. A child conceived by a brother or uncle would in this way bear the family resemblance and so no one would know that the husband had failed in his

Faiths

fundamental duty as a man. He himself might not know it if the arrangement had been made at the request of a frustrated wife or his own mother. An apparently fertile marriage thus survived as the public mask, enabling a man who was heterosexually impotent to maintain his social standing and the all-important descendants.

In cases where sexual failings or transgressions became known, explanations, punishments, cures and other interventions first had to be assessed by elders in consultation with healers and religious leaders according to the level of the potential threat. For minor sexual transgressions, the punishment could be as little as public mockery (caught masturbating, ha!). More serious offences could require the performance of regret, and payment of compensation to the family of the 'victim' or to the offended ancestors through gifts to a shrine. In the case of a man who committed adultery, for example, the worry was that disapproving ancestors would punish the whole family by visiting illness and even death upon the wife's next child. A formal confession to the wife would prevent that and restore harmony.

Acts that offended sensitive social lines of rank, age and totem (incest) drew increasingly harsh condemnations. Incest was a particularly strong taboo in much of Africa and deeply repugnant to the ancestors. As such it brought punishments ranging from exile to death. A male commoner would for the same reasons probably want to think twice or three times before accepting an invitation to share a mat with a bored junior wife of a powerful polygynous chief.

If and when illicit sexual acts were revealed to have taken place, it was critical to determine not only the status of the parties involved (totem, age, rank, gender, etc.) but also what was the cause of the deed. Physical need could explain some cases, men being lusty by nature and women legitimately requiring sexual intercourse for their health and well-being. When those needs were evidently and unjustly unmet, the harms could be offset by restoring the order of natural justice. Most commonly, a man might commit adultery because his wife could not get pregnant or her period of lactation and abstinence went on a bit too long. The cause was understood as not very blameworthy, but he would still be expected to make amends by marrying the girl he had seduced or perhaps requesting (with all the proper rituals and exchanges) another girl from her family to relieve his natural needs (and to show respect).

Other transgressions, however, were so flagrantly against norms that they could only be understood as arising from the intervention by one of the many different types of unseen powers. The most feared of these were witchcraft and sorcery. An act such as bestiality by a married man would typically be explained in these terms, and would have demanded his cleansing from the community by exile or even death.

Same-sex sexual behaviour traditionally had several possible causes and, consequently, no single response or dogmatic condemnation. Some common themes have been recorded across the continent. Traditional healers interviewed in the course of this research (*n'angas* in chiShona) gave similar explanations to those offered by *sangomas* among the Ndebele and Zulu, *ngakas* among the BaSotho, *ngangas* among the Kongo and *amkopo* among the Akan people of Ghana, among many others referenced in the ethnography. These included, in the first place, that same-sex sexual experimentation and bestiality among adolescent boys were simply a normal part of growing up, through which, and far out of the public gaze, they tested their physicality and learned how proper *hetero*sexual roles could be performed (basically active, insertive, regular). A boy's interest in such experimentation would pass with time, hastened, if necessary, by the mockery of peers or a discreet talking-to by elders, and confirmed through formal initiation and eventual marriage (a process that could extend for many years beyond physical adolescence). It was also understood that 'accidents' could happen when sleeping bachelors huddled together against the cold, especially after an evening of much beer or palm wine.

Unmarried girls also engaged in a type of sex play/education. *Kusenga* (among the Shona, *puxa-puxa* in central Mozambique, but also widely reported throughout eastern and southern Africa –

Bagnol and Mariano 2011) was the practice of manually stretching their labia majora through constant pulling. A girl, after instruction by a godmother, might spend hours at *kusenga* alone or with help from a close friend to achieve the appropriate aesthetic appearance. Never for a moment would it be doubted that the activity was for anything other than the pleasure of the future husband and, perhaps, to ensure the health of future children. As with boys, intimate relationships between girls were expected to wither away as the duties and pleasures of social maturity and marriage took hold. Should such intimate friendships continue among mature women, it was not necessarily a problem provided they were discreet and all other conjugal obligations continued to be fulfilled. The prevailing homosociality of village life would have made such relationships largely invisible.

What we today would now term homosexual orientation or transgender identity was also not necessarily an offence but a respected attribute if caused by certain types of spirit possession and manifest in certain ways. This would have included rare cases of physiologically ambiguous genitals (hermaphroditism or intersex). Possession by a spirit or spirits of the opposite sex was another cause, as in the case of Nkabinde discussed in the previous chapter. A child showing strong signs of such possession would be apprenticed to learn the arts of divination and healing. As time went on, the male spirit who occupied a female body would show himself in increasingly masculine characteristics in the woman even to the point of insisting that she wear men's clothing. The same could happen the other way around when a female ancestor possessed a male body. The more flamboyant the man's effemininity, the more successful the *n'anga/sangoma* was likely to be in his (that is, her) trade. Abstaining from sex with a woman would be essential to that success, lest the female ancestor be offended and withdraw her wisdom.

Such explanations of cause removed blame from an individual who did not conform to the heterosexual norm. In the case of same-sex couples possessed by benign and not so powerful ancestors, they could live together as husband and wife without attracting much more condemnation than gently mocking humour. In the case of a powerful ancestor, whose ability to heal was manifest in the successes of the *n'anga*, it brought respect or perhaps a healthy dose of fear. Sexual and gender difference or rebelliousness might also be disapproved of but accommodated by steering the affected people to socio-economic niches where they performed specialized services often relating to hospitality or dancing, the *bori* cult among the Hausa being one example. People so possessed could play an important role for the whole of society, mediating conflicts or enabling outlets for psychological and emotional stresses among the properly married majority. Chimaraoke Izugbara goes so far as to make the remarkable claim that 'Among the Dagbara of Burkina Faso, gays, lesbians and transgendered people are considered key to society's psychic balance' (2011: 544), although of course those terms would not have had any meaning in a pre-twentieth-century setting.

Rare cases of flagrant and persistent homosexual behaviour that could not be explained by ancestral or other spirit possession were naturally regarded with much greater concern. Some contemporary Zimbabweans claim that execution was the norm on account of the great danger wilful homosexuality posed to the community. As one traditional herbalist told University of Zimbabwe researcher Rudo Chigweshe, 'The traditional society believes that homosexuality pollutes the country. A lot of misfortunes, for example, droughts, hunger and diseases we are having in Zimbabwe are being caused by this evil thing' (Chigweshe 1996: 45). It seems, however, that ambiguity about cause acted as a powerful restraint against capital punishment. What if the unrepentant, incurable, violent man in such a case were accused of sorcery when in fact he was really possessed by a transient 'stranger spirit' (*shave*)? If executed rather than appeased by the proper rituals, that man's spirit could return as an 'avenging spirit' (*ngozi*) to inflict misery on his persecutors and their families, perhaps for generations to come. Likewise, what if it were not sorcery (a conscious act of evil) but witchcraft (whereby a witch works through a third person to effect his or her evil agenda

Faiths

without that person approving or even being aware of the evil)? There were less dangerous ways to deal with witches than to persecute them, and elders thus sometimes went to great lengths to avoid finding the 'proof' needed to justify an execution.

And was it sorcery when ritual male–male sexual acts were intended to invoke a protective or enriching medicine (*muti*)? Purposefully to break a sexual taboo was to invite direct intervention by powerful spirits, but it might be understandable if the intent was to cure an otherwise incurable disease or persistent misfortune. As one Shona scholar expressed it, 'for medicinal purposes a brother and sister may mate' (R. P. Hatendi, cited in Epprecht 2006: 43). Breaking the male–male taboo was even more powerful as a cure for impotence, to improve soil fertility, or to advance political and economic ambitions. Among the Pangwe of present-day Cameroon, the practice was known simply as 'wealth medicine' (Tessman 1998 [1921]). Anal penetration by, or of, cult priests has also been reported as a form of initiation to the cult (transfer of knowledge, power) among the Yoruba and Ovimbundu peoples (Matory 2005, for example). The patriarchal and gerontocratic nature of most African societies meant that the initiates or other young men at the receiving end of the rite would have had little option but to submit to the demands of their elders. Resistance, or making a public scene about it, would have caused far more indignity for one and all, as well as negated the hoped-for benefits of the act.

Traditional religions and beliefs did not simply die out with the coming of colonialism, capitalism and new religions. Yes, in some cases people abandoned the old ways and became fervent converts to Christianity or puritanical forms of Islam that demanded the repression of 'lewd' practices. More commonly, however, people adapted the old to the new, sometimes simply applying new terms ('saints', 'djinns', '*masheitani*') for old concepts. There is considerable evidence from around the continent that this idea of male–male sex for 'medicine' has been adapted for modern conditions, for example. This has been documented among men who seek protection from industrial accidents or want to improve their chances of a raise in pay. As one informant told Eduardo Antonio in a Zimbabwean prison in the mid-1990s, 'the reason he had sex with a young man was because a *sangoma* had instructed him, after communicating with the prisoner's ancestors, to do so in order to secure his position at work' (Antonio 1997: 306). As I discuss in the next chapter, rumours abound about such medicine put to the service of political ambitions. This ancient belief may also partly explain the widespread stereotype that homosexuals in Africa are elites, and another reason to be feared. It is not just that they prostitute themselves to rich foreigners, this thinking goes, but that the nature of their sexual acts itself attracts wealth to them by tapping into the power of the occult.

None of this is to claim that same-sex genital relationships were commonplace in traditional African religions. It is simply to say that they happened, they were known to happen, and they were not regarded with dogmatic, transhistorical revulsion. The key was to maintain or strengthen the lineage, which in most cases was not particularly endangered by acts and relationships that took place outside the public gaze. In some cases, which I will elaborate in the next chapter, they could actually serve the broader social good on the understanding that the sexuality or gender identity so expressed was not for an individual to decide but, rather, was a manifestation of the will of the community across the lines of living and dead. There were sophisticated ways to ensure everyone understood this, not least of all, strategic silence.

§

In 2011 the Nigerian Senate passed a bill criminalizing same-sex marriage and gay clubs (homosexual acts, or 'unnatural offences', as the penal code puts it, were already illegal). One Dr Chima Okereke of the Global Success Ministry used the occasion to celebrate Africa as nothing less than 'God's own continent'. In expressing this view, Okereke joined a chorus of prominent Christian leaders across Africa who have harshly condemned homosexuality and who steadfastly reject appeals to respect sexual orientation either as a human right, or as a God-given attribute. African theologians have also taken a lead role in what is effectively a schism of the worldwide Anglican community. The breakaway 'Primates Council' created following the Global Anglican Futures conference in Jerusalem (July 2009) was headed by Nigeria's Archbishop Peter Akinola, and no fewer than seven of its eight councillors hailed from Africa. In a rare show of ecumenism, the Orthodox, Catholic and Protestant churches in Ethiopia in 2009 joined to call upon the Ethiopian state to prohibit same-sex marriage in the national constitution, and in 2011 disrupted an international conference to discuss public health initiatives for men who have sex with men.

This appearance of a common front across so wide and complex a region as Africa, and between such historically disunited if not openly hostile branches of Christianity, is based on remarkably thin pickings from their shared sacred text, the Bible. 'Six bullets' justify absolute intolerance as being God's will – that is, a mere six verses or groups of verses out of the thousands in the text. This includes two of only a single sentence in length (Leviticus 18:22 and 20:13) situated within long lists of how to behave, including instructions about diet and clothing that are now almost universally ignored; two where sodomy and male prostitution are lumped together in lists of other acts abhorrent to God (1 Corinthians 6:9 and 1 Timothy 1:10), and a fifth list of 'vile affections', 'that which is unseemly' and 'things which are not convenient' that hinges on an assumed understanding of 'the natural use of woman' (Romans 1:25–8, King James translation). The sixth and most substantive 'bullet' is the account of moral crimes and punishments against the people of Sodom and Gomorrah, including for homosexual lust and rape (Genesis 19:1–29). Leviticus specifies death by stoning for the guilty individuals, while Genesis indicates mass annihilation as more appropriate, an act of God which in recent times has been interpreted to justify non-intervention against HIV/AIDS among gay men.

Male–male lust is mentioned as 'vile' in one other Old Testament story (the Levite in Gibeah – Judges 19:16–29). However, probably because of its ambiguity as much as its stunning barbarism, this story does not get as much attention from homophobes as

78

the other six mentions. Indeed, as I will discuss in more detail below, this story is a bit confusing. The men of Gibeah who express homosexual lust are not the ones God punishes, but rather, it is the *female victim* of their *hetero*sexual lusts who pays the price for the men's bad behaviour.

Notwithstanding these bullets, a great many African lgbti turn to the Bible for comfort against the prejudices (and other stresses) that they encounter in their lives. Some simply ignore the selective homophobia their ministers preach and focus on the broader message of God's love for all who embrace the spirit of the faith. Others turn to Christian churches that openly welcome lgbti and explicitly reject interpretations of scripture that condemn homosexual orientation. In Africa today this includes the Rainbow Church of God in Nigeria, Other Sheep East Africa based in Nairobi, the Hope and Unity Metropolitan Community Church and the Deo Gloria Family Church in South Africa. Some African leaders of more mainstream churches have also interpreted the Bible in an lgbti-friendly way. Anglican archbishop Desmond Tutu is probably the most famous example. Tutu, who won a Nobel Peace Prize for his role in the struggle against racial oppression, has gone so far as to call it 'the ultimate blasphemy' when people use the Bible to stir up fear and hatred against sexual minorities (Tutu 1996, 1997). In this view, taking the Bible to be the literal truth is a form of idolatry or fetishism (worship of a thing), which breaches a fundamental commandment rather than one item on otherwise obscure, complicated and culturally archaic lists.

My goal is not to debate the theology behind these differing approaches. But it is helpful quickly to summarize the main arguments in favour of gay-friendly interpretations of scripture, if only for the benefit of those Christian lgbti and their families who worry that they are straying from a central message of the Bible if they refuse to condemn or 'cure' themselves. Then I want to examine the different influences upon Christian churches that have made them more or less homophobic over time. Might there be ways to influence those influences in the present to steer non-literalist churches in gay-friendly directions?

Faiths

The first point to underscore is that the word 'homosexuality' does not appear anywhere in the original versions of scripture because, of course, that word did not exist until 1869, two to three thousand years after Leviticus, Corinthians, etc., were written. Scholars of the original languages of these texts (ancient Hebrew and Greek) say that the words used there do not actually mean homosexuality as an orientation the way we use it today. They refer instead to same-sex prostitution or ritual sex acts (homo- *and* heterosexual) for occult purposes such as increasing soil fertility. Temple prostitution was an ancient Semitic practice that recalls the 'wealth medicine' beliefs in Africa noted above. It provided an obvious focus for Jews to define themselves as morally distinct from (and superior to) their neighbours. The stories of Sodom and Gomorrah meanwhile describe a range of crimes of which homosexual desire in and of itself is not necessarily the worst. Rather, rape, attempted rape of non-humans (angels) and violation of the rules of hospitality are the main focus of condemnation. The interpretation of these texts to apply specifically to homosexual acts dates from the time of St Thomas Aquinas – that is, more than a thousand years after Peter's epistles to the Romans.

Understanding these translation issues and the wider textual context of the 'bullets' opens the door to accepting mutual, loving, honest same-sex relationships as equivalently honourable to mutual, loving, honest heterosexual relationships. It would invite people, like the eunuch of Ethiopia discussed below, to find God's love despite the fact that they cannot have heterosexual relations. This is precisely what happened for a long period in the history of the Church in Europe. Same-sex unions were blessed in church ceremonies for hundreds of years, with cases documented from as late as the eighteenth century, after which that sacrament was definitively suppressed.

Secondly, the harsh punishments described in the Old Testament have to be understood in the historical context of the times when it was written. Not only did that context include ritual male–male sex, slavery, concubinage and brutal violence as more or less normal aspects of daily life, it also included patriarchal control over women's sexuality and a degree of callousness regarding women's humanity that can only be repugnant in today's world. It is worth recalling the Levite in Gibeah story to illustrate this point. In it (Judges 19:16–29), a Jewish man first has problems with his concubine, who 'played the whore against him' then ran off to her father. He got her back, but on their way home they ended up in the village of Gibeah with no place to stay. A kind man offered them hospitality for the night. Then, however, the townsmen of Gibeah arrived at the door demanding to have sex with the male stranger. The host refused to give up his guest for such purposes. Instead, he offered the townsmen his own virgin daughter and his guest's concubine for them to do with as they wished. They opted for the latter, raping her all night long and leaving her at death's door. The stranger took her home but atoned for the evil by killing her. He then cut her body into twelve pieces which he sent around as a lesson to the twelve tribes of Israel. What lesson, I wonder, except that women's and girls' lives and dignity have no inherent value, and that it is normal, indeed approved by no less than God himself, that women and girls should be sacrificed to preserve men's honour?

Thirdly (although I am sure there are more points still), most Christians would agree that the teachings of the Old Testament prophets were superseded by the teachings of Jesus as recorded in the New Testament. Jesus himself had nothing to say on the topic of same-sex sexuality, a strange oversight if it was so important. Moreover, in general terms his teachings directly contradict the notion that ostracizing or punishing people based on sexual orientation is a holy and honourable thing to do.

There is, in fact, at least one quite strong indirect allusion to the need to honour homosexual orientation as a God-given attribute. I am not going to claim that the parable of the Ethiopian eunuch (Acts 8:26–39) is a case of a gay African man receiving the blessing of the apostle Philip in the year 34 of the Christian era (although some gay Christians do plausibly make that case). But this story of a black eunuch who converts to Christianity is pertinent both to the concept of gay-friendly theology, and to my argument that Africans of two thousand years ago were well aware that not everyone fitted the heterosexual norm. The term eunuch refers to a courtly practice found throughout pre-Islamic western Asia (and hence to Axum, the ancestral kingdom of Abyssinia, and later the Ethiopian empire). Literally, eunuch means a man whose testicles have been removed. However, it has also commonly been used to mean a 'passive sodomite' or naturally effeminate male who could be trusted by the king with his wives and treasure (with or without castration). The Ethiopian in this parable seems to fit the description, all the more so since the scripture that inspires him to convert to Christianity is Isaiah's prophecy (Isaiah 53:10): the oppressed, despised and socially outcast will receive 'the pleasure of the Lord'.

I do not want to belabour the issue. Rather, for the remainder of this section I want to focus on the non-theological factors that have played a role in causing different churches to take different positions at different times during the long history of Christianity in Africa. Understanding the economic and political contexts that make homophobia more or less attractive to African preachers and their audiences can help us to identify where best to direct our efforts to counter the current appeal of homophobia to so many of the Christian faithful.

Let us begin with the common error that people often make in thinking that Christianity was introduced to Africa by European missionaries. On the contrary, it came directly from one of Jesus's disciples (Mark) and it is thus considerably older in Africa than it is in England or France. It is also worth noting that several of the key figures in the development of Christian thinking in western Europe came from Africa, including St Augustine of Hippo. Augustine, like the founders of the Coptic Church established in Egypt in the first century after Christ, took what today we would call a sex-negative interpretation of scripture. They downplayed the parable of the Ethiopian eunuch and the erotic poetry of the psalms, for example, while stressing the view that sex for any purpose other than procreation within legal marriage was sinful. This included same-sex relations, of course, but also masturbation and even sex for pleasure between husband and wife. Even with procreation in mind within a legal marriage, sex was *still* disapproved of to the extent that it clouded the mind and hampered spiritual contemplation. Abstinence from sex was necessary for the attainment of true spiritual clarity, a belief that eventually led to the prohibition against marriage among the religious leadership.

The ascetic (self-punishing), monastic (secluded, celibate) tradition in Egypt was especially strong. But why would early African Christians have developed such a restrictive and disapproving view of human sexuality? One argument is that it came from a desire by African theologians to align themselves against the ruling elites and dominant cultures of the day. The Roman and Byzantine empires in particular were by that time notorious for their uninhibited sexuality, at least among the ruling classes. There were as well the lingering folk practices of the ancient Jews and other Semitic peoples who had occupied the cities of the southern Mediterranean, including, as noted above, ritual male–male sex. Centuries of political domination by foreigners (Romans, Arabs, Mamelukes, Turks, French) were not conducive to mellowing the stern moralism of the Church on this issue, particularly since some of those conquerors were infamous for using male rape as a deliberate strategy to humiliate men defeated in battle. The Coptic Church thus survived as a popular religion in part by emphasizing its role of protecting its persecuted Egyptian flock from the perceived moral degeneracy of outsiders and non-believers. Once in place, moreover, the monastic tradition generated its own sexual tensions that required policing. Men in exclusive, close contact with men over long periods of time tend to develop emotional attachments that can lead to physical temptation. David Greenberg mentions prohibitions from the fourth century against bringing boys into monasteries and against any kind of physical touching between monks precisely to prevent carnal distractions from prayerful meditation (Greenberg 1988: 284).

Coptic missionaries travelled from Egypt to Nubia (in modern-day Sudan) and Axum (in modern-day Eritrea and Ethiopia). Over the centuries their influence became entrenched up to the level of political institutions – Nubian armies fought alongside Europeans in the crusades to conquer Jerusalem. Christianity was largely extinguished in Nubia, however, following the triumph of Muslim invaders in the fourteenth century. In the case of Axum and its successor kingdoms, the Church was then cut off from the rest of the Christian world. Over the centuries, its theologians turned increasingly to Old Testament scripture to create a popular, national religion among the Amharic and Tigrayan people. The Old Testament, after all, with its clear lists and harsh punishments, with its vivid descriptions of tribal society including polygyny, levirate marriage, animal sacrifices and war, and with its explicit mentions of Ethiopia, speaks a lot more directly to peasant farmers and herders than the more urbane, often ambiguous New. Gravitating towards the ancient Jewish doctrines, the Ethiopian Church then successfully defined itself as a pillar of moral strength against 'barbarous tribes' within the empire, Muslims encroaching its borders, and against flirtations by the nobility with foreign ideas (such as, briefly, the Catholic faith proselytized by Portuguese missionaries in the seventeenth century). Those traditions became intimately linked to the power of the 'Solomonic' state of Abyssinia, which relied upon Orthodox monks to administer the far-flung regions. A male-dominated society with rigidly enforced gender roles was not only justified by scripture, but closely watched over by an institution associated with Amharic and Tigrayan national identity.

The first Europeans to promote Christianity in Africa south of the Sahara were Portuguese missionaries who, together with explorers, slave traders and conquistadores, introduced Roman Catholicism in the fifteenth to seventeenth centuries. Church dogma at that time still drew heavily on the Augustinian tradition – that is, prohibiting as sinful all sex outside of heterosexual marriage, and honouring celibacy among a learned elite. Smaller sins such as masturbation could be atoned for by an act of private confession to the priest. The so-called 'nefarious sin' of sodomy, however, was punishable by death. Indeed, during the Counter-Reformation against the Protestant breakaways, special courts were set up to find and try such moral threats, including among Africans enslaved in the Portuguese colonies. The cruelty of those courts, however, belied their fundamental and growing weaknesses. The Inquisition could not stop the progressive decline in the authority of the Church during those centuries of overseas expansion and capitalist development. Its ability to impose discipline, sexual and otherwise, on the Portuguese royal household and state officials was extremely limited. Its ability to control its own priests and mariners in faraway places, let alone convince sceptical Africans to change their ways, was even less. The impact of this early phase of Catholicism on African attitudes towards sexuality was thus minimal, and indeed, the Portuguese were eventually expelled or 'went native' in their main footholds in the interior of the continent.

A fascinating exception to that trend was in the old Kongo kingdom of northern Angola. The Kongo people had followed their king when he voluntarily converted to Catholicism soon after the first arrival of the Portuguese mission (1491). Kongo remained an independent ally of Portugal rather than a colony. Kongolese Catholicism then developed over the following centuries as a syncretic religion that included the veneration of ancestors along with the orthodox sacraments such as baptism. For a while the kingdom prospered, with a capital city built somewhat in the European style. By the late eighteenth century, however, Kongo had broken into warring factions which, encouraged by the Portuguese, preyed on each other for captives to sell into slavery. The city of San Salvador, with its fortifications and great stone cathedral, was abandoned and fell into ruin.

A number of messianic or prophetic figures arose in this context promising salvation, none more dramatically than Dona Beatriz Kimpa Vita. Baptized Catholic, Dona Beatriz as a young woman had had visions that she was possessed by ancestral Kongolese spirits. Both her marriages quickly failed on account of these possessions, and she became an *nganga* (traditional healer) in the familiar pattern. Around 1704, however, she experienced possession by a male Italian saint from the thirteenth century.

Faiths

St Anthony allowed her direct contact with God, who instructed her to preach a revised form of Christianity to her people. The message was that Kongo was being punished for its people's bad behaviour (primarily greed, jealousy and treachery). It needed moral regeneration to win back the pleasure of God. This would lead to political reunification of the warring factions, an end to the slave trade and Portuguese meddling that was devastating the region, and prosperity for the common people who suffered so much under the misrule of their nobility and foreign backers.

Among Dona Beatriz's specific teachings was that Mary, Jesus and his apostles were all black, which added a powerful spice to her anti-Portuguese message. She also claimed to have powers to heal, especially infertility. When she reclaimed the old capital city and started preaching from the ruins of the cathedral, people flocked to her as if to a messiah. Her popularity also understandably attracted the less welcome attentions of the Portuguese and their local slave-trading allies. Her enemies eventually captured her and put her on trial for heresy. Both she and her male 'concubine' (her accusers used this odd choice of word) were burnt to death as punishment. Although her followers rose up in mass defiance, they too were crushed in battle in the following months, and sold off in thousands as slaves for export. Yet even then the spirit of resistance lived on to inspire other independent African churches both in the region and in the Americas, where many of her defeated followers ended up. Notably, the first phase of the great slave uprising that led to the Haitian revolution was led by a Kongolese Christian. In Kongo itself, Dona Beatriz's mantle as a prophet was later taken up by a man named Simon Kimbangu. Kimbangu echoed her message of moral regeneration among Africans as a necessary first step to ridding the country of the burden of European rule, a message that earned him nearly three decades in and out of prisons on the Belgian side of the border.

We do not have a good record of Dona Beatriz's specific teachings about gender and sexuality. However, we can infer from her message of moral regeneration, from her emphasis on chastity among youth and teachers, and from the later puritanical ideas of Kimbangu, that she would not have been particularly tolerant of sexual freedom. As for her own inability to fit the marital ideal as a woman and mother, this was due to her respect for the male spirit who possessed her. After her capture by the Portuguese, she first explained her one childbirth as an immaculate conception (that is, no man was involved). But she later regretted that birth as the cause of her downfall. Her sins were to first allow a man to rob her of her chastity and subsequently to conceal that sin from her followers, hence earning God's wrath.

Was Dona Beatriz transgendered? Who knows; perhaps, but does it matter? What is really pertinent to us today was her insistence that the Bible should not be read in a literalist and dogmatic way. God would judge us on the purity of our intentions, she said, not on our ability to follow rules and regulations set down in foreign languages by faraway people. As her prayer *Salve Antoniana* put it: 'Marriage serves nothing, it is the intention that God takes. Baptism serves nothing, it is the intention that God takes. Confession serves nothing, it is the intention that God takes. Prayer serves nothing, it is the intention that God wants. Good works serve nothing, it is the intention that God wants' (reproduced in Thornton 1998). Good intentions – love, selflessness, honesty, honouring the integrity of the community – supersede the hypocritical performance of piety. To extrapolate from there to today's debate, the performance of heterosexual marriage to hide homosexual affairs would be more sinful than the open and honest expression of homosexual orientation (intention).

Such a heresy, and indeed Christianity in any form, was little known outside of Kongo, Abyssinia and the coastal trading posts. It was only with the Protestant evangelical movement at the tail end of the eighteenth century that the foundations were laid for the rise of Christianity on a mass scale in Africa. Beginning with the London Missionary Society, but later including emancipated slaves from American churches, the Protestants advocated relatively radical new ideas about individual morality, respectable gender roles, and sexual propriety. These ideas often came tied to the promise of material wealth and worldly status: follow the basic message of self-discipline, monogamy, modesty and self-improvement through literacy, then not only would salvation await in the next life in heaven, but prosperity would also follow in this one on earth.

Most Africans who first heard this promise were healthily sceptical. To people who were social outcasts in African societies, however, such as divorced women and widows, accused witches, twins, exiles, slaves, the infertile, refugees from war, and so on, the Protestant message was attractive for obvious reasons. Those converts embraced both the moral teachings and the new technical skills and literacy that Protestant missionaries also brought with them and propagated through their schools. These men and women then often went on to become clerks, teachers, evangelists, progressive farmers and others at the core of a modernizing or 'assimilated' African elite during the early years of colonial rule. In the later years of the colonial era, they became the intellectual and political spearhead of the nationalist movements for independence in most of Africa south of the Sahara.

Protestants tended to be hostile to many aspects of African customs concerning gender and sexuality, which they saw as the work of the Devil, including polygynous marriage, child betrothals, concubinage, levirate marriage, girls' labial stretching, 'marriage by cattle' (bride price), female genital cutting, adolescent sex play, 'lewd' dances and music, beer drinking, and initiation ceremonies. Converts were expected to renounce those customs. The Protestants also raised the bar in terms of punishment for transgressions. Traditional religions tended to emphasize appeasement and negotiation with the ancestors, using trial and error to determine the correct mix of compensation or sacrifice to atone for sexual indiscretions. By contrast, Protestants brought news of eternal damnation. They closed down even the possibility of negotiating with God that Catholicism offers through the concept of confession and penance. Moreover, as if the prospect of hellfire weren't bad enough, moral breaches such as adultery or marriage by cattle resulted in ostracism from the small Christian community. That in turn closed the door to any hope of advancement in the colonial social and economic hierarchy. The stakes were high, in this world and the next, for the aspiring African middle class to attain and maintain their respectability according to the principles of this imported religion.

The successes of the Protestants by the late nineteenth century inspired a new generation of modernizing Catholic priests and nuns to compete to win African souls, and to rejoin the story with an aggressive expansion of their schooling system in the twentieth century. The thrust of the combined missionary efforts at cultural transformation was against 'primitive' or 'Satanic' heterosexual customs and the presumed oppression of African women by men. However, male–male sexual relations among Africans were also the target of attack in those cases where they were more or less openly acknowledged in African societies. In Evans-Pritchard's famous account of same-sex practices among the Azande, his informants make it clear that those practices were associated with the pagan past and had died away under the influence of modernization and Christianization (Evans-Pritchard 1970). Elsewhere on the continent, Christian missionaries played a key role in erasing traditional knowledge about same-sex erotic relationships, and even the words to describe them. It was the missionaries and their African evangelists who created the first generation of dictionaries of African languages. They did not, with rare exceptions, include translations of indigenous terms for same-sex sexuality. Whether that was because they never learned these shameful words or whether they self-censored for the sake of decency, we don't know for sure.

Yet at the same time as leading the charge against same-sex sexuality, the European missionaries also created new institutions wherein new forms of disapproved sexual relations could emerge in secret. These included theological schools, monasteries, convents and boarding schools strictly segregated by gender. It may be that some European priests, ministers, nuns or lay teachers took advantage of the situation to sexually exploit the African children in their charge, an accusation sometimes made in African nationalist literature, and which even today still crops up in occasional scandals. Such abuse would most likely have had a scarring effect on the victims' sense of sexuality that could have been passed on to subsequent generations. The research still needs to be done, and may be especially important to healing in those cases where the victims went on to become political or religious leaders. We do know, however, that single-sex boarding schools did give rise to new forms of sexuality among African boys and girls upon their own initiative. These too may have been exploitative and abusive in some cases, but African-initiated relationships were probably more often a quite positive experience. Lacking the kind of traditional outlets for adolescent heterosexual play or court-ship, schoolboys and -girls turned to each other for intimacy in extremely alienating environments, and to act out the roles for future heterosexual relationships.

For girls especially such relationships provided a safe way to experiment with the ideals of modern courtship (safe meaning no possibility of pregnancy and the family shame that would entail). Anthropologists who documented the phenomenon from the 1950s found that the girls in so-called 'mummy–baby' or 'amachicken' relationships did not regard them as sexual or themselves as lesbian (if they even knew what that word meant). Rather, they saw the relationships as a way to practise approved gender roles (dominant, gift-giving masculinity and coy, gift-receiving femininity). The mummies and babies alike thus prepared themselves for heterosexual dating and marriages after matriculation.

Many Africans, of course, resisted the imported Christian cul-ture of respectability. Despite the many achievements of European and American missionaries, and despite their professed commit-ment to a universal notion of humanity, as a group those men and women were as flawed as the societies they came from. They often treated their African converts as if they were children, and sometimes with an outright racist attitude. Moreover, despite their promises to improve Africans' lives through education and capitalist enterprise, missionary idealism very often hit the brick wall of the colonial political economy. No amount of Bible study could compensate for the poverty and racialist laws that drove African men to abandon their family obligations in favour of far-distant employment or the temptations of city life. No amount of prayer could stop African women from selling sex if that's what they needed to do to survive.

As in the cases of Dona Beatriz and Simon Kimbangu, the failures of the mainstream or mission-descended churches to resolve the injustices of colonialism and capitalism led some Africans to break away from imported faiths to form their own independent churches. As the terms Zionist, Ethiopian and Pentecostal suggest, these breakaway churches tended to look backwards towards the Old Testament, the Pentecost, for spiritual guidance. Why is easy enough to discern, and for the same reasons as impelled the Orthodox Church in Ethiopia. The Old Testament has a militarism that resonates with people angered by injustice. The Old Testament is also a lot more explicit about what can and cannot be done to remain holy and to regain the favour of God. That favour was presumably lost in the dispiriting rise in prostitution, family breakdown, loss of culture and more that everyone could see in the burgeoning colonial towns. Adhering to the stern moral code laid down in Leviticus thus became not just an expression of truer African spirituality, but a political act, an act of resistance against the alienating relationships that cash and colonial racism had engendered. From the late nineteenth century probably thousands of these independent churches sprang up all around the continent. Typically these were led by a single strongly charismatic leader with claims to have healing powers through his (and in rare cases, her) own idiosyncratically defined doctrine. One other common feature of such churches was the preference for polygyny, as indeed was the norm in Old Testament times just as it was in traditional African societies.

Two other streams of Christian thought have shaped today's debates about homosexuality in Africa, the Charismatic, Evangelical or Born Again movement and liberation theology. Charismatics were first reported in Nigeria in early 1970. The other terms are widely used to capture the sense of joy, renewal and spreading of the word that they enjoin under a myriad of local church names. By now, Charismatics comprise the fasting-growing set of Christian denominations on the continent, attracting the attention of a new generation of missionaries, this time mostly from the United States (more on this phenomenon later). Like the Zionists, Charismatics arose to provide spiritual comfort against the disappointments that the mainstream churches seemed uninterested in or incapable of addressing. In this case it was primarily the widespread, growing disillusionment with the heady promises that accompanied economic development and political independence. Where Charismatics differ from earlier independent churches is in their emphasis on individual salvation and self-healing rather than following a Moses-like figure out of the wilderness. One of the keys to that salvation is through sexual discipline. In that message the Charismatics are often sharply critical both of aspects of the Old Testament and of traditional African culture. They are adamantly against polygyny, for example, and stress that a husband not only had to remain faithful to his one wife, but had to defend her against pressure from the extended family to agree to more wives (for more children).

Charismatics see themselves very much as modernizers, but by no means do they ally themselves with liberal interpretations of scripture that were starting to come out of the West in the 1970s. They are, notably, strongly against homosexuality, which they do not accept is an orientation but rather see as a lifestyle choice or form of addiction (that is, taking physical pleasure without showing social responsibility). As such they maintain it can be 'cured' through a combination of prayer, group therapy and a buddy system closely along the lines of Alcoholics Anonymous. This is an important distinction from the thundering denunciations of the older churches. It suggests that Christian fellowship is better served by outreach to help homosexuals recover or convert rather than ostracizing or punishing them.

Interestingly, within heterosexual monogamous marriage, Charismatics tend to assert a quite strongly sex-positive position, emphasizing the need for both husband and wife to achieve sexual pleasure. To that extent they dissent from the older missionary legacy of prudishness and fear of female sexual pleasure, as well as the deeper cultural taboos about public discussion of sexuality. Moreover, while pro-family, they recognize that too many pregnancies can undermine the health and happiness of the wife and put tremendous stress on the husband, the provider. Too many pregnancies too close together are thus a threat to the stability of marriage and a source of temptation to sin. Hence they advocate birth control in tandem with education, counselling and public discussion to open people's minds to the possibilities of sexual play. Of course, such play is strictly meant to be confined to the heterosexual marital union. However, celebrating the notion of sexuality distinct from reproduction is a huge advance from the procreation-only messages of the older churches. On that basis, and on the visceral emotiveness of sermons, singing and speaking in tongues, the Charismatics (Born Agains, Evangelicals) tend to attract a lot of (closeted) African lgbti.

Some of the mainstream churches kept their eyes and ears firmly shut while all these changes were unfolding. Notoriously, for example, the Dutch Reformed Church in southern Africa continued to cite the Bible as a justification for white supremacy – and the gathering violence needed to maintain it – right through to the 1990s. A significant element of the leadership, however, began to question the way Christian doctrine could be used to excuse such profound injustices. So-called liberation theology also expressed deepening concern about the growing gap between rich and poor that seemed to follow upon unfettered forms of capitalism. They noted as well that gender-based violence often intensified as structural adjustment programmes spread throughout the continent in the 1980s. These injustices could not be explained, let alone resolved, through literalist interpretations of the Bible. Rather, sacred texts needed to be read and understood metaphorically, especially with regard to gender and sexuality. In that spirit, prominent leaders such as Allan Boesak of the NGK (the Coloured branch of the Dutch Reformed Church) began to link the fight for justice against racial and class oppression with feminist and gay liberation struggles. Many gay rights groups in the West meanwhile saw the affinity between South Africans' fight against racism and their own hopes for dignity and equal rights. Within South Africa, small white-dominated lgbti groups moved decisively to place anti-racism at the top of their political agenda. The leading liberation movement (the African National Congress) recognized this support as early as 1987 when Thabo Mbeki, then the ANC Director of Information, assured the international press that a future ANC government would respect sexual orientation as a human right. The first major religious leader to explicitly endorse that view was Archbishop Desmond Tutu of the Cape Town diocese, soon followed by others lobbying in favour of the sexual orientation clause in the country's first democratic constitution.

South Africans do not have a monopoly on liberation theology on the continent, and indeed, a number of Christian leaders elsewhere in Africa have stood up to defend victims of homophobic hatred. Former Anglican bishop Christopher Ssenyonja of Uganda, notably, has been a leader in the movement to stop that country's proposed anti-homosexuality bill, and he has been outspokenly critical of American missionaries who propagate homophobic interpretations of the Bible in Africa. The Reverend Kapya Kaoma, an Anglican minister from Zambia, is another important leader who has written eloquently on the threat posed to Africans by the American Christian right. He has called upon African 'progressives' of all stripes to join with allies in the West to resist American neoconservative interventions to inflame homophobia, Islamophobia and other prejudices in Africa (more on this in the next chapter). Several gay-affirming independent churches have sprung up in places like Nigeria and Kenya, while individual priests have sometimes defied their church doctrine in order to minister to the health and emotional needs of same-sex-practising people, above all on the HIV/AIDS front.

The prevailing trend in Africa, unfortunately, seems to have shifted dramatically, even cruelly, in the opposite direction in the last decade. Ssenyonja is a tragic case in point. For continuing

94

to administer with compassion to openly gay people in Uganda against the direct orders of his superiors, Ssenyonja was not only barred from the Church he had served for thirty-four years, he was denied his pension. How to explain such meanness in the name of Christ?

I am going to save this question until the next chapter, since I believe the meanness and the turn to homophobic literalism we have seen in recent years can only be understood in relation to changes in the political economy. Let me therefore leave Christianity for a moment and turn to a brief overview of the third major faith in Africa, Islam.

'Arabs' and Islam

The term 'Arabs' has often been applied very loosely in Africa to include Swahili, Berbers, Nubians, Persians, Gujaratis and other liminal peoples seen as distinct from black Africans (or 'real Negroes' in the language of European colonialists). Rather than race or ethnicity, it is the practices/interpretations of Islam and self-identification with Arabic or Middle Eastern culture which set them apart. Homosexuality is one of those supposedly defining cultural issues. Indeed, 'Arabs' and Islam more broadly have a very strong, albeit often contradictory reputation in Africa when it comes to homosexuality, as indeed they do in the West. For many non-Muslim Africans, 'Arabs' and Islam are associated with violence and sexual exploitation. It was not just a question of homosexual rape during war, as Diop maintained happened in the case of the Moroccans who conquered Songhai in the sixteenth century, or the enslavement, castration and export of African boys and young men as eunuchs to the Muslim empires of Egypt and western Asia, as happened from the Christian states of Nubia for hundreds of years. 'Arab' traders also had a reputation for enjoying if not promoting male–male sexual relationships, with sometimes disastrous outcomes for Africans (the case of the martyrdom of Ugandan Christians, which I will discuss in the next chapter, comes to mind). During the colonial era, Muslim rulers and soldiers were also commonly co-opted to serve European

Faiths

colonial interests and had a reputation for abusing that power as middlemen. It is no coincidence that in his angry novel *Two Thousand Seasons*, Ayi Kwei Armah calls African homosexuals askaris, the Swahili term for mercenaries in the colonial army or police. To this day, a common belief is that the only parts of Africa where homosexuality can be found are those areas with large Muslim populations.

As for Western attitudes, a very long tradition in European culture accuses Muslims of sexual deviance and corruption. Edward Said influentially described this as Orientalism, which he saw as a key element in the West's efforts to forge its own distinctive cultural identity in the eighteenth and nineteenth centuries. Much of this Orientalist imagery focused on the supposed heterosexual licence found in the courts of Muslim elites (concubines, harems), the explicit attention to sexual details and carnal enjoyment in much Islamic writing (including the Qur'an), the relative ease with which Muslims could divorce, and the fact that men (in some embellished traditions) could take multiple wives, including 'temporary wives' for a night of pleasure while travelling. But homosexual licence was also part of Orientalist lore. Perverted and predatory Arabs in that lore were thought to pose a danger to naive black Africans, an image that played a role in morally justifying European conquest of Africa (to protect the 'real Negroes'). The notion of the easily available Arab male also played a role in the emergence of the Maghreb (Morocco, Algeria and Tunisia) as destinations of choice for homosexual refugees from persecution in Europe in the late nineteenth century, Oscar Wilde perhaps most famously. Cities like Tangier and Fez were glamorized by the first generation of out gay American authors in the post-Second World War era, and remained an attraction for gay tourists from the West well into the 1980s, if not to some extent still.

Yet on the other hand, Islam has a reputation today for extreme homophobia. The Qur'an, it is widely maintained, is even more explicit and unrelenting in its denunciation of homosexuality than the Bible. Islamic law (shari'a) purportedly names specific punishments such as one hundred lashes with a whip, stoning to death and tossing off a high tower to be followed by everlasting torment in hell. Flowing from that, homosexual relations carry the death penalty in several Muslim-majority states, including Mauritania, Sudan and twelve states in northern Nigeria where versions of shari'a are in force. In recent years, Muslim leaders have vied with Christian leaders to make the most violently homophobic threats. President Yahya Jammeh of Gambia, notably, while positioning himself as a pious Muslim, warned that he would 'cut off the head' of any homosexual who did not leave the country within twenty-four hours. Such extremism is commonly justified on the grounds of protecting Muslims from HIV/AIDS through 'holy war' against permissive, supposedly Western values (in which argument, not only homosexuals but all people with HIV are heavily stigmatized; see Badri 1997 as a much-cited scholarly example). With Boko Haram now threatening to blow up primary schools in its drive to impose shari'a law on the non-Muslim majority of Nigeria, with al-Qaeda-linked Tuareg militants wreaking havoc in hitherto famously tolerant Mali, with mobs in Senegal desecrating the graves and disinterred bodies of alleged homosexuals, and with a Salafist minority in the Egyptian parliament that wants to cover up the pyramids, the extremists certainly seem to be gaining ground.

Which, then, is it? Is Islam in Africa a 'gay-friendly' or a homophobic force? For the remainder of this chapter I want to review that contradictory evidence – again, not to get bogged down in theology. Rather, the goal is to encourage thinking about the complex history of Islam in Africa on this topic, including the changing ways in which theology has been interpreted or adapted in specific cultural, economic and political circumstances. Indeed, the answer to my rhetorical question above is both. All of the contradictory points made above are strongly supported by documentary evidence stretching back to the beginning of Islam in Africa. What does that mean for engaging politicians like Jammeh, or ideologues like Malik Badri? Can it help us to imagine what Khalid Duran (1993) calls the 'theological accommodation'

Faiths

or 'ultimate', reformed Islam that is needed to fight the gathering strength of homophobia (and misogyny)? Here my hope is simply to temper the hint of fear and stereotyping of Islam (that is, Islamophobia) that sometimes creeps into the debate, and help us to reflect on the potential for moderate, non-literalist forms of Islam to support the movement for erotic justice.

Let us begin with the notion that 'Arabs' had a relatively accommodating view of homosexualities, at least under certain conditions. This was not entirely an Orientalist fantasy. In a very long literary tradition in the wider Islamic world, male Muslim authors themselves wrote considerably about the topic with humour and praise for same-sex desire when expressed by a man towards 'beardless youth'. The fact that words describing different types of same-sex relationship derived from Arabic and Persian appear in Swahili and several other African languages also suggests an influence from the Islamic heartland on the African continent. The concept of effeminate or transgendered men in service to elite Muslim families and offered as a gesture of hospitality by the host to his visitors (*mukhanatheen*) was known in Muhammad's time, and still lives on in the role of *gor djiguen* in Senegal. The community of effeminate men known as *'yan daudu* in Kano, who also perform sexual services for ostensibly straight men either as sex workers themselves or procurers of female sex workers, includes members who strongly identify as devout Muslims, who give alms, and who travel to Mecca for the haj (Gaudio 2009).

Within the parameters of highly gendered culture, the *'yan daudu* allow for loving, playful, respectful and potentially mutual same-sex relationships in the spirit, they say, that Muhammad himself commended for the full achievement of human spirituality. They sometimes find themselves having to perform sex work to make ends meet, for which they believe Allah's compassion will see them through. To the sympathetic ethnographer, this comes across as rather sex positive. In other cases, however, accounts of same-sex sexuality among Muslim Africans suggest a profound sex-negativity and prevalence of psychologically alienating practices. The first – to my knowledge – academic study of psychosocial influences on sexuality in an African Muslim society (Morocco) describes pervasive man–boy rape in the name of piety in religious schools. Serhane (2000 [1996]) also describes highly eroticized female–female relationships and spaces in which boys are allowed almost to the age of puberty, the *hammam* or public bath above all.

How is any of this possible if shari'a unambiguously forbids same-sex sexual relationships? That is easy to answer: it doesn't. Shari'a is in fact much more complicated than generally understood by non-Muslims and there are alternative ways of reading even the most sacred components of it. We can start at the level of translation. Islam holds that the most sacred text, the Qur'an, is only accurate in its original Arabic as dictated by Allah to Muhammad. Stage one, then, is to render that archaic and highly allegorical language into modern Arabic; stage two to translate it into other languages accessible to followers worldwide. Even the most careful translations therefore inevitably introduce inaccuracies, and are often hotly disputed. What, then, of bad translations? According to one Nigerian commentator on the shari'a as translated into Hausa in the state of Zamfara, 'bad' would seem to be an understatement. It 'shows every sign of hasty drafting, incorrect cross-referencing, incorrect and defective wording, omissions and contradictions' (Ayuba 2011: 263).

Yet even literally accurate translations can hardly be said to be crystal clear and free of ambiguity. Bearing in mind that the Qur'an provides but one part of shari'a, its 114 chapters contain remarkably little on the subject. There is a single possible reference to lesbian sex (Sura 4:15) but that depends entirely on how one understands 'lewdness', 'an indecency' or 'base act', the usual translations of *al-fahisha*. The two most explicit references to male–male sexuality are a bit less vague: 'Do you come to the males of created being, and leave alone the wives that your Lord has created for you?' (Sura 26:165–7, Jones translation 2007), and 'Do you approach men in lust, rather than women?' (Sura 27:54). These appear among a total of six references to male–male lust found within the numerous reiterations of the story of the destruction of Sodom and Gomorrah. Yet as in the biblical account of the same event, that story is open to interpretation about which sin or collection of sins was most abhorrent, and indeed, several of the retellings of the story do not mention male–male lust at all (37:133–8, for example). Was the crime of the Sodomites that they put their penis in the wrong orifice, or was it the violence they used against guests to do so? Was it that they were unclean and miserly? Was it that the offence was done by straight men, betraying their true nature as heterosexual? Was it the practice of castration or vasectomies on slaves? Was it that the offence was committed between social equals rather than between men and non-men (slaves, eunuchs, boys and non-believers who wouldn't matter if penetrated)? Did it condemn male–male anal intercourse only? In other words, were homosexual acts wrong in all cases or only when they involved violence, the betrayal of the principle of hospitality to strangers, lack of respect for social hierarchies, or flouting the primacy of Arab men's sense of masculine dignity as unpenetrable?

The fiery destruction of the 'people of Lut' (or Liwat, the one moral man whose name ironically has come to mean 'homosexuality' in Arabic) certainly contrasts sharply with the one other direct reference to the issue outside the Sodom and Gomorrah story. Sura 4:16 says 'If two of you [male] commit it [referring back to *al-fahisha* in the previous verse, meaning an indecency, implicitly with each other], then punish them both.' But it then goes on to say, 'And if they repent and make amends, turn from them. God is Relenting and Compassionate.' Compounding the uncertainty are allusions to erotic desire by men for adolescent boys as a simple fact of life, the presence of boys as well as virgin girls as a sensuous reward in paradise, and an acknowledgement that Allah created people who 'have no desire [for women]' (24:31, also translated by Malik as 'ineffectual', and by Kugle as men 'who have no guile with women', meaning incapable of consummating heterosexual union). How can one not respect that which Allah created?

Such uncertainties, as with numerous other topics obscured

in the poetic language of the Qur'an, or by the contradictions between sura written in different periods of Muhammad's life, created the need for Muhammad and his followers to deduce meanings and elaborate clearer moral instructions. Muhammad himself proposed the concept of abrogation (*naskh* and *mansukh*), by which his later writings rendered earlier, contradictory ones void. The later sayings were then collected together over the following two centuries and edited with third-party accounts into the Hadith, which comprises the rest of the shari'a. The most explicit injunctions against homosexuality and punishments are taken from here – that is, they are not the direct and indisputable word of Allah but the word of human interpreters, however revered.

The Hadith too can be obscure and open to further interpretation, not least of all since no fewer than seven slightly variant 'readings' have been approved as canonical (that is, acceptable to base legal decision upon; Jones 2007: 19). Not surprisingly, deep disputes between Islamic scholars quickly arose about how much of the Hadith is compatible with the Sunna, or broader cultural traditions of moral behaviour among Muhammad's people. Smallish doctrinal disputes then sometimes flared into political conflict. Doctrinal differences sometimes also followed after political conflicts as a way of retroactively justifying the violence. The Sunni/Shi'a schism perhaps most notoriously began with a brutal act of treachery in a contestation over claims to leadership of the first Arab caliphate, and only subsequently acquired theological meaning.

The passing of time made literalist readings even more problematic. New technology, changing social relations and the spread of Islam throughout non-Arab cultures stretched the ability of scholars to make comprehensible analogies between Hadith or Sunna among the ancient Arabs and the contemporary situation in their own countries. Hence, Islamic scholars over the centuries developed a large body of legal rulings (*fiqh*) and lists of moral crimes (*Kaba'ir* or 'Enormities') to guide the interpretation of shari'a in a way that would be suitable and understandable to the context of their day.

Faiths

Some Muslim scholars today cite these documents to support their homophobia. Taleb (2007: 38), for example, cites a fourteenth-century scholar of the Hadith to justify prohibition of lesbianism in Nigeria. Yet this too remains disputed. In the first place, while most of the Enormities do indeed include same-sex relations as sinful, not all of them do. Further nuances creep in between the extremes of what is forbidden and lawful behaviours by categorizing them as either recommended, reprehensible or indifferent. The social rank of the person being penetrated and his or her legal relationship to the penetrator, rather than the act of penetration itself, usually determined which category applied. Many of the Enormities thus found same-sex relations reprehensible between social equals but tacitly condoned the use of slaves however one wished as indifferent.

A further issue still is the ranking of sins. According to Ali (2006), all of the Enormities place same-sex relations below heterosexual intercourse outside of legal marriage or concubinage (*zina*) in importance. The penalty for *zina* was death, and it is easy to see how this arose in relation to the culture of family honour, and particularly masculine honour in the Arab and Berber worlds. The need to protect the virginity of daughters, the modesty of wives and hence the good reputation of the family over which the husband presided was paramount. Temptations to commit *zina* therefore had to be reduced by practices that kept boys and girls, men and women apart in all but the most controlled, carefully watched settings. Strictly enforced segregation by sex meant people spent long periods of time without any prospects of heterosexual relations. By many accounts, this gave rise to same-sex relations (and, for adolescent boys, to bestiality) as the lesser of two evils.

Shari'a also stresses that bearing false witness or spreading unfounded allegations about the morals of other people are grievous sins to be avoided at all costs. *'Yan daudu* may therefore admit to being sinners on account of their sex lives. But they take some pride in at least being honest about it. In expressing this view to American researcher Rudolf Gaudio, his informants made it clear that the bigger sinners before the eyes of Allah are the 'big men' who 'do the deed' in private but in public denounce homosexuality as an abomination.

Islam has no single theological doctrine enforced by an authority structure. It is a contract between the individual and Allah. For many Muslims, any attempt to impose a singular dogma or theocratic state that enforces one interpretation of scripture that transcends history and context contravenes the central messages of scripture. The Ismaili branch of the Shiite family, for example, which remains popular on the Swahili coast, explicitly rejects a literalist interpretation of the Qur'an, Hadith, *fiqh* and the Enormities. In place of such literalism they favour the constant renewal or reinterpretation of these revered texts for each generation by spiritually gifted imams.

History, of course, is full of examples of leaders who did impose a single theological doctrine married to the power of the state. The concept of jihad applies in this case. Jihad is commonly mistranslated in the West as 'holy war', and in the literal sense can mean taking up arms to defend the 'true' interpretation of Islam against those who would corrupt it. But jihad can also, indeed *should*, also be applied privately in one's relationship with Allah. Struggle in that sense is to remain honest and pious in one's day-to-day life, even under the rule of hypocrites and oppressors. *Itijihad* is a further refinement of this concept to mean intellectual struggle. How to read complex, contradictory sacred texts to glean lessons that can be applied in an ethical way, appropriate to specific lived contexts? The principal guiding ethic is not war but social justice, which includes respect for minorities and a fair distribution of wealth among other things.

The latter point perhaps goes to the heart of the issue. The founder of Queer Jihad put it this way. According to him (an American convert) in Islam there is only one God:

Acknowledge this God; submit to this God. Do good to others and build just, fair societies. Don't cheat people in your business dealings. Be moderate in all that you do. Avoid intoxicants and lewdness [meaning *public* offences to modesty]. Help

Faiths

103

widows and orphans. Remember that you were created by Al-lah, and unto Allah you will return – and you will be asked to render an account of yourself. (Sulayman X 1999)

Judgement, in short, should be left for Allah, not some self-appointed earthly intermediaries. For that reason, feminist Islamic scholar Kecia Ali has described the requirement not to expose sinful behaviour of others as the first of Islam's two 'most salient principles' (Ali 2006: 78). The second is that it is a greater moral offence to deny certain rules than discreetly to break them. This leads to what Stephen O. Murray has aptly termed 'the will not to know' if or when rules are being broken. To emphasize this, shari'a law puts the bar very high indeed for an allegation of male–male sexual misconduct to be upheld. Four responsible adult eyewitnesses to the act must publicly swear to have seen penetration, on pain of punishment (eighty lashes) should this prove false. Eighty lashes is a strong incentive to 'don't ask, don't tell'.

This ethic is by no means exclusively Islamic. Indeed, it suggests a refinement of the traditional value of not seeing or naming certain things that might disturb the peace. Signe Arnfred's informant among the *tariqas* of Ihla de Moçambique, Abdallah, made almost exactly that point with respect to another disapproved deed, *zina*, and he is worth citing at length for his articulate way of putting it in a positive light:

> The men of the coast do not supervise their women too closely.
> As long as they behave well in public they close their eyes
> to what else is going on. Adultery is a normal situation, it is
> nothing new. The clever woman might have a lover, but in
> order for the husband not to notice, she will show him even
> more than usual, and the husband who has a girlfriend in town
> will do the same thing. This is the behaviour of wise and well-
> behaved men and women. Discretion is an important capacity.
> On the coast adultery is a way of life, it is part of our culture.
> There is more enjoyment and more fun in these extra-marital
> relations, and if husband and wife behave well, it will very
> rarely be those that provoke divorce. (Arnfred 2011: 284)

This is an important point to recall when people characterize Islam as a monolithic and inflexible cultural regime. In fact, as Islam expanded into Africa, it often simply papered over or refined pre-Islamic practices. Provided converts obeyed the five pillars of Islam (or most of them anyway), they were generally left to follow their traditional practices and beliefs. The Arab conquerors of North Africa, for example, quickly accommodated with Berber culture in what came to be known as Kharijism. Existing spirits were renamed djinns and *sheitani*, and charms and spells were taken from the Qur'an rather than (or in addition to) older sources. This adaptability explains how the Qur'anic injunction to modesty was used to justify pre-existing extreme forms of female genital cutting in parts of north-east Africa, while barely requiring torso cover-up in parts of West Africa. It explains as well the continued existence under Islam of women's autonomies from men in traditionally matrilineal societies such as the Makhuwa (Makua) of northern Mozambique (ibid.). It may also explain a practice noted from Morocco that sounds a lot like the 'wealth medicine' concept found elsewhere in non-Islamic Africa: Qur'anic teachers who justify what effectively amounts to rape of their male pupils as a means to teach deeper knowledge of the sacred text. In Abdelhak Serhane's words, 'the sperm of the *faqih* includes a dose of intelligence and divine benediction, which is desirable in that the Qur'anic teacher transmits it directly to the pupil' (Serhane 2000 [1996]: 44, my translation).

The dominant form of Islam that emerged in most of Africa, Sufism, is particularly amenable to such cultural adaptability. Sufism stresses individual attainment of the experience of Allah's love through a direct, mystical experience. That experience can come through private meditation, fasting, repetitive prayer or a physical trance induced by whirling. *Tariqas* or 'brotherhoods' (which could include women in leadership positions) not only help with spiritual guidance but offer mutual assistance through the daily struggles of life. Pre-Islamic possession cults such as *zar* (Sudan) and *bori* (Nigeria) also lived on under Sufism. In some cases, men and women so possessed act out the desires of foreign or even opposite sex spirits. This allows for some creative blame-shifting for transgressive behaviour. In Larsen's study (2008), for example, otherwise decent Muslims in Zanzibar took up drinking alcohol when visited by the spirits of Christians from Madagascar. Similarly, contemporary Islamists denounce homosexuality among the *'yan daudu* as a pre-Islamic abomination (*bori*) that the Christian British and their Sufi allies had corruptly allowed to flourish, and hardliners would now like to see them expunged in a 'pure' Islamic state.

A number of modern Sufi theologians have spoken out against such claims and the Islamic right more generally, calling instead for radical reform of shari'a in line with an international human rights and gender equality ethic. Why? Because romantic love is one path to mystical union with Allah, surrendering oneself to the passion of connection with another person. Such love, such surrender, such union cannot be fully achieved when the relationship between individuals is skewed by a power imbalance or the injustices and taboos structured into patriarchal cultures. Sudanese teacher Ustadh Mahmud Muhammed Taha, notably, did not call for sexual orientation as a human right. However, after a spiritual epiphany in the 1950s, he began to emphasize gender justice in his writings and judgements. This included women's emancipation from patriarchal controls and the redistribution of wealth to be achieved through democratic socialism within a federal state. Taha applied this striking blend of Sufism, feminism, anti-Arab chauvinism and Marxism to a political movement which remained active through three decades of independence (the Republican Party). Ultimately, and specifically for opposing the Sudanese state's brutal imposition of a reactionary interpretation of shari'a upon non-Muslims, Taha was accused of apostasy and then executed for sedition in 1985.

These days it seems almost incredible that a revered Islamic teacher, who had been imprisoned by the British for protesting against colonial rule, could become a martyr for, among other things, calling for women's equality with men and equal rights for all citizens regardless of their religious beliefs, race or ethnicity.

No doubt, Taha was a controversial figure in Sudan with a modest following throughout his years of political activism. But the government was fearful enough of his popularity that it had his body buried secretly in the desert so that it could never become the focus of a political movement. Yet the idea of a feminist-inspired, 'depatriarchalized' Islam lived on, and indeed has achieved some stunning successes in recent years outside Sudan. The Family Code in Morocco adopted in 2004 is perhaps the most remarkable, overturning – in the name of shari'a principles – 1,400 years of patriarchal domestic power linked to an autocratic monarchy claiming descent from Muhammad (Pruzen 2011). We should also note the successes of Nigerian feminists in using the Qur'an to thwart the application of misogynist interpretations of shari'a (Badran 2011).

§

Let us not be misty-eyed about the African past. *Ubuntu* does not mean liberal democracy or communal egalitarianism, while the term African humanism misrepresents the patriarchal nature of most African societies. Those societies were in fact often highly stratified by age, by gender, by rank, by caste and by other social lines. Slavery and pawnship were commonplace, and violence against those who stepped out of their assigned role could be severe and arbitrary. Similarly, matriliny, human rights and democratic socialism may theoretically be possible under Sufi practice, but so too are local forms of patriarchal authority, female genital cutting and superstitions. The types of same-sex relationships described above, meanwhile, whether traditional or in new institutional settings such as the industrial compounds and boarding schools, do not always fit very well with the modern concepts of homosexuality, gay or lgbti. On the contrary, if they were transported to a modern context, we would be hard pressed to distinguish some of them from rape or child abuse. In almost all cases, those same-sex relationships overlapped with heterosexual marriage and reproduction without disrupting the norms of senior heterosexual male dominance and kinship networks.

Faiths

Indeed, they often explicitly reinforced those norms provided the relationships remained discreet (not talked about or seen) and discrete (kept separate from and not interfering with the needs of family, kin and nation).

That said, however, as long as proper roles and status were correctly acknowledged and social etiquette was maintained, *Ubuntu* allowed for pragmatic adjustments to take account of people's diverse characters and attributes as people. Africans had many words, symbols and myths to explain and categorize such diversity, or simply to turn a blind eye to it. Whether understanding themselves as traditional, Christian, Islamic or creative combinations of the three, Africans have a long history of bending the rules to accommodate the quirks of human behaviour and desire, especially when those quirks were recurrent.

I am not suggesting that those ways of bending the rules and of enabling discreet/discrete same-sex relationships could or should be elevated to a place of pride under today's expectations of human rights. However, understanding how religions in the past explained and accommodated the fact of sexual diversity in spite of the general commandment towards heterosexual marriage and reproduction might be helpful for today's debates. For example, that history shows that traditional religions, Christianity and Islam are clearly far more complicated than hardliners would have us believe. It tells us as well that Africans have often resisted hardline interpretations of what it means to be faithful coming from outside of Africa. That applies to the idea that the repression of all forms of same-sex desire has greater social merit than holding family together or defending broader ethical principles such as compassion, justice and modesty about the limitations of human knowledge.

Of course, it would be wrong to interpret *Ubuntu* as inherently or historically 'gay friendly', but the potential is certainly there. That potential is something many lgbti in Africa today intuitively appreciate, and which might be tapped into as a source of strength and solidarity for future activism.

4 | Sex and the state

For most African lgbti today, the state is an enemy. Its police harass and extort from them, its media slander them, its institutions block their attempts to organize and to educate themselves about safer sex and other life skills, its politicians encourage vigilantism against them. Yet the African state will be essential to challenging cultural attitudes and facilitating the achievement of sexual rights and gender justice. Who else is going to reform and enforce the law to protect people against extortion and discrimination? Revise and deliver new national curricula on sexuality education? Guard public health against homosexually transmitted infections? Counter an influx of profit-seeking charlatans from the United States or dogmatists and Salafist jihadis coming to Africa to peddle their homophobic ideologies?

This then raises two questions. How and why exactly did African states of today come to be so homophobic, and, knowing that, can we find ways to win allies within state structures who can begin turning the ship around? I will deal with the second question in the next chapter. Here, let me focus on factors that have contributed to so many African states coming to see homosexuality as a threat to national values, if not national security. Understanding that history is critical to developing strategies for change.

Pre-colonial states

The oldest states in Africa were in the Nile river valley (Egypt, Nubia, Meroe) and along the Red Sea (Axum). These developed independently, but over time they became closely engaged through trade with other societies of the region and foreign influences upon them became apparent. By two thousand years ago, both Egypt and Axum were significantly 'Hellenized' – that is, ruled by elites who identified culturally with Greece. This was reflected in patriarchal gender relations that followed Mediterranean and western Asian patterns, including the practice of dowry rather than bride price. Another aspect of Hellenistic culture of that time was the idealization of same-sex sexuality and love as being more refined and conducive to spiritual uplift than obligatory heterosexual reproduction. Love spells and charms to help women attract and hold their female lovers have been found from Hellenistic Egypt. Male–male sexual bonds were meanwhile thought to strengthen the cohesion and fighting ability of warriors, and indeed, the greatest military conqueror of the age, Alexander of Macedon, was both married to a woman and well known for his love of men and eunuchs. As I argued in the previous chapter, this aspect of elite culture in Egypt and Axum may partly explain the ascetic, anti-homosexuality trend in early Christianity as it took root in those countries, sheltering its people from foreign morals.

In Africa south of the Sahara states have existed for over a thousand years but in significantly different forms. Unlike ancient Egypt, Axum, and even less than in Europe and much of Asia, a common feature of African states south of the Sahara was their decentralized, multi-ethnic, and multi-linguistic nature. It is not that African *mansas*, *mutapas*, *kabakas* and other big chiefs, kings and emperors would not have appreciated and probably have abused the kinds of centralized power of someone like Alexander or Qin Shihuang or Tamerlane. It is that they lacked one of the most crucial technologies to achieve that power – the warhorse. Horses get sick and die quickly in most of Africa south of the Sahara, and zebras just don't cut it as a means to extend military force. Lacking such means, Africa's vast spaces and unenclosable borders were an open invitation for unhappy subjects to migrate away. African history is consequently full of breakaway states and the rise and fall not just of splinter kingdoms but of entire peoples ('tribes', if you will) taking on new identities as they migrated in search of security and justice.

African rulers thus had to convince rather than compel their subjects to remain loyal and to stay put. This was to have a profound impact on the cultural forms that gender and sexuality have taken over the ages, and the ways that state power depended upon its ability to control its subjects' sexuality.

Public generosity was one crucial strategy for African rulers to woo their male subjects. For that, they depended heavily upon their ability to command women's labour, both productive and reproductive. To have many children was to gain a labour asset, as well as a means to secure alliances through marriage across kinship lines. Moreover, women performed most agricultural labour plus tasks such as cooking and brewing beer. Surplus from that production at the family level could then be used by the head of the household/lineage to offer as an incentive to attract other men to perform communal labour. The men's labour so secured enabled the lineage head to amass a further surplus which he could redistribute as a proof of his generosity and to help the poor through the lean times. As the number of his subjects and the extent of his power increased, men's labour could also be directed to the task of kidnapping pawns, slaves and wives from the neighbours, both to increase production internally and, later, for the export of people in exchange for guns.

Women's sexuality was a political asset as well in that many wives meant many children and (hopefully) loyal kin. Big men could take very many wives, reportedly hundreds and even thousands in some cases. Their status varied from the Great Wife, who might hold significant political power behind the scenes, to lowly concubines or chattels. The latter could be offered as a sexual present to visiting men – if a pregnancy resulted, it was not a problem since the offspring would be 'owned' by the patriarch who had paid bride wealth. Female chattels could also be given to men as wives in reward for service.

Most African rulers were men, but women sometimes became rulers in their own right. Angola in the time of Dona Beatriz of Kongo seemed to produce a lot of them, who even passed on their powers to female relatives across generations. The 'Rain Queen' of the Lovedu people of South Africa, and Ahebi Ugbabe, 'the female king of colonial Nigeria', are better-known examples. Such female rulers took wives to the same political ends as male rulers did, and used much the same marriage rituals and exchanges of gifts and cattle between families. The intention of such woman–woman marriages was not to celebrate sexual union or mutuality between lesbian women. Far from it. Rather, the 'female husband' or 'female king' would pay bride wealth to the family of the bride to bind that family to her rule. The wife would then get pregnant by a male proxy designated by the female husband. The resulting children belonged to and enriched the husband's lineage for her to marry off as she determined.

Pageantry and ritual provided the other major non-military path to securing a loyal network of subjects who could enable a ruler to secure or further to expand his sphere of influence. This included dramatic demonstrations of material wealth through awesome public buildings, celebrations and rituals that blurred the lines between religion and politics. African kings were generally not considered to be deities themselves, but were intermediaries with the most powerful ancestors, gods and other spirits. Their authority depended upon their ability to ensure that those spirits brought rain, fertility and prosperity to the people. Should the people be stubborn, unruly or immoral, however, rulers could invoke the ancestors to punish them with drought or other calamities. (It worked the other way as well, and natural calamities might be evidence of the ruler's unfitness to rule.)

Beliefs about the relationship between sexuality and spirituality played an important role in this cultivation of mystery around political elites, and hence in the development and functioning of African states. Ritual incest, notably, was one of the practices that irrevocably placed the Shona *mutapa* outside the realm of normal humanity. The intent was not to produce offspring, for which purpose there were many other wives. Rather, the role of incestuous marriage was symbolically to 'fortify installation' against rival claimants to the status of *mutapa*. What regular human would dare break such a profound taboo? Also, and similar to the effeminacy of the male spirit mediums or healers noted in the previous chapter, some of the most powerful kings among

Nguni-speaking peoples of early nineteenth-century South Africa sometimes performed as if possessed of a feminine spirit – Dingiswayo and Shaka were both reported to have complained of having menstrual cramps. Abstinence or sex with males were thought to have had specific powers to prepare men for battle, as reported among the Azande in Central Africa/Sudan, the Tutsi kingdoms of the Great Lakes, and the Zulu, Ndebele and other Nguni kingdoms in southern Africa. In the latter, the ruler's ability to control his subjects' sexuality was critical to the process of state formation in the late eighteenth and early nineteenth centuries. Under Shaka, Mzilikazi and others, men were strictly not allowed to marry until they had proved themselves in battle and won the leader's permission. Small chieftaincies were unified in that way into large kingdoms and confederacies.

Notions of female pollution could also require men to protect themselves, at the very least by abstinence around the times of menstruation and parturition (breastfeeding). This was yet another incentive for polygyny for those men who could afford it. But it could also assume political importance on important ritual occasions. Donald Donham's analysis of the *ashtime* role in Maale society of southern Ethiopia reveals a case in point. *Ashtime* (which Donham translates as male 'transvestites', but it would probably be more accurate to say transgendered) performed domestic labour and ritual functions in the king's court. The king, as 'the male principle incarnate', had to be shielded from pollution by female sexuality at key moments in the ritual life of the nation. Men who approached him after having had sex with their wives endangered his purity as a symbolic figure. Hence, they should either abstain altogether or have sex with an *ashtime* in order to protect the health of the nation. Achebe (2011) describes something similar to protect the 'female masculinity' of the *eze* (king) Ugbabe – only virgin girls could serve her food.

The spread of Islam brought new forms of political organization to Africa south of the Sahara. Sometimes this came by direct conquest but more commonly it was through the gradual spread of ideas and economic prosperity arising from Muslims' domination of trade with the wider world. Beginning with Kanem and ancient Ghana 1,200 to 1,300 years ago, Muslims established distinctive state forms known as emirates, sultanates, caliphates and pachaliks in much of the West African Sahel and Sudan. From the 800s they also established smaller city-states southwards along the east coast (Mogadishu, Zanzibar, Kilwa, Sofala, and so on). In many cases this started out with a puritanical ethic that allowed the Muslim minority to set itself morally apart from the culture of the majority kafirs (unbelievers). A typical pattern over time, however, was to soften the edges between Islam and traditional practices, both cultural and political. The Moorish traveller Ibn Batutta, for example, famously recorded what struck him as a scandalously loose interpretation of Qur'anic expectations about modesty in Mali. *Mansa* Musa of Mali was reportedly surprised to learn that Islam limited the number of wives a man could have to four – he had travelled to Mecca in 1324 with a retinue of hundreds of his own wives. The *mai* of Bornu, to give an example from the political realm, practised a form of concealment from the public eye inherited from the pre-Islamic times. Sunni Ali of Songhai mixed Islamic prayers with pre-Islamic rites and idols to consolidate his power over the sprawling Songhai empire in the fifteenth century.

Despite the continuity of many pre-Islamic lineages or other economic redistribution practices, and despite the Islamic requirement to give alms, Muslim-dominated states tended over time to concentrate power and wealth in a tiny, urban, literate elite. Modest segregated quarters for Muslim traders gave rise to rich courts with large harems of wives and concubines. Elite privacy and the honour of the male head of household had to be protected by physical seclusion and close guardianship over the women. The preference for the latter task was for male eunuch slaves. Eunuchs were presumed to be impotent and hence without the risk of impregnating the women or holding their own dangerous political ambitions. But eunuchs were not necessarily as sexless as presumed, and harems acquired a reputation for sexual licence, both among the bored and lonely women in seclusion and between the eunuchs and the emir or his guests. The word widely used to mean 'homosexual' in Wolof today (*gor djiguen*) has its origins in a caste of 'natural eunuchs' – that is, not actually castrated but effeminate boys who served in rich households. Similar language recalls similar origins among the Swahili – *basha* (from Turkish *pasha* for 'lord') connoting the penetrator, and *mahanisi* (from Arabic *xanith* or *khanith*) meaning the passive partner, servant or 'third sex' available for hire.

A recurrent pattern in the history of Islam in West Africa and Sudan was for reformist clerics to lead jihads intended to purify the state and society from such perceived looseness. The rise of the Sokoto caliphate in the early nineteenth century drew significant impetus from Fulani Muslims' anger at abuses and indignities women suffered under kafir or nominal Islamic rule (Mack 2011). According to an Egyptian general who was captured by Mahdist jihadists in Sudan in the 1880s, one of the reasons for the Mahdi's success was that he tapped into popular anger at the paederastic practices of Sudan's Egyptian and Turkish rulers (Jacob 2005). In another infamous case from around the same period of time, popular backlash against the ruler's homosexual behaviour and cruelty resulted in the rise of a jihadist faction in the court, civil war, and a revolution that eventually swept Christians into power. It is an important story commemorated today by a national shrine in Uganda, and a huge annual celebration of Christian martyrs as national saints.

The story goes as follows. Mutesa I, the *kabaka* or king of Buganda, had by the late 1860s converted to an eclectic form of Islam as part of his strategy to modernize and expand the kingdom. He nonetheless maintained many traditional practices, including large-scale polygyny to extend his patronage networks throughout the kingdom. Mutesa also allowed European missionaries to establish schools and a presence in the royal court, calculating that Europeans provided access to better guns than the Zanzibaris. It was a volatile mix, and when his young son Mwanga became *kabaka* in 1884 the politics of religion, kinship and sexuality at the court exploded. Mwanga was an autocrat who both exploited the *kabaka*'s traditional practice of grand polygyny (he had at least sixteen formal wives) and felt entitled to command the sexuality of young men under his authority. When Christian pages at court refused to submit to that command, he had some dozens of them executed. Turmoil ensued, with a faction of Muslim purists seeking to impose a hard line against the Christians, traditionalists and wobbly Muslims alike (for example, requiring male circumcision for all males, as well as seeking Mwanga's overthrow). The turmoil was such that, with the looming danger of Egyptian or German intervention in a strategic area, the British stepped in to impose their own preferred *kabaka*. Muslims were marginalized from influence and Mwanga died in exile, a convert to Christianity. Although later repatriated and buried with honour along with Buganda's other *kabakas*, he is widely recalled as the man whose corruption into bisexuality by Muslim traders from Zanzibar set the stage for the kingdom's subordination under colonial rule.

Another important aspect of Islamic societies is that they tended to depend heavily on slaves. Slaves provided domestic service for elites, including as concubines, entertainers and the aforementioned eunuchs. Slaves could also be chattels either for sale into export or for the production of commodities on domestic plantations and mines. For the purposes of our discussion here, however, their role as professional warriors is most interesting. In a number of Islamic states slaves served as a caste of elite soldiers who, in some cases, actually became powerful enough to pose a threat to the political leadership. They were discouraged from ambitions in that direction by, among other things, a ban on marriage and families who might lead them to feel independent of the patronage of the ruler. The Mamelukes of Egypt and Sudan were the classic case, and are worth recalling here for several reasons. The Mamelukes were men imported into Africa mainly from Central Asia, the Caucasus region and the Balkans – that is, from among 'white folks', to use an anachronistic term. A Turkish Mameluke effectively ruled in Egypt from as early as 868, although in the later years of that dynasty, black Mamelukes played a key role in government. They were defeated in 905 by invading Arab armies but the system was retained. Mamelukes lived together in barracks in the encampment that became Cairo, conducted endless military training, and fought fiercely to defend *dar al-Islam* from its many enemies. While they could marry women, neither their wives nor children could inherit any wealth or property. As such, the Mamelukes were a 'one-generation nobility'. Their ranks were constantly refilled not by producing their own children, but by purchasing and attracting recruits.

The Mamelukes were also notorious for being 'addicted to homosexuality' (Murray and Roscoe 1997: 161), primarily with eunuchs imported from elsewhere in Africa rather than each other. That tendency did not seem to compromise their potency as a military force. On the contrary, a Mameluke army liberated Jerusalem and the Levant from the remnants of Christian crusader kingdoms, and in 1250 defeated the combined European armies of the seventh crusade in North Africa. Soon after, they dealt a similar fate to the invading Mongols from the east, and then seized power over Egypt in a *coup d'état* in 1260. In the early fourteenth century, Mamelukes shattered the independence of the Christian kingdoms of Nubia, thus extending the realm of Islam far to the south into present-day Sudan. Their refusal to adopt modern, 'unmanly' weapons such as muskets and cannons eventually led to their defeat and removal from power by the Turks. But as late as the early nineteenth century Mamelukes still provided the backbone of Egypt's military, and even a battalion fighting in Napoleon's army in Europe. The Mameluke system finally ended owing not to homosexual scandal or demographic drought, but through a very focused bloodbath conducted at the order of Egypt's modernizing ruler in 1811.

So who cares about a group of boy- or eunuch-loving white guys in Egypt, massacred to extinction over two hundred years ago? They certainly do not prove the existence of gays or homosexual orientation in African history. As Stephen O. Murray first argued, however, their history is pertinent to today's debates in at least one important way. It confounds arguments one often hears to

117

oppose sexual minority rights – notably, that same-sex sexuality is not sustainable for a nation owing to lack of reproduction, or that homosexuality somehow leads to the decline of military strength, national vigour or civilization in general. The Mamelukes ruled an extensive empire for two and a half centuries, while their system lasted virtually a thousand years, longer than almost any other state institution on the continent. A distinctive culture of masculinity that celebrated old-fashioned equestrian warrior skills, patronage of the arts and allegiance to the faith was renewed each generation without lineage ties. Moreover, the Mamelukes were not just militarily successful but provided the stability for Islamic Egypt's 'Golden Age', the period lasting until the devastation of the Black Death in the 1350s. It was an age when Cairo was the centre of a global network of trade, export production, scientific invention and Islamic learning. Cairo under early Mameluke rule was, in the words of the great Arab historian Ibn Khaldun, 'metropolis of the universe, garden of the world, swarming core of the human species' (cited in Iliffe 1997: 47).

Colonialism

Europeans who came to Africa five-hundred-plus years ago were for the most part neither keen nor able to establish much more than tiny trading outposts along the coasts. They struck alliances and played one African king off against another to win commercial advantages. Attempts to secure territorial control mostly ended in defeat, demoralization by illness or, as in the case of the feudal estates of central Mozambique, progressive 'Africanization' as Portuguese landholders married into local families. The notable exceptions were the self-declared Boer republics established by Dutch- and French-descended settlers who migrated into desirable lands on the southern African highveld, and the Turkish-Egyptian colonization of Sudan from 1820. Even here, the settlers in South Africa only truly entrenched themselves with the assistance of African and mixed-race allies in the late nineteenth century; the Arabs in Sudan with the aid of the British in 1898.

This long history of political weakness sometimes gets forgotten in blanket denunciations of 'five centuries of colonial rule' in which Africans are largely reduced to hapless victims. For others, colonialism may be remembered as bad, but it ended decades ago. Obsessively flogging a dead horse detracts attention from urgent contemporary problems. I would argue, however, that the colonial period set the stage for many of those contemporary problems, in part by the very weakness and complexity of its structures. Indeed, even after Europeans carved Africa up into vast empires in the last decades of the nineteenth century, they crucially depended upon African collaborators to keep the system afloat. The British (in hindsight) called this system Indirect Rule, but the other powers had similar techniques for using Africans to do much of the dirty work of colonialism: gather taxes, enforce labour recruitment, and carry out the many other unpleasant tasks needed to shore up foreign powers to the profit of foreign corporations. This is not to detract from the crimes of European colonialists and their looting business practices. It is just to say that we need to consider the ways in which Europeans incorporated African traditional elites into the system, inventing them first if need be. These had several long-term consequences, including upon gender and sexuality.

First, as alluded to in Chapter 3, rulers in Africa had traditionally had checks and balances against abuse of power. In many cases there had been no chiefs at all but government by consensus of the elders, including post-menopausal women. Consensus was achieved through debate but also by close consultation with the ancestral and other spirits through mediums adept at the arts of selling compromise. Under colonial rule, many of those traditional constraints were removed. Co-opted (or created) chiefs were given extensive new powers as local enforcers or bureaucrats with little interest in abiding by the second-hand opinions of the ancestors, or need to do so. The 'Native Administration' was also given positive incentives from the colonial authority to squeeze their people for personal gain (for example, by 'tax farming' – the more taxes you collect, the more you get to keep personally). Another big traditional check on abuse of power was removed by the imposition of borders. Subjects' ability to pick up and move away from a bad chief was thereby sharply curtailed. Along with cooperative imams, emirs and other Muslim leaders, locally empowered chiefs were freer than before to indulge themselves without regard to old standards of consensus, morality or restraint.

Secondly, the new colonial masters needed to keep subjugated peoples from becoming politicized or forming a common front to oppose the system. Divide and rule by ethnicity was one favoured tactic. In addition, the colonialists sought to minimize unrest by 'scientifically' managing existing social relations, religious beliefs and the practice of law. Customs and practices that were offensive to European sensibilities were outright banned (witchcraft and child marriage, notably), and the most serious crimes were referred to European courts. But otherwise Africans who remained in the rural areas were basically allowed to keep their old ways. The problem was, how to know what the 'real customs' were in order to write them down with scientific confidence? Who were the real custodians of knowledge about these matters? And how to square the new chiefs with the old or, to put it another way, how to find traditions that justified a bureaucratized local authority or other expedient adaptations? This was where anthropology came in, a new scholarly discipline that flowered in the 1920s and 1930s. Once famously referred to as the 'handmaiden of colonialism', anthropology provided the information needed to legitimize a patriarchal tribal authority that served the new system while continuing to provide a cultural buffer for people against the stresses created by an increasingly cash-based economy, and the related breakdown of the moral economy of honour.

For the first few decades, the anthropology (and ethno-psychiatry, another new and closely related 'science') was not very sophisticated. Find the man who looked like the chief or who said he was the chief and ask him (through an interpreter) what the customs of his people were. Write them down. Make them the law to be referred to in all future cases applying to all the people in the neighbourhood who seemed to speak roughly the same language or whom the chief said belonged to him. Use this to block African-controlled innovations that might disturb colonialist prerogatives.

From those crude beginnings, and with slowly improving sophistication, a body of expertise was built up to define exactly who each tribe was, who and what they prayed to, how they married, raised their children and buried their dead, among other day-to-day concerns. The research was so convincing that by the 1950s it was not uncommon for European experts to lecture African chiefs on what their 'real customs' were. In the process, however, flexible, negotiable traditions were codified as inflexible customary or 'Native law'. Ambiguities in African cultures concerning gender and sexuality, such as discussed in the previous chapter, were clarified into more easily managed either/or categories. Subtleties and silences were given explicit names and definitions, assessed for their functions, and preserved for future study in museums of ethnography and colonial governance.

Native Administration comprised an important cog in the wheel of cost-efficient exploitation of a colony's natural resources. Efficient in the years following colonial occupation meant a) the rapid construction of infrastructure across vast spaces and technically challenging terrain, b) the rapid clearance of forests, swamps and wild animals and the preparation of select lands for commercial crops, herds and white settlement, and c) the extraction of mineral or other wealth from the land at as low a cost as possible. Slave labour could of course no longer be condoned, so other means to attract or coerce Africans to do these tasks had to be organized. Indentured labour was one way (long-term contracts, wages payable on completion); alcohol as a recruiting tool was another. However, the requirement to pay taxes in cash was probably the most effective incentive to get African men to sign up for wage labour. The bottom line in all these projects was to keep costs down by not having to compensate the men for the costs of reproduction – that is, to pass responsibility for the care and upkeep of their families as much as possible on to the unpaid labour of African women. This required keeping the women and children in the rural areas where they could feed themselves while the men were away. An added bonus was that it avoided the costs of providing a normal urban infrastructure with family homes, schools and hospitals in the industrial or commercial centres. The chiefs, backed by Europeans with thick, erudite monographs demonstrating the appropriateness of women's perpetual subservience to men, were useful for keeping the lid on the kinds of social strains that inevitably began to appear when the men left for long stints of work hundreds or even thousands of kilometres away.

Where the chiefs were almost useless, however, was on the town side of the migrant labour equation. Here, a more modern architecture of control had to be erected, including police, *askaris* and 'boss boys'. In addition to maintaining discipline among the men and boys who came to work on colonial projects, African police were essential to the task of keeping African women out of the new urban centres. In much of West Africa urban centres pre-dated colonial rule and women dominated market trade. Attempting to exclude them was an impossible task. In the settler colonies of East, Central and southern Africa, however, the colonialists achieved a remarkable accomplishment that lasted well into the mid-twentieth century: cities where 80 or even 90 per cent of the population was male. The few women who were there, often illegally, commonly survived by selling beer and sex in negotiated relationships. So-called loose women or *femmes libres* and their many partners in turn gave rise to an epidemic of sexually transmitted diseases, the most feared of which was syphilis. With no effective treatment available until the 1950s, infection condemned people to infertility, social disgrace and death, not unlike HIV in the 1990s.

Colonial states faced with this situation were compelled to assume an ever-increasing role in policing Africans' sexuality – keeping women away from town, keeping migrant men away from local women, finding and destroying the places where men and women could meet to drink, dance and have sex, and mitigating (at as low a cost as possible) the health and demographic impacts of the migrant labour system. The police and military, of course, could easily exacerbate the problems – the French thus allowed their African conscripts (*tirailleurs Sénégalais*) to bring wives and children along on military campaigns. Some states (Belgium in particular) meanwhile invested in 'stabilizing' an African urban labour force, providing model homes, recreation facilities, social welfare and a complex bureaucracy that allowed a small percentage of the population to settle with family in town. Prisons, closed industrial compounds, juvenile workhouses and psychiatric hospitals (which scarcely differed from each other in the early days) also provided new institutions for the containment of sexual unruliness.

These new instruments and strategies of control in turn gave rise to new forms of disapproved behaviours that eventually re-cycled back into the urban population – for example, through criminal gangs. The kidnapping and rape of girls by young men was one such widely rued behaviour. Young men's ability to earn cash wages freed them from a sense of obligation to parents and community, and threatened the fraught social compact. Less talked about were new forms of male–male relationships. The best-documented cases of the latter were the so-called 'mine marriages' between men and boys in the industrial compounds of Johannesburg in the early 1900s. Migrant men away from their families for months, or even years, at a time, who were afraid to engage in relations with unattached women in town, took younger men or boys as servants and 'wives' for the duration of their contracts so that they could return home healthy and unencumbered by the expenses of a town family.

New laws were imported and refined to catch the new offences. The British, for example, simply copied a law developed in its other big colonial possession, India, that criminalized an act of penetration 'against the order of nature'. Over the decades they added new terms such as 'indecent assault', 'gross indecency', 'soliciting' and '*crimen injuria*' in order to extend the reach of the law to catch consenting, private and non-penetrative acts that the state disapproved of.

A third big change brought by the colonial system is that it stimulated the rise of a small class of mixed-race and/or culturally assimilated, literate Africans sometimes called (including by themselves) progressives, modernizers, educated elites, tea-drinkers and *ama-respectables*. In the case of the French, African *assimilés* could become French citizens with the right to vote and even to sit in the French parliament. Educated elites everywhere played an important role in the developing colonial bureaucracy, school systems and urban social welfare. For the most part, however, they were largely frozen out of the real power structure. Their ability to establish themselves as an economic bourgeoisie was meanwhile undercut by legal restrictions on property ownership, by discriminatory pricing for agricultural products, low salaries and structures that favoured the stranglehold on capitalist trade by non-African minorities. Perhaps even more frustrating, educated Africans were commonly subjected to humiliation at the hands of racist and/or paternalist whites, often tarred with the brush of Africans' supposedly unbridled or primitive sexuality (as proved by the ethnography!). Small wonder that men and women from this class grew restive, indeed very angry in some cases, at the restrictions, injustices and slanders ranged against them. They became the core of the African nationalist movement for independence from colonialism.

Yet at the same time, educated Africans were deeply affected by the colonial ideology of respectability. The generation that emerged as political leaders in the 1930s to 1950s was often the second or third to be educated in the mission school system. European, Christian, middle-class values were part of their family upbringing and something they often very profoundly admired. This was especially so when those values were set against either the retrograde and thuggish chiefs promoted under native authority or the culture of alcohol and freewheeling sexuality among the working class in the cities. African progressives may have been furious at the racism and hypocrisy of European individuals in Africa. However, the ideology of respectability as a marker of modernity and progress remained powerfully attractive to those Africans hoping to rise above both the crumbling traditional moral economy on the one hand, and rampant urban indiscipline on the other.

The main focus of the cult of respectability was the performance of monogamous marriage, with a judiciously fertile wife largely confined to the domestic and churchgoer sphere and a husband who demonstrated his masculine persona of duty, earning power, self-control and paternal authority. Without question many happy and prosperous unions on this model took place over the decades. Poverty, however, was the most obvious threat to Christian marriage, and adultery one of its most common manifestations. This in turn was taken by colonialists as a proof that the African middle class was simply not ready to assume the reins of government.

Same-sex sexuality did not enter into the discussion in any serious way. In part this reflected traditional taboos, but it also reflected colonial and Christian missionary influences. Remember, the late nineteenth and early twentieth centuries were a time of gathering 'scientific' as well as cultural and religious homophobia in Europe. European settlers and missionaries in the colonies brought intolerance of homosexuality with them. Not only was such intolerance important to the performance of their personal respectability, it was also often directly linked to the cause of nation- and empire-building. Homosexuality was equated with effeminacy and weakness in men, whereas a virile masculinity was needed to confront the enemies of the nation/ empire. The dangers of lesbianism were also implicit in the belief that European women were needed as mothers to raise the next generation of imperial patriots and to settle the wild African frontier. It was not a topic commonly raised in public discourse, but the message was conveyed clearly enough through extremely harsh punishments, public humiliation and ostracism of white men caught letting down the side (see Newell 2006 for a close study of one such renegade in colonial southern Nigeria).

The message that homosexuality was not just disgraceful but politically unacceptable also occasionally came through in colonial interventions against Africans whose behaviour cast doubt on the so-called civilizing mission. Such was the case in Belgian-ruled Rwanda in 1930. Léon-Paul Classe was the top church official in the colony at that time. He appealed to the state through the press in Belgium (and presumably behind closed doors as well) to have King Musinga, its central instrument in the native administration, removed from office. Why? Classe claimed that Musinga's flagrant moral breaches brought the Church and Belgian colonial rule into disrepute in the eyes of its enemies (Germany, no doubt, from whom the Belgians had recently taken over responsibility for Rwanda). Musinga's moral breaches included his alleged sexual affairs with young men and boys at the royal court, which, reputedly, had been a long-standing perk of office among the Tutsi aristocracy.

Colonialist homophobia clearly had white supremacy close to its heart. As an ideology, however, it otherwise fitted very well with African middle-class aspirations to assume leadership of the colonial state. In the Rwanda scandal, Classe was said to have been secretly informed of Musinga's behaviour by African Christians who were his rivals at court. The appeal of the ideology is also evident in its continuity from 'tea-drinkers' to radicals in the emerging African nationalist movement. Some of the most influential voices from the 1930s made precisely that point – homosexuality was a threat not just to the survival of the African family but to African dignity in the face of the affronts of colonial racism. To the extent that it existed among blacks at all, they argued, homosexuality was introduced to Africa by whites, one more reason to reject European rule and culture. Jomo Kenyatta (1961 [1938]) was the first African intellectual to explicitly express this view, holding up his people's 'normal' sexuality (heterosexual missionary position only) as a source of pride when set beside confused and perverse Europeans. Even more influentially, Frantz Fanon argued in the 1950s that a revolutionary movement in Africa needed black men to stand up against European men's hatred of blacks arising from their (not always) 'repressed homosexual' desires. In the Cold War era, hardline Marxist-Leninists and Maoists joined in the refrain, characterizing homosexuality as a symptom of Western, capitalist, bourgeois decadence, a betrayal of Africa's toiling masses.

To be sure, homosexuality was never a major theme in the liberation struggle, the subject of fiery speeches on the campaign trail or bloody retribution on the battlefields. Rather, it was more like a footnote, a few scattered letters to the editor, or a subtle subtext in pro-independence politics. Gaudio found denunciations of the 'yan daudu, for example, together with certain lewd dances and prostitution, in letters in newspapers from the 1950s. These were linked to criticism of the emir (British puppet) for not defending northern Nigeria's Muslim nature against corrupting colonial and southern influences. From retrospective comments by a wide range of nationalist leaders from that generation, we can infer that similar politicized homophobia has deep roots in the nationalist project. That includes the obvious, explicitly homophobic denunciations by leaders like Julius Nyerere. But it was also subsumed within the culture of womanizing, 'warrior' masculinity performed by leaders like Kwame Nkrumah, Idi Amin and, yes, by his own belated admission, Nelson Mandela. The theme crops up as well in a genre of African nationalist fiction from the era, wherein heroic male African characters consume women sexually, and white women in particular, as if to cock a snook at white men. It was a masculinity that allowed no room for doubt about African heterosexuality lest such doubt feed into the colonial propaganda of African indiscipline and immaturity.

As it happened, of course, outside of southern Africa formal colonial rule collapsed much faster than almost anyone had expected. In the euphoria of independence, and all the frustrations and calamities that so often followed quickly afterwards, anxieties about the theoretical dangers of homosexuality to the body politic took a back seat to other more immediately obvious and pressing concerns. By numerous accounts there was actually a small flowering of gay or gayish urban scenes in the early post-colonial period – a short-lived 'heaven' in the case of Namibia in the early 1990s, according to one lgbti activist (Currier 2012: 45; see also Le Pape and Vidal 1984 on Abidjan in the 1960s and 1970s).

In the next section, I want to examine what happened to close these milieux down (somewhat), and specifically what changes to the state from the 1970s to the 1990s laid the groundwork for the re-emergence of political homophobia in its contemporary, harsher-than-ever forms.

The post-colonial blues

Under economic and political pressure from the African nationalist movement, the United Nations and the Cold War superpowers, most of the European powers in Africa after the Second World War sped up the pace to hand power over to Africans. Decolonization for most of the continent thus unfolded in a process that might be described as somewhere between rushed and precipitous. Twelve French colonies were granted their independence on a single day in 1960. The Belgians left Rwanda, Burundi and Congo in criminal haste soon after. The British devolved a bit more gradually, but even there, few would have correctly predicted in 1950 that almost all of the colonial empire would be gone by 1966. The Portuguese were an exception, hanging on through the use of extreme violence. When they finally did give up, however, their departure was even speedier than the others. Scarcely more than a year passed between the coup that toppled the Portuguese government in 1974 and the attainment of independence for Angola, Mozambique, Guinea-Bissau and Cape Verde.

In the rush, African leaders had much to do to meet their people's high hopes, not least of all cleaning up the mess departing settlers left. They also scrambled to expand the rudimentary and highly skewed education, health and social welfare infrastructures that the colonialists had built. Policing sexuality was low on the list of priorities. Indeed, because it was reminiscent of colonial obsessions, policing sexuality tended to be neglected altogether. In most cases the new regimes did not even bother to revise the pertinent laws. They simply kept them on the books as inherited but then generally ignored them. This has resulted in some striking anachronisms. Today, for example, Britain's first colony in West Africa, Sierra Leone, retains language that pre-dates Britain's own modernization of its sodomy laws in 1860. The language is so archaic ('abominable crime of buggery, committed either with mankind or with any animal') that American officials researching it in 2010 found that local lawyers 'could not recall a case in which the law had been applied'.

An interesting exception to that rule is Cameroon. There the newly independent government introduced a national criminal code in 1970 which included a brand-new law prohibiting male–male sex. Such a law was justified in part by the need to unify the country, which had inherited Britain's anti-sodomy law in the anglophone part but none in the former French mandate. There were, moreover, lingering, deep divisions between the predominantly Muslim north and the Christian or traditional-ist south of the country that were papered over to some extent by the state's demonstration of a moral fibre that most faith practitioners could agree upon. It has also been speculated that independent Cameroon's first president, Ahmadou Ahijo, had calculated political reasons for wanting to be seen as tough on homosexuality. Rumour had it that he himself enjoyed sex with men, and indeed, allegations linked him to the last French governor. Those rumours resurfaced in 2005 when one of the leading figures from the defeated revolutionary left during the independence struggle claimed that Cameroon's current neocolo-nial dependency could be directly traced to French manipulation of Ahijo's sexuality. The anti-homosexuality law of 1970 was in this view a mere smokescreen to hide his failure as an African patriot (Nyeck 2013).

There is little evidence that the tougher law was ever enforced, and in the main cities of Cameroon, as elsewhere on the con-tinent, small gay scenes or milieux took root. The 1970s also saw a small flowering of 'gay-friendly' fiction by African authors such as Yambo Ouologuem of Mali and Yulisa Amadu Maddy of Sierra Leone, fiction in which the homosexual African character in some cases shows greater moral integrity than the corrupt, violent or womanizing men around him. In the popular press the topic of homosexuality meanwhile made for either easy humour at the foibles of white people, or for serious education. Kenda Mutongi's analysis of letters to the advice column in the influential style magazine *Drum* through to 1980 reveals both young Africans struggling to understand their uncertain sexuality, and the magazine responding with sometimes surprising empathy. In Abidjan, the popular weekly *Ivoire-Dimanche* ran a story in 1983 that almost celebrated the modern style of a flamboyant drag queen and his transvestite cabaret (Nguyen 2005).

Two major exceptions to this pattern were Ethiopia and the states of southern Africa where whites hung on to power. Ethiopia had successfully withstood conquest during the partition of Africa in the nineteenth century, and suffered only six years of Italian misrule from 1935. The emperor returned to power in 1942, quickly restored the old institutions of the feudal state and violently repressed peasant and non-Amharic insurrections. The Orthodox Church was also restored as the state religion and de facto local authority in the rural areas where the vast majority of the population lived. Not only was the Church the extremely conservative guardian of public morality and national identity, the Ethiopian government also promoted itself as the spiritual heart of pan-Africanism and African identity, a conservative bulwark against presumably corrosive Western values. To be sure, with American patronage through the 1950s and 1960s, the capital city of Addis Ababa modernized quite rapidly and we can guess (absolutely no research has been done) that extremely discreet spaces for same-sex encounters were established there. Any slim hope of liberalization, however, was dashed by the revolution of 1974. The Orthodox Church was disestablished, but the new political leadership adopted a crude, repressive form of Marxism-Leninism as the new state ideology that was in some ways even worse, including a pro-natalist policy for its 'patriotic' wars against ethnic secessionists. When this regime in its turn fell (1991), the ostensibly democratic successors replicated much of the old pattern, including the widespread torture and killing of political dissidents, and new 'patriotic' wars against its Muslim neighbours. It was, in short, a social and political climate that made freedom of speech let alone freedom of association around sexuality almost impossible.

In southern Africa, the militarization of white settler populations introduced another dynamic. The apartheid regime in the 1970s stepped up its efforts to prepare young white and biracial men to defend the country against a supposed 'total onslaught' of communists and other Africans bent on the destruction of Western civilization on the continent. In addition to relentless propaganda promoting an idealized heterosexual fighting man, the military embarked upon a secret programme known as the aVersion Project. The aim was to 'cure' suspected homosexuals of their treacherous feelings using psychotherapy and drugs. New laws enabled police to arrest people for an expanding number of same-sex crimes, including lesbian sex and even the possession of sex toys. The pressure to have white and coloured people's bodies conform to their assigned gender roles and identities was so high that South Africa emerged as one of the leaders in the world for sex-change operations for transgendered people, heavily subsidized by the state.

The irony in all this is that the abuses committed in the name of Christian civilization and white rule helped to mobilize a generation of same-sex-attracted people into political activism. White South African conscripts who came out as gay in the late 1980s played a leading role in transforming the small, partying-oriented gay associations of the time into a political movement linked to the broader struggle against racial capitalism. A further irony is that the apartheid state's obsession with policing white sexuality directly fed into that old trope of African nationalist ideology – that is, whites were the main source of homosexual contagion in Africa. The first important use of that trope for political advantage came during the 1990 trial of Winnie Mandela, the 'mother of the nation'. In her defence against charges of kidnapping and murder, she alleged that she had only been trying to protect a defenceless African boy from molestation by a white sexual predator. The argument won her passionate support in the black townships, although, for want of evidence, it failed to convince the court. It may in fact have helped to mobilize the lgbti community to fight harder for the constitutional rights they eventually achieved.

What was it about the South African state that made the transition to embrace sexual minority rights possible, even in a period of tremendous political and civil strife? The long answer to that requires a book, and indeed, several excellent ones explore that remarkable story. The short answer is not because there are so many white people in South Africa. Rather, it boils down to three main factors that may or may not be replicable in other parts of the continent: a) democratic institutions with checks and balances on executive and 'tribal' authorities which, however corrupted and weakened by decades of racialist ideology, still functioned well enough to allow relatively free political expression and association; b) a vibrant and self-confident civil society with allies in the West and friends within the main political parties, including both the ruling party and the presumptive ruling party; and c) an extremely delicate balance between parties whose major constituencies lay in distinct ethnic minorities. In the fraught negotiations for a new constitution, the protection of minority rights assumed a greater salience than was the case in most other political transitions in Africa.

The Zimbabwe case illustrates how difficult it could be for other African countries to follow the South African path. Zimbabwe started with many similarities to South Africa, including (up to the mid-1960s) a respected parliamentary tradition, an independent judiciary and a circumscribed but nonetheless relatively strong civil society that allowed space for the expression of liberal social views. Yes, this was largely restricted to the white minority, whose failure to adhere to stated liberal, Christian values eventually led blacks to take up armed struggle against it. During the 1970s, that bitter war pitted a militarized white minority against African nationalist movements which drew upon Marxism-Leninism, Christian theology and traditional beliefs to justify and mobilize for violence. Yet following a negotiated peace settlement and subsequent democratic elections in 1980, the winning party (ZANU) promised to respect the rule of law, private property, ethnic minorities and the principle of reconciliation between old enemies. The racist and sexist laws of the previous regime were quickly repealed in the spirit of human rights and citizenship for all, including women's legal emancipation from traditional patriarchal authority. There was a massive expansion of the education and health systems in the rural areas and for the historically underserved black majority. Life expectancy in that first decade increased by six years (from fifty-eight to sixty-four, one of the best on the continent). And the prime minister, later president, Robert Mugabe, emerged as a model of statesmanship and a leader among the front-line states in the struggle to liberate South Africa from apartheid. Indeed, many South Africans, including white gays and lesbians fleeing repression or conscription in their own country, came to Zimbabwe in the mid-eighties to enjoy the relative freedom it offered. A small, white-dominated gay scene flourished in the capital city during the first decade of independence, and an association to promote awareness and rights for sexual minorities was formed in 1989: Gays and Lesbians of Zimbabwe. The first gay-identified black men joined soon after and the first known black lesbian/bisexual in the country came out in 1993 (Polyanna Magwiro).

The Zimbabwean state appeared strong enough at that time to withstand the shock. So what happened two years later to make the president suddenly choose to put his reputation as a statesman at risk internationally and to court public dismay domestically by hyperbolically, repeatedly, embarrassingly denouncing homosexuals ('worse than pigs and dogs' in his most famous quote)? A number of personalized theories have been put forward to answer that, including Mugabe's bruised ego at being upstaged as the regional African liberation star by Nelson Mandela. Other possible factors were crass electoral politics which hinted at an attack on whites in general, Mugabe's Roman Catholic conscience belatedly coming out, and to hide his own homosexual affairs (the opposition party MP who spent Christmas 2011 in prison for floating that last theory would probably agree it was not particularly helpful). Yet if the political homophobia was idiosyncratically unique to Mugabe and Zimbabwe's colonial/Christian heritage, how to explain the very similar outbursts that followed in country after country and continue to this day in places with no history of white settlement or democratic elections or Christian missions? Are there lessons we can learn from the Zimbabwean turn that may be helpful for African lgbti and allies elsewhere?

To answer that, we need to understand the meaning of ESAP or *Ehe, Satani Ari Pano* ('yes indeed, the devil is among us'). The devil being referred to in this classically dark Shona pun is not homosexuality at all, but Zimbabwe's Economic Structural Adjustment Programme. ESAP was launched in 1991 on essentially the same neoliberal principles as were beginning to squeeze countries all across Africa and the global South more broadly. Although couched in the language of economic reform, structural adjustment directly targeted and profoundly threatened African states and political systems, and in the process created a thriving market for demagoguery.

To appreciate the impact of ESAP we need to recall Zimbabwe's sometimes bittersweet successes in its first decade of independence. These were achieved under the rubric of so-called scientific socialism, leavened with a dash of Christian liberation theology and targeted repression against old rivals, all taken with a pragmatic grain of African salt. Scientific socialism allowed a great deal of capitalist enterprise and protected white commercial farmers from land expropriation. It also included heavy state involvement to manage the economy and finance the expansion of health, social welfare and education to the majority population. Taxes were high, there were currency controls, central plans, high tariffs on imports, sometimes scarce consumer goods, subsidies for staple products such as maize, agricultural marketing boards that protected small farmers from the vagaries of world market prices, and sometimes critical shortages of inputs to maintain industrial productivity. There was plenty of wiggle room for an underground economy and ingenious jerry-rigging. Wages in the parastatals (government-owned and -managed enterprises in key economic sectors such as steel production) were grossly uncompetitive compared to similar sectors in Asia, in part because they employed unionized workers. But the key point is, they did employ people.

Personally, living in Zimbabwe in the mid-1980s as a high school teacher was a wonderful experience in spite of the obstacles and absurdities that scientific socialism sometimes created. The high payroll taxes and frequent irritation at how difficult it could be to get car parts for the old banger were more than offset by the spirit of pulling together for social change. The inherited infrastructure was solid, and the new health and education systems promised great things. The true extent of violence against Ndebele people in the country's south-west was generally unknown, and in any case, by 1987 a political solution had been reached which brought the two main liberation parties together in a Patriotic Front. Yet one could sense the frustration growing as the eighties drew to a close, particularly at the inability of the economy to generate enough jobs to absorb all the new school-leavers. The level of government debt was ballooning.

Zimbabwe held out longer against the 'Washington consensus' than most African countries. However, the abandonment of state socialist principles by old allies in Tanzania and Mozambique, not to mention the USSR and China, increased the pressure on Mugabe to relent to advice from Zimbabwe's principal donors. In return for new funding to relieve the debt crisis, Zimbabwe would liberalize its economy. This meant, basically, withdrawing the state from interference with the free market. Mugabe probably felt the deal would stimulate the economy out of its semi-stagnation, and indeed, for a small number of people there was an immediate positive effect. Mostly white commercial farmers were now able to import cheap vehicles, machinery and agricultural inputs, to ramp up exports of specialized products such as flowers, and to keep profits from their exports in foreign currency. Politically well-connected black elites picked up government-owned assets sold off for a song, and stimulated a building and consumption boom in the low-density suburbs.

For the majority of the population, by contrast, a stunning, long-term crisis exploded. Free primary healthcare and schooling were replaced by service user fees. Local manufacturers went bankrupt in the face of cheap imported goods. State employees were made redundant and unemployment soared. As the Zimbabwe dollar crashed, the costs of imported fuel and other hard currency items rocketed, spreading inflation through the economy and bloating the foreign debt. It was the perfect recipe for alienation, food insecurity, unemployment, street crime and street kids, gender-based violence, the proliferation of slum housing conditions, and survival sex (sex for cash). These in turn all poured fuel on the tuberculosis and HIV/AIDS co-epidemic just then beginning to take off. By the end of the decade, Zimbabwe's average life expectancy at birth had fallen to thirty-seven years, the lowest in the world.

The main political opposition party, Movement for Democratic Change, and the current prime minister, Morgan Tsvangirai, owe their rise to their leadership of the labour movement through the unfolding ESAP catastrophe. By 1995 Mugabe was keenly aware of his vulnerability in this respect. Unlike other African countries which took their neoliberal medicine *after* a prolonged period of crisis, Zimbabwe took its meds *before*. It was a choice, and no amount of blaming the IMF could hide how well the people in the ruling party who had made that choice were doing as the majority fell into misery. Attacking gays and lesbians during the presidential election campaign in 1995 was thus a diversion, however implausible, calculated to stem the haemorrhaging of political support away from the president. Given that the crisis is still not resolved, and indeed has become progressively worse, the diversion can be trotted out at convenience. This included, in 2012, as one of several red herrings to allow ZANU to sabotage negotiations for a new constitution. It denounced drafters' proposal for no discrimination based on 'circumstances of birth' as 'trickery and deceit' to sneak gay rights into the constitution against the democratic wishes of the mass of the population which ZANU claims to embody.

Every African country went through some form of ESAP. The acronyms and morbid humour varied from place to place, but the neoliberal mantra remained the same: short-term pain for long-term gain. Unfortunately for the theory, most people do not become more liberal minded as their family, tribal or national pies shrink. They often behave in irrational and even unscrupulous ways. Some families pillage the belongings of widowed daughters-in-law, some men abandon their families, some traffic in children, many look for someone to blame and hate for the misery they feel. Embattled elites and factions within elites in adjusting countries commonly seized upon the latter instinct, mostly by directing demagogic language to scapegoat ethnic or national minorities, Rwanda being the extreme case, but see also the anti-foreign rhetoric in Nigeria. A lot of anger could also be directed at the West. Mugabe was particularly skilled at portraying Africa as a victim, and gays and lesbians as proxies of the victimizers.

Few of the other adjusting countries even had sexual rights associations that could be inflated to such a threat. The idea nonetheless touched some very old and widespread anxieties. Who had not heard whispers about the occult power of same-sex sexuality and of metaphysical collective punishments against the people? Who had not heard of cases of Western tourists or priests or their African proxies exploiting Africans? Everyone suffers when individuals misbehave. To that extent, the political homophobia made sense to people under siege by unseen forces, whether those forces were called ancestors, zombies, the West or global markets.

The reference to zombies is not a bad joke, although 'demons' is probably the more common choice of word people use to understand the unseen forces at work. Indeed, one other pronounced effect of the economic crisis and the contraction of the state has been the spectacular rise in popularity of fundamentalist Christian churches and Islamist movements. Both promise to ease people's suffering in the crisis and to step in with community and social supports where government, markets and the old (mainline) religious institutions have so profoundly failed.

The new faiths also offer sometimes quite explicit and pointed political critiques of the elites who facilitated, and profited from, structural adjustment. The mainstream churches and moderate imams were often closely linked by family or other ties to the political leadership that got the country into trouble in the first place. The mainlines suddenly faced an existential struggle to account for themselves and to retain the loyalty of their members.

Competition for souls is a very old story in Africa, but it has unquestionably intensified in recent years as the promises of development/adjustment/globalization/(preferred jargon here) have proved so hollow to so many. This competition frequently requires the severe simplification of religious teachings. The Lord's Resistance Army boiled its message down to the ten commandments in its struggle against the Ugandan state. Others have turned to literalist interpretations and rote repetition of the easiest selections from the sacred texts, turning away from more difficult metaphorical and contextualized readings, and neglecting the history of complex debates about sexuality among theologians and traditional healers. In places where sectarian tensions between Muslims and Christians are on the boil and heading for open violence, leaders in the respective communities face intense pressures to appear strong, certain and morally clear. The space for reflection on the ambiguities and diversity of the human condition has been sharply narrowed.

Not surprisingly, African politicians are behind some of this turn to fundamentalisms, manipulating the situation for their own political advantage and making it difficult for humanistic interpretations of faith to compete. The Archbishop of Khartoum in the Episcopal Church of Sudan, for example, came under attack by a rival within the church for allegedly taking 'gay money' and favouring the ordination of gays and lesbians. The rumour was that the rival was backed by the government in Khartoum in order to undermine the Church, hence to weaken the appeal of secession in the Christian south while promoting its own Islamist agenda and dirty war in Darfur. In Uganda, the government of Yoweri Museveni has used moralistic Christian rhetoric to justify its militarized, repressive, highly conservative agenda in the fight against the LRA, the AIDS crisis and domestic political enemies. In Gambia, a man who came to power by the barrel of the gun and who has since the mid-1990s presided over an expansion of a sex tourism 'industry' (among many other glaring structural adjustment outcomes), in the run-up to presidential elections in 2008 suddenly cloaked himself in references to shari'a law and Islamic justice. A pattern begins to emerge.

§

One other state has had a profound impact upon the politics of sexuality in contemporary Africa, that being the United States. I do not want to focus too much attention there, and hence add to that irritating habit of casting blame on 'imperialists' for all of African history, and of making Africans the perpetual victims of others rather than captains of their own fate. But people sometimes treat political homophobia in Africa in isolation from external pressures. I want to remind them that American influence on this issue has been significant – and has been changing in dangerous ways.

The big stereotype is that the USA is the main exporter of perversion to the rest of the world. San Francisco was ground zero for gay liberation and 'Gay Related Immune Deficiency' (the early, misleading term for AIDS). Los Angeles is the main source of pornography in the world, and has long been at the forefront of a global cultural industry that now churns out a raft of gay-friendly movies and homonormative television characters. New York City is the headquarters of the 'gay international' (ILGA, IGLHRC, *The Rachel Maddow Show*, the United Nations and such). Washington under President Barack Obama began to assert an intrusive sexual and reproductive rights foreign policy, threatening to cut off its development assistance to human rights violators, and even hosting African gay rights activists at the White House. When politicians greeted the passing of Nigeria's Prohibition of Same-Sex Marriage Bill by exclaiming 'Africa for the Africans', they were making the point that state-backed homophobia in

Nigeria was a legitimate way to stand up to US cultural and other imperialism.

The impact of American sexual liberalism on Africa is, however, more assumed and asserted than studied and substantiated. The high-sounding rhetoric and flashy pop culture in fact tend to blind people to what has been a far more significant impact in the opposite direction, a not-so-discreet shoring up of the forces that have been most active in promoting homophobic policy and violence. The recent export of gay-friendly cultural products like *Will and Grace* and Lady Gaga, for example, must be assessed against what is far more prevalent in Africa: homophobic and misogynistic hip hop or gangsta culture, and hand-me-down scientific homophobia embedded in much psychiatric theory.

With specific respect to the state, we need to start by recalling that the USA over the last three decades has indirectly fomented homophobia by cultivating many of the anti-democratic tendencies in Africa discussed in the previous section. As noted, the Washington consensus around neoliberal economic policy pulled the rug out from under the state in Africa. Americans were thus the main architects and most vigorous cheerleaders of the catastrophic structural adjustment programmes that create conditions in which intolerance flourishes and African politicians clutch at whatever scapegoat straws they calculate might work. But there is an even older narrative that sometimes gets forgotten. During the Cold War the USA supported many of Africa's most odious dictators. Its policy of 'constructive engagement' with South Africa prolonged the life of white supremacist regimes there, in Zimbabwe, Namibia, and in neighbouring Portuguese colonies. When the latter collapsed, it covertly intervened in civil wars that resulted in hundreds of thousands of deaths. We should add to this that US foreign policy in the Middle East and the Horn of Africa has long provided political fuel to radical Islamist groups that are undermining the cultural tolerance found in more traditional forms of Sufism as widely practised in Africa. The recent war in Libya is germane here in that it quite directly abetted the rise to power of al-Qaeda-linked secessionists in Mali and the spread of hardline shari'a to a whole new swathe of West Africa. To be fair, the USA also strongly backed the liberalization of family law in its ally, Morocco, although ironically this may have helped to stabilize the monarchy in the face of other pressures to democratize.

The legacy of US government moralism in the struggle against HIV/AIDS also continues to intrude on the debates. The President's Emergency Program for AIDS Relief (PEPFAR) poured billions of dollars into prevention and treatment programmes. Even George W. Bush's enemies will often cite it as a success – perhaps his only one – credited with averting over a million deaths. The money, however, came with strings attached, including the infamous 'gag rule'. This prohibited any organization that 'promoted' sex work or abortion from receiving funds – such organizations were often the only ones in some countries which understood what sexual minority rights were and were sympathetic if not actively engaged in that struggle. PEPFAR did advocate the ABC approach to prevention (abstain, be faithful, and condomize), but it placed a high minimum requirement for spending on abstinence programmes. This resulted in hundreds of millions of dollars going to faith-based groups, some of which denied the effectiveness and morality of condoms. According to Robert Thornton (2009), PEPFAR officials in Uganda tried to repress evidence that contradicted their rosy claims about the effectiveness of the abstinence approach. His, and others', conclusion is that by fudging the evidence and strengthening anti-human rights groups, the USA may have contributed to the resurgence of HIV/AIDS in Uganda in the last decade. More to the point here, US taxpayer money also went to groups that openly promoted anti-homosexuality education. Through USAID, Americans lent a secular, scientific veneer to organizations that unabashedly discriminated against people on the basis of their sexuality (Ugandan Christian University, for one well-funded example).

Undoubtedly, the victories of Barack Obama in 2008 and 2012 were major setbacks for social conservatives in the USA, and a frustration for some of their international activities. The most egregious strings in PEPFAR have now been removed. The US State Department began collecting intelligence on the state of lgbti rights in Africa in 2008, producing its first annual report the following year. The Wikileaks documents show that US officials met with sexual rights activists where they exist, sought advice from them on how to help them in their struggles against human rights violations and for public health, and intervened at the highest level of government to urge restraint on leaders like Yoweri Museveni in Uganda. And yet, a close read of those documents also reveals a striking degree of mildness and respect for African leaders' needs to save political face. While American diplomats raised the anti-homosexuality bill with Museveni several times in 2009/10, the American embassy in turn passed on his request for the US administration to tone down its language and let him handle the issue quietly. When President Jammeh of Gambia conceded he had made a speech threatening to 'cut off the heads' of homosexuals, the American ambassador 'suggested that sometimes the choice of words can be left to interpretation and care should be taken when speaking in public'. Of course, these documents do not reveal the whole behind-the-scenes story, but they do not support the claim that the USA is aggressively twisting arms to promote gay rights.

Ironically, or perhaps infuriatingly would be a better term, the very successes of the sexual rights movement in the USA are contributing to the strength of its opponents in Africa. The Christian right remains an extremely powerful political force in the USA. It is constantly threatening to overturn abortion rights, state funding for contraception and other sexual health interventions. It has scored significant successes to 'balance' science-based sexuality education programmes in favour of so-called evolutionary science. It has been highly active in the fight to defeat sexual minority rights in the USA, including by plebiscites to overturn legislation of same-sex marriages and assiduously mobilizing to unseat Obama from office. The inescapable fact remains, however, that the Christian right has been generally losing such battles on the domestic front. Bans on same-sex marriage achieved through plebiscites or state congress have been overturned through the court system. Leading spokesmen and -women on the Christian right, including the 2012 presidential candidates, have been the target of unprecedented ridicule in the mainstream media. To offset some of that, they often feel obliged to deny that they are homophobic. The Christian right is also losing the battle to defend the homophobic hard line in a growing number of mainline Protestant churches in the USA. The Lutheran and Episcopal churches, notably, now allow the ordination of openly gay and lesbian ministers and perform same-sex weddings.

In this context, Africa has emerged as a new battleground for America's 'culture wars', a field made ripe for the export of discredited ideas from the USA by the demoralizing impacts of bad governance and economic structural adjustment. We can be sure that there are many sincere, joyous, selfless and compassionate people involved in the evangelical project. Yet there have also been deeply cynical interventions by Americans in African affairs under the guise of moral rearmament or family values. The more African Christians know about their supposed friends on this issue, the better.

The Christian right in the USA has long regarded Africa with interest. It was an enthusiastic defender of Ronald Reagan's policy of 'constructive engagement' with apartheid, and an apologist for white minority rule through such organizations as the Institute for Religion and Democracy. Indeed, the IRD was founded in 1981 precisely to oppose the National (also the World) Council of Churches' policy of support for the liberation struggle against apartheid. One of its early 'successes' was to slander the NCC for supposedly using congregant donations to fund African Marxist 'terrorists' (in its terms; Clarkson 2006). In more recent times, the IRD has been an unwavering supporter of Israel. It is scathing in its criticism of the 'religious left' for expressing doubts about the wisdom of the USA and allies bombing Sudan, Iraq and Libya. One of the rare issues on which the IRD is not harshly critical of Obama is his commitment to fight the remnants of the Lord's Resistance Army, which used to cause havoc in northern Uganda.

Uganda in fact appears to be ground zero in the current battle for hearts and minds. The seeds for this were planted as far back as 1986. Despite his socialist rhetoric, the US government at that time regarded Yoweri Museveni as a potential ally in the region and reopened its aid programme. Christian evangelists joined the effort to rebuild the country in the aftermath of war, among them Bob Hunter, a former member of the Ford (Republican) and Carter (Democrat) administrations and subsequently a leading figure in the Fellowship, or Family. The Family is commonly described as fundamentalist, secretive, neoconservative and a leading force in the Christian right, notable for its strong focus on recruiting influential political leaders. Hunter, by his own account, quickly struck up a friendship with Uganda's new president and his wife, Janet, and over the next two decades facilitated burgeoning links between Uganda and other conservative American churches, institutes and politicians. Among the latter is Republican Senator James Inhofe, perhaps best known for his role as a climate change denialist, but also claiming to be the most knowledgeable man in Congress about Africa. These evangelical organizations were often very well connected with the political establishment in the United States, including the aforementioned Institute for Religion and Democracy, the Saddleback Church (said to be the largest in the country, whose pastor, Rick Warren, gave the prayer at President Obama's inauguration) and Pepperdine University. Pepperdine is a self-described Christian institution whose best-known faculty member is the man who led the Whitewater investigation into Bill and Hillary Clinton's alleged corrupt dealings in the mid-1990s, Kenneth Starr.

Millions of dollars flowed into Uganda to support such activities as the establishment of the Uganda Christian University, the travel of conservative Ugandan theologians to and throughout the USA to study and to 'cast out demons', among other activities, as well as more typical health and social welfare projects. A notable success came with Janet Museveni's conversion to a Born Again. Following the Family model in Washington, DC, in 1999 she launched a National Prayer Breakfast for Ugandans to repent of their immoral behaviour. Uganda meanwhile did indeed emerge as a key US ally in Africa, receiving hundreds of millions of dollars in aid, including military training. Uganda has 'peacekeeping' troops in Somalia to fight the Islamist insurrection there, while the USA now has a small brigade of troops based in Uganda. This is ostensibly to assist in the hunt for the LRA but also, we might reasonably surmise, to stand watch over the development of the region's new-found oil riches.

Anti-homosexuality has always been a key component of Christian right theology. It became explicit in Uganda beginning in the late 1990s with a number of speeches by President Museveni. Martin Ssempa, a confidant of Janet Museveni, was meanwhile a frequent visitor to the Saddleback Church in the early 2000s, where he lectured Americans on the supposed successes of Uganda's AIDS prevention through abstinence and heterosexual monogamy. The US connection, however, only really became widely apparent in 2009. In that year, three prominent American speakers attended an event in Kampala called the Seminar on Exposing the Homosexual Agenda. Scott Lively, Dan Schmierer and Caleb Lee Brundridge all claimed to be able to coach or cure homosexuals back to heterosexuality. They came to advise Ugandans both on how to do that and on the nature of the threat posed to the country by Western homosexuals (said to be recruiting Ugandans to their cause). Family-backed Ugandans took up the struggle soon after in a national anti-homosexual campaign that included Ssempa publicly airing explicit gay pornography. Ssempa then collaborated with political ally David Bahati, who introduced the Anti-Homosexuality Bill to parliament in April 2009.

The USA–Uganda connection has gained considerable attention in the USA owing in large measure to the investigative work of Jeff Sharlet and talk show host Rachel Maddow. Ssempa himself became known through a YouTube video that has received millions of hits. Zambian researcher Kapya Kaoma has meanwhile shown that the US evangelicals are also active elsewhere on the continent in sometimes quite brazen, albeit covert ways. Most remarkable to me was his revelation that the IRD doctored a statement by Reverend Jerry Kulah of Liberia to turn Kulah's vague call for moral renewal into a specific attack on liberal-minded Methodism (the United Methodist Church is one of the churches in the USA that has been wavering on the issue of ordaining gay ministers). The IRD also used Kulah's name to introduce the concept of a 'massive silent invasion of Islam' in Africa that appealed primarily to its US audience (Kaoma 2009: 20). Kaoma provided other examples of American ghost writers behind some African theologians' denunciations of liberal interpretations of scripture on homosexuality; the systematic buying of Africans' votes to block reform in the Episcopal, Anglican, United Methodist and moderate wing of the Baptist churches in the USA; the indoctrination of African leaders in the abstinence approach to HIV/AIDS using bowdlerized science to discredit condoms as a prophylaxis; and promotion of the idea that homosexuality, abortion and sexuality education are part of a Western neocolonialist project. The American Center for Law and Justice, founded by televangelist and former apartheid and Mobutu apologist Pat Robertson, now has regional offices in Kenya and Zimbabwe. It advises political leaders on how to frame laws and constitutions so as to block sexual minority and women's rights claims, while drawing attention to the persecution of African Christians by Muslims (Kaoma 2012).

The Christian right in Africa is no doubt using American evangelists and their very deep pockets to achieve its own objectives: to provide social services that African governments are unable or uninterested in doing, to promote local church brands against rivals, and to distract attention from political repression and corruption in the regimes that nurture them (and to which they are in many cases closely linked by social and family ties). However, it is abundantly evident that American anti-gay evangelists are exploiting popular naivety in Africa on this issue and using Africans in their own battles in the USA. How? By encouraging extremism in Africa, radical American anti-gay activists can pose as moderates in comparison. Citing African theologians gives heft to what otherwise often looks like a losing fight in the USA. The

IRD statement on marriage, for example, leads with a statement by 'African Christian leaders' as a preamble to mocking gay Episcopal minister Gene Robinson, a strong supporter of human rights in Uganda. Subsidized travel for African delegates has helped to pack theological conferences with opponents of reform and stalled decision-making on that issue in several mainline churches in the US. One hopes not to be too cynical, but there is a consumer side to all this as well, with US Christian television networks streaming throughout Africa selling products as well as righteousness. The IRD prompts people on how to donate a portion of their estate in their wills (suggesting $15,000, 12 per cent, a home or jewellery) among other cash appeals for its so-called charitable activities. While that appeal is presumably directed primarily at Americans, the lack of financial transparency in US-backed African evangelical churches is a serious cause for concern.

The Christian right in the USA is not the only foreign actor directly implicated in the rise of homophobic ideologies in Africa, and we may rightly wonder at the role of Saudi Arabia or Iran in promoting the Islamic right. That is a research project still to be done. It is important to recall, however, that the stereotype of the USA as the main and consistent proponent of sexual minority rights is not factually correct. That in turn raises a further important question of where people in the USA and elsewhere in the West should be focusing their attention in their will to support African lgbti.

§

Sex has had a long political career in Africa, thousands of years if one considers the role of marriage in forging alliances between powerful families and securing men's loyalty to the state. The ritual breaking of taboos (incest, 'wealth medicine') has been a relatively common practice that enhanced the mystery of power. Control over the sexuality of slaves, including self-control if we consider the highly successful Mameluke masculinity, has played an important role in state formation throughout the continent.

Set against those thousands of years, colonialism seems like a blip in time. Yet colonialism had very profound and lasting impacts upon African sexualities which continued to shape political institutions and discourses in the decades following independence. Among other things, explicitly homophobic ideology became entrenched in African nationalist discourse. On the other hand, the colonial period also created new spaces for Africans to experiment with new types of relationships and expressions of gender and sexuality. Some of these became the milieux or discreet homosexual scenes of the early post-independence period. Whether they might have evolved to become more visible and more accepted by the general population is an open question. Outside of South Africa, however, and even there only fitfully, such a development never happened. Political malaise and corruption, unresolved ethnic or other conflicts, and deteriorating economic conditions undermined the ability of African states to provide social welfare and to argue for sexual minority rights. Indeed, by the mid-1990s the situation was ripe for African leaders to scapegoat minorities and foreigners for their own culpability in the multilayered crisis. Ironically, seeking allies in the religious right, leaders like Museveni have opened doors for canny Americans to propagate new and increasingly explicit forms of homophobia, and to enlist Africans in a US domestic 'culture war'. What I would like to show in the final chapter is how people are now targeting – or avoiding – the state in their strategies to promote sexual health and rights.

5 | Struggles and strategies

In the current climate, many same-sex-practising people opt to remain in, to return to or to adapt traditional forms of discretion that allow them to avoid attention, including by secretive, de facto bisexuality. This desire to keep a low profile is understandable, and a case can certainly be made that 'don't ask, don't tell' is more effective for preserving freedoms in many places than litigation or lobbying for rights could ever be. In the context of high rates of HIV/AIDS, however, this strategy is decidedly risky, not just directly in health terms but also in its potential to engender an even fiercer backlash against sexual minorities (spreading disease to the moral majority!). More and more Africans are accepting the need actively to engage the debates and come out from behind the veils of secrecy or denial.

The newish activism comes in many forms. Research, or the *ethical* pursuit of new knowledge that may be applied to efforts to change policy, social attitudes or cultural beliefs, is one obvious one dear to my own heart. Feminists also made the point some time ago that we should consider building personal relationships based on honesty, self-worth and respect for the integrity of others as a form of activism critical to the struggle for human rights. The focus of this chapter, however, is on the two most obviously public fields of activist engagement. They share the common long-term goals of attaining human rights and social justice, but differ on how best to press their cases forward in the face of public scepticism or the hostility of the state and other institutions. On the one hand are those who emphasize rights in principle, and on the other those who use the language of public health to make the rights argument in less obviously confrontational terms.

With respect to the first strategy, I look first at a few of the major turning points in the history of sexual rights activism in Africa – it is older than you might think. I will also elaborate upon what sexual minority rights might eventually, potentially, entail. In practice, African lgbti have tended to make quite modest claims (the simple right to privacy, notably). But there is no denying that the full panoply of sexual and reproductive rights suggests a fairly radical transformation of society, governance and political economy. It can be helpful to think about the full panoply for ideas on how to link sexual minority rights to the broader objective of social justice for all.

An explicit rights strategy remains hotly contested even in some of the most established and developed democracies in the world. In most of Africa today the transformation it implies is not just daunting; just to enumerate the necessary changes can incite a strong reaction. How, then, to advance those long-term rights/ justice arguments past the door of disapproving gatekeepers? One of the main strategies towards that end is to link advocacy for the health of sexual minorities to the achievement of health for all. The second section of the chapter focuses on that, and in particular on the strategic use of euphemism and technocratic language to get the rights foot in the door of public discourse.

There are risks in both approaches, but I hope to show that real successes are not just possible but are happening today in ways and in places that challenge the doom-and-gloom analysis that often predominates in the media. I also want to make the point that activists, donors and researchers from the West have played and will continue to play an important role in this struggle. In the future, their ability to contribute will require greater patience and respect for distinctive aspects of the African context than has sometimes been the case to date.

Rights activism

'Stonewall' is shorthand for 'the start of the gay liberation movement', so named because of a riot and political organizing that followed a police raid on the New York City gay bar, Stonewall.

Every country has (or will have!) its own Stonewall, an event that galvanizes lgbti into political consciousness and activism in some form or another.

It has been said that 'Africa's Stonewall' took place in a leafy suburb of Johannesburg in 1966 – that is, three years before the New York version. The police had raided a private house after a tip that men were behaving lewdly with other men. Indeed they were: hundreds were caught, ten men arrested, and much scandal splashed across the headlines. For these were not just any men. They were white men, in many cases from elite families. The scandal led to a proposal to increase police powers to investigate such parties and crack down on homosexuality in general. This in turn sparked the establishment of the Legal Reform Movement to lobby for an end to police harassment of consenting adult relationships. It sought the reform of discriminatory laws based on new scientific knowledge about homosexuality then emerging from the West but interpreted in South Africa by such scholars as Louis Freed and Renée Liddicoat.

A parliamentary committee was set up to investigate the issues, taking evidence from a wide range of witnesses, including police and concerned citizens on both sides of the debate. The main concern of the committee was the presumed danger to society posed by homosexual (presumed effeminate) white men. This reflected long-standing anxieties about the sustainability of white minority rule in South Africa. Would effeminate white men have the backbone to defeat black revolution? While most of the debate focused on existing laws against 'sodomy' and 'unnatural offences' directed almost exclusively against men, women who loved women added their voices to the demand for sexual rights. Among the petitioners was Durban author Mary Renault. Unbeknown to the vast majority of South Africans, Renault was already something of a hero to gay men in the West on account of her quietly subversive portrayals of male–male love and sexual relationships in her novels set in ancient Greece.

The Forest Town raid and subsequent reaction were un-questionably important events that succeeded in placing sexual minority rights directly in the public eye for the first time in Africa. However, there are three big problems with celebrating it as 'Africa's Stonewall'. First, unlike the real Stonewall, the Forest Town raids did not succeed in bringing about legal reform or spark a national movement for change. On the contrary, through the 1970s and 1980s, the apartheid regime actually introduced new repressive laws, including some aimed directly at lesbians. The reform movement simply melted away.

Secondly, the focus on South Africa as taking the lead on this issue feeds into the notion of South African exceptionalism – that is, the presumption that South Africa is always and self-evidently ahead of the rest of the continent. To put it negatively, as often happens, South Africa is 'too white' to be 'really African' and therefore irrelevant to the debates in Uganda or Senegal. In fact, much of Africa in 1966 already had what the reform movement was arguing for. As far back as 1791, the revolution-ary government of France removed the old laws against sodomy and 'crimes against nature' from its penal code. The new code applied directly to France's four communes in Senegal but was later established throughout the French empire as it expanded over West Africa and Madagascar. Portugal also decriminalized same-sex acts long before there was any kind of homosexual rights movement (indeed, even before the word homosexual had been invented). Although both Portugal and France later recriminal-ized sodomy (1886 and 1941, respectively), there is little evidence that the renewed hostility to homosexuality in the metropoles was institutionalized in their African colonies. This may partly explain why relatively open 'gay scenes' existed in places like Lourenço Marques (Maputo), Tangier, Abidjan and Dakar. Taking into account that Belgium extended similar laws over today's Democratic Republic of Congo, Rwanda and Burundi, it can be seen that many independent African countries inherited a rela-tively progressive legal code in comparison to the former British colonies like South Africa and Uganda.

Thirdly, the history of the Law Reform Movement simply does not resonate very well in Africa today, or even among the majority of black lgbti in South Africa. Just look closely at the hidden subtext of the narrative: middle-class white people complain about discrimination while enjoying the material benefits of a system of exploitation and human rights abuses against black people. Their lack of attention to the wider injustices in their society meant that the movement for sexual minority rights did not gain credibility among black South Africans for at least two more decades. Indeed, Stonewall for black South Africans might more accurately be identified as a cluster of less dramatic events in the mid-1980s: the coming out of anti-apartheid leader Simon Nkoli, the expulsion of the white-dominated GASA from the International Lesbian and Gay Association, and the explicit acknowledgement of gays' rights to privacy and freedom from discrimination by Thabo Mbeki, the eventual president of the country.

I would like to recall, then, another event that may be more interesting to lgbti activists in Nigeria, Botswana or Burundi today. This is not to suggest it as a Stonewall moment or model of activism, but simply as a demonstration of the power of sexuality to mobilize people even under extremely repressive conditions. It is a story of working-class black men successfully resisting the power of the colonial state, thwarting the efforts of their white employers, and thumbing their noses at the moralistic campaigns of homophobic Christian missionaries. To what purpose? To defend the right to have male–male sexual relations and even marriages as they desired. That story pre-dates Africa's so-called Stonewall by almost five decades.

In the previous chapter I mentioned the emergence of the practice of 'mine marriage' or *nkotshane*, as it came to be known in several of the major languages of southern Africa. By most contemporary accounts the practice first appeared among the Tsonga or Shangaan people of southern Mozambique in the late 1890s. These men migrated in large numbers to work in the gold mines of the Johannesburg area, where they were housed in large, male-only compounds. By 1896 there were an estimated 30,000 Tsonga men in the city to ninety Tsonga women (Harries 1994: 323). Many of those women had multiple partners and as a result acquired sexually transmitted infections. The men themselves certainly saw it that way and so, to protect their earnings and health for an eventual successful return home, they began taking their boy servants or other younger men as sexual partners. Over time the practice became normalized along the following pattern. The boys and young men arrived at the compounds, were taken up by (or sought out) an older patron who gave them protection and gifts in exchange for thigh sex (that is, no anal penetration). As the young men matured and had earnings enough to buy gifts for their own *nkotshane*, they would graduate from the passive to the active role. Sometimes the unions were celebrated with dancing and such feasts as were possible in the context of barracks life. At the end of their contracts, they would return home *sans* syphilis and without any obligations to a town family, enabling them to marry and build a respected family in the rural areas with land and cattle.

The mining companies and the South African government knew about this practice almost from the beginning but generally tolerated it as the lesser of several evils arising from their need for abundant and extremely cheap male labour. Attempts to suppress it were generally half-hearted and intended mostly to demonstrate probity to missionary critics or scandalized chiefs in the rural areas. In October 1919, however, a 'police boy' from Lesotho named Alfred Maama overstepped the limit of what the mine owners could turn a blind eye to. Maama had effectively kidnapped and was raping a young boy in the compound at Brakpan mine. The boy, Mokete, finally escaped and reported the abuse. The company laid charges against Maama. But to its surprise Maama and no fewer than forty-four of his supporters put down their tools and left the mine in protest. The company was forced to back down to get them back, reinstating Maama to his position and tacitly acknowledging his men's 'right' to take boy-wives in return for Maama paying a fine.

Clearly, Maama does not qualify as a gay rights activist, and the *nkotshane* system is not something anyone today would advocate. This anecdote nonetheless speaks to the potential for a determined minority to win concessions even from an oppressive state and 'totalizing institutions' such as the huge mining corporations. My point is that there are probably other such events in every African country, perhaps hushed up as a scandal. While they might not be directly pertinent to today's debates about rights or gender equality, they could trip up stereotypes of identity, culture or nature more effectively than the chronological progress-to-rights narrative. It's something to look for.

To return to the progress narrative in a more recognizable form, however, we do need to go back again to the white folks of South Africa, English-speakers above all. More than any other 'tribe' on the continent, white anglophone South Africans tended to keep a close eye on cultural developments in the West. Johannesburg in particular long styled itself as a modern, Western, cosmopolitan city. By the early 1970s, things were changing rapidly in the West. Those were what reporter Randy Shilts (1987) called the 'glory days', a period of mass coming out from the closet of Cold War homophobia but before the fearful onset of HIV. A subculture emerged in places like London, San Francisco and New York City that celebrated sexual freedom, experimented with new acts and relationships, and proudly, openly displayed that freedom to the world. It was not long before some white South Africans began to seek the same and to organize themselves into often colourfully named associations that could amplify their voices. GAIDE, Lambda, GASA, TOGS (a sports-themed group), LILACS and numerous others sought to create safe spaces and to promote self-esteem in the context of South Africa's intensifying political homophobia in the late 1970s and early 1980s.

The history from that point has been well told elsewhere (Gevisser and Cameron 1994, notably, and Hoad et al. 2005). Here let me just sketch the main trends: white-dominated associations that looked primarily to the West for inspiration split into rival groups in the mid-1980s. People of colour like Simon Nkoli, Bev Ditsie and Alfred Machela, plus whites who were critical of apartheid, such as anti-conscription campaigner Ivan Toms and Sheila Lapinsky, formed their own associations. Rather than mutual social support or the cultivation of self-esteem, they placed their priority on ending the system of racial discrimination in the country. This was, of course, eventually successful, but in the meantime many activists left South Africa as exiles, including to neighbouring Zimbabwe, where they contributed to the establishment of a rights movement in a second African country. Gays and Lesbians of Zimbabwe subsequently went through a similar wrenching process of debate about race and politics, a debate sharpened as government in that country took a sharply divergent path towards human rights from South Africa's. By 1997, however, GALZ had emerged as a predominantly black, professionally run association and became a leader in promoting sexual minority rights in the region. Before the end of the decade, GALZ had supported activists in Botswana and Namibia in forming their own associations. The launch of Behind the Mask in 2000 then presaged a flowering of new activist groups across the continent. By the end of the first decade of the millennium, the majority of African countries had some form of sexual rights association, usually based in the capital or other large cities.

It would be an exaggeration to call it a movement in the sense of coordinated initiatives, but leaders from the different associations do meet to share experiences and to strategize for winning sexual minority rights at the level of national constitutions and the African Commission for Peoples' and Human Rights. A 2010 conference in Cape Town on the 'Struggle for equality' was a noteworthy event in that respect, bringing together over a hundred activists, scholars, journalists and government officials from around the continent. It did not result in a unifying manifesto, but a consensus emerged that lgbti rights had to be pursued in a wide range of fora both in and outside the courts and in alliance with other civil society groups (and sympathetic branches of government – Palitza 2011). Another virtual network cohered to produce a moving volume that highlights the diversity of people and forms of activism across the continent (Ekine and Abbas 2013).

In addition to the widening geographic circle of sexual minority rights activism, there is a growing number of venues and instruments available for the task, from local courts and bureaucracies to national parliaments and constitutional courts. As discussed above and in Chapter 1, activists may now also circumvent their own recalcitrant or obstructive lawmakers by taking their appeals to the international system, including the African Commission on Human and Peoples' Rights and the (so far untried) African Court of Justice. The SMUG case in the USA (see below), and South Africa at the United Nations, take the issue to an even bigger stage, albeit with a considerable risk of provoking nationalist reaction.

The rights path has unquestionably seen the most impressive successes in South Africa. Since the principle of non-discrimination on the basis of sexual orientation was enshrined in its constitution in 1996, activists have pressed the state to bring the country's laws and national HIV/AIDS prevention and education policies in line with (and in some case surpassing) global best practices. Activists in a small number of other African countries are beginning to move in this direction as well – a gay man in Botswana (Caine Youngman, supported by the Botswana Network for Ethics in Law) sought to sue his government to force the overturn of the sodomy law on constitutional grounds, while discrimination on the basis of sexual orientation has been declared illegal in the workplace (but not elsewhere) in both Botswana and Mozambique. The African Commission has meanwhile been disappointing for its failure to provide leadership on the sexual orientation question. Yet even in their frustration, rights activists have remarked on its potential. For example, Wendy Isaack, legal adviser to the National Coalition for Gay and Lesbian Equality with a special interest in the rights of African migrants and asylum seekers in South Africa, angrily denounced the Commission's refusal in 2010 to grant observer status to the Coalition of African Lesbians. But she also noted that:

What makes the Commission's decision especially ironic and devastating is that for the last five years, it has been one of the most meaningful political spaces for extra-national engagement on the protection of human rights of sexual minorities in

Africa. For most African lesbian and gay people, organised civil groups and human rights defenders working on different issues ranging from women's rights, sexual and reproductive rights and HIV and AIDS issues, the sessions of the African Commission provided the space for building solidarity and collective organising around human rights issues of concern to Africans. (Isaack 2010)

The kind of frustration Isaack alludes to here is also evident when trying to take state officials and police to task in South Africa. Rights on paper are frequently not enforced in practice. Moreover, very few of the rights-oriented associations in South Africa, let alone in less developed countries in Africa, have the wherewithal to take their grievances to court, to monitor abuses, or to lobby government for reform. When only a single friendly lawyer is willing to speak out and defend the lgbti community against gross human rights abuses (as was long the case in Cameroon), it is understandable that the rights arguments are often expressed in a reactive, ad hoc manner, if at all. Compromising on key principles has consequently emerged as an important interim strategy. Zimbabwean lawyer Derek Matyschak's advice to lgbti people on how to protect themselves against extortion or blackmail is an example (Matyschak 2011). That advice steps away from the principled position of equal rights and freedoms for all citizens, at least until the police can be relied upon to understand and defend that position. He advises lgbti not to have sex with someone not known well, and to avoid attire or places that might attract the attention of extortionists. However, this is not to promote the closet. On the contrary, Matyschak also advises blackmail targets to compel their blackmailers to be explicit with their accusations and, if possible, document them. This in effect outs the accusers and their otherwise mostly invisible crime. By so doing, lgbti not only scare some blackmailers off but they also contribute to the wider campaign of raising awareness of the issue, and of the community's existence, among the police and the public.

The 'gay international' has been instrumental in developing such responses, in helping African associations to network and professionalize, and in funding research to support rights claims. Global solidarity associations such as Human Rights Watch, ILGA and the International Lesbian and Gay Human Rights Commission (IGLHRC) have also played a significant role, lobbying donor governments to be alert to the issues. In the case of the US-based Political Research Associates, they have helped to reveal the activities of the 'homophobia international' (Kaoma 2012). The hope is that knowledge of those activities will make it easier for African statesmen and -women to distance themselves from the more extreme US evangelicals. After all, what self-respecting African leader would want to be seen as a dupe or pawn of American fanatics, climate change deniers and Holocaust revisionists?

The international support for sexual minority rights will undoubtedly continue for the foreseeable future, albeit with a major shift from the early days of solidarity. That is, over the past few years, leadership of the 'gay international' has become no longer strictly Western. Particularly with the 2009 victory of the Naz Foundation in challenging India's sodomy laws, effective leadership is increasingly coming from the global South. The fact that South Africa's co-sponsor for the UN resolution on sexual orientation was Brazil rather than Norway or the USA is symbolically extremely important. Another noteworthy development is that African activists are no longer passive recipients of the fruits of rights victories in the West. They are taking the fight directly to the West. A suit filed by SMUG in a federal court in Massachusetts will be a case to watch. SMUG is using American federal law to hold Scott Lively and four Ugandan 'co-conspirators' (including Martin Ssempa and David Bahati) accountable for the homophobic violence they have allegedly fuelled. Should SMUG win it will have done an important service for Americans concerned about the role of Lively and his ilk in fomenting homophobia in the USA.

How these debates unfold in different African countries is highly unpredictable and dependent upon countless factors rooted in history, local cultures and the relative strengths or weaknesses of civil society and political leadership. Who would have thought Uganda and Malawi would have taken such divergent paths as now appears to be happening? Rights, in other words, will emerge from local struggles in an organic way that reflects the art of the possible in differing circumstances. They won't be imposed let alone enforced from outside, whatever opponents may say about 'human rights imperialism'. It may nonetheless be helpful to consider how international law could inform future campaigns for rights in Africa as a reference point. How could the general principles laid out in broad, global statements be interpreted and applied in specific local debates some time in the future, keeping a particular eye open to identifying commonalities with other rights-seeking groups?

We can look to three main documents as a short cut to understanding the vision arising out of six decades of international law. The first is the 2006 Yogakarta Principles (O'Flaherty and Fisher 2008), which is not a formal treaty but a set of guidelines developed by leading legal scholars on how to apply the Universal Declaration of Human Rights and other international treaties and covenants so that these would explicitly include sexual minorities and gender identity. One of the authors was South African Constitutional Court justice Edwin Cameron. The second document (UN 2011b) has an African as its lead author, UN Special Rapporteur Margaret Sekaggya, a Ugandan lawyer specifically concerned with the rights of people who advocate for human rights. And the third document is *HIV and the Law: Risks, Rights and Health* (Global Commission on HIV and the Law 2012), drawn up by a group with a large global South majority, including a prominent African contingent (Festus Mogae, Sylvia Tamale, Miram K. Were, Shereen El Feki and Bience Gawanas). Based upon close studies of legal and policy precedents from around the world, these documents allow us to become quite specific about what an extensive definition of sexual rights *might* include, subject, of course, to the normal give and take and compromises, and notwithstanding the provisions that democratic governance allows. In no particular order (and in any case, they are all mutually supportive), we can imagine:

- The right not to have sex at all. Principally this would apply to children and to wives or girlfriends who want a break from sex with their husband/boyfriend and do not want to be raped in the name of conjugal duty or a date. It would respect lgbti who wish to remain celibate, and protect them from coerced heterosexual marriages. The state would need to take actions to obviate survival sex for anyone, however they identify. It also implies an obligation by the state to protect men and boys from unwanted homosexual sex, including by rape or out of hunger in prisons, or as an act of terror/war.
- The right to privacy. Aside from the obvious freedom from surveillance and intrusive questions, this would include the right to remain anonymous or in the closet if desired (meaning freedom from unwanted outing by police, healthcare providers, blackmailers, jilted lovers, lgbti activists, and so on). It would respect people's desire not to be publicly identified as male or female (allowing, for example, a category of other, trans, *sangoma* or something else appropriately vague on passports and other administrative documents).
- The right to protection. Everyone needs protection from persecution and harassment by the state, of course, but this right also obliges the state to protect people from those who commit or incite violence or promote stigma and abuse specifically on the basis of sexuality and gender identity. There is, for example, a debate about whether so-called corrective rape should be distinguished as a hate crime with harsher penalties than 'normal' rape, but the right to protection would at a minimum require that police and other state officials are proactively equipped to deal with the distinctive needs of lgbti victims of sexual violence.
- The right to health, obliging the state to protect all citizens against public health threats that derive from sexuality and gender-based violence, and to promote conditions that favour good health, mental as well as physical. In addition to all the obvious, globally recognized public health imperatives, in the African case this should probably also prioritize

protection of people from quacks who profit by peddling fraudulent 'cures' that exploit people's fears, ignorance or self-doubt (reconversion therapy, as a notable example), and protection of healthcare providers or religious leaders from pressure to break confidentiality of their lgbti confidants.

- Further to the above, the right to health would recognize the specific health risks entailed by incarceration, minimally requiring the provision of condoms in prisons but ideally addressing the conditions of living within prisons that heighten health risks. It would recognize as well the legitimate specific needs of transgendered people who desire counselling to effect sex-change surgery. No one would argue that the latter should be a priority for public health budgets, but neither should it be dismissed as a decadent Western thing. In no country in the world today are more of these operations conducted than in the Islamic Republic of Iran. The Iran experience suggests that meeting a larger unmet need than generally assumed may generate its own human rights abuses and further health problems that will need to be assessed on the basis of evidence.
- The right to freedom of peaceable assembly, association and protest. This would apply, for example, to parades, social clubs, counselling services, lobbying initiatives, public demonstrations, faith and other solidarity groups in alliance with transnational networks. It would allow lgbti groups to freely participate in other associational or institutional life – for example, as observers at the African Commission on Human and Peoples' Rights or as commentators on constitution-making processes.
- The right to freedom of opinion and expression. This would apply to newsletters, educational material, social media, art and any other public statement. States at present often justify denial of this right by asserting their need to protect the majority population from 'obscenity'. The state, however, should not be able to arbitrarily define depictions or discussions of homosexual acts and relationships as obscene when those same acts/relationships between heterosexuals are not. Similarly,

freedom of expression should extend to choice of attire. Laws that prohibit transvestism will need to be scrapped.

- The right to receive the best available (scientifically valid) information about sexuality. This means the state is obliged to ensure honest and age-appropriate education for children so that they will know and be prepared to take up their rights upon reaching adulthood. Such education should empower people with accurate knowledge to protect their health, and to enable them to discern (and reject) false claims about human sexuality. Many of the latter have been discussed already (occult beliefs, for example), but one could also mention the commonplace assertion made by opponents of sexual rights that sexuality education, the HPV vaccine or condoms will increase promiscuity and health risks. It would be incumbent on such education to proactively raise awareness of and combat stigma.
- The right to develop and discuss new human rights ideas, taking account of new scientific discoveries, new technology and new rights as articulated elsewhere in the world.
- The right to solicit and access funding for advocacy for human rights, including from foreign sources, as explicitly affirmed in the commentary on Article 13 of the Declaration on Human Rights Defenders (UN 2011b: 96). Restrictions on foreign funding are a major tactic used by governments to obstruct or undermine the work of NGOs and civil society groups such as lgbti activists. This right would provide critical support in much of Africa for most of the above-mentioned rights, and indeed, one could argue that it promotes those rights in the West as well (the SMUG case in the USA would be a case in point).
- The right to equality before the law. This means that a same-sex act should be treated in law and policy in the exact same way as the same act would be if performed between heterosexuals, beginning with the presumption of innocence for the accused. If consenting oral and anal sex are illegal between two men, then those acts must be made equally illegal between a man and a woman (more sensibly, those acts would be decriminalized for everyone); the state must treat a criminal act such as

rape or extortion against lgbti at least the same as it would treat similar acts against heterosexuals – I say at least since provision might be made for the added virulence of hate in crimes against lgbti. If heterosexual individuals can access sexual and reproductive health services, then the same provision must be made for non-heterosexuals. If heterosexual women can wear trousers, then why can transwomen not wear dresses? Marriage, inheritance, child custody, spousal benefits ... the list of current discriminatory laws, customs, practices and policies is a long one that will need to be rectified so that lgbti individuals, couples, parents, employees (etc.) are not discriminated against.

- The right to freedom of movement and asylum. By this, reasonable fear of persecution on the basis of sexual orientation becomes legitimate grounds for seeking and attaining refugee status, together with fear of genital mutilation, rape and other acts of sexual violence tacitly or explicitly condoned by the state.

- The right to participate in cultural and family life. On the latter, I would include the ability to freely choose if, when and with whom to get pregnant, equitable access to reproductive healthcare, the ability to safely terminate a pregnancy (abortion), and the right to refuse coerced abortion or sterilization (as is reportedly a commonplace occurrence for HIV-positive expectant mothers). This is simply to say that 'reproductive rights' are not, as often assumed, only a majority heterosexual concern. Many lgbti people desire to have families, including by natural means.

- The right to 'redress and accountability', meaning that victims of homophobic acts, fraud or policy failures in any of the areas discussed above would be able to sue the victimizers or state actors who betray or neglect their obligations. It would enable lgbti, other civil society groups and whistler-blowers within government to hold governments accountable to the documents they have signed (including international human rights conventions) and laws they have passed or constitutions they have enshrined (yet cynically ignore).

No doubt the list could go on, and it unquestionably will as African activists strengthen their networks and solidary links, and build the confidence and means to press cases. Of course, there are huge obstacles, including the political appointment of court jurists and the vague or heteronormative language used in so many constitutions and indeed in the African Charter on Human and Peoples' Rights itself ('normal family', 'community values', for example). Moreover, an approach emphasizing human rights and full disclosure in confrontation with the state or powerful religious groups is expensive, financially and emotionally. The risks can easily outweigh what may amount to mostly symbolic victories – even where willing, African states typically lack the capacity or bureaucratic heft to put human rights principles into practice on many issues, not just in the case of lgbti. In the next section, therefore, I want to look at an alternative approach that has been gaining ground quickly as a way to further the rights agenda without naming it as such.

Public health

A public health approach to promoting sexual rights and, hence, enabling or abetting the development of politically self-confident gay identities is not new in global terms, having been deployed with varying degrees of effectiveness in contexts as diverse as 1980s San Francisco, 1990s Thailand and Brazil, and 2000s India and China. Can it work today in Africa? And does it necessarily fuel 'gay identity migration' from the West, as Matthew Roberts once optimistically predicted in time for 'Stonewall 50' (i.e. 2019)? In this section, I examine specific initiatives that are using somewhat covert means to challenge prevalent homophobic or silencing cultures, and so preparing the ground for future human rights victories.

The basic argument is that homophobic laws and social stigma drive people to hide sexual feelings and choices that do not conform to heterosexual norms. Moralizing at people and threatening them with death does not, in fact, work very well to stop people from expressing their sexuality as feels right according to their own sense of gender identity and sexual orientation. Rather, they conduct same-sex relations furtively to avoid the stigma, often hiding behind concurrent heterosexual relationships, which obviously expands the circle of people at risk of sexually transmitted infections. Owing to the lack of frank and honest education about the full range of human sexuality, the status quo also exposes people to death by ignorance. The classic case is men who responsibly wear condoms when they have vaginal sex with women but do not wear condoms when they have anal sex with men since they have never been informed of the (significantly higher) risks. Removing homophobic laws and working to reduce stigmatizing public attitudes thus acts as a form of harm reduction. It removes the incentives for secrecy and concurrent 'masking' relationships, while providing knowledge necessary for people to make responsible decisions. Putting the emphasis on public health, harm reduction and science reduces the potential of social backlash and political demagoguery around morals.

The successes of this approach in bringing down HIV prevalence have been clear and compelling enough to make it strongly recommended by such global actors as the World Health Organization, UNAIDS and the World Bank. The International Gay and Lesbian Human Rights Commission (IGLHRC) made an important early intervention with its report on the failures of virtually all African countries – even South Africa – to help African msm protect themselves against HIV (Johnson 2007). Even more significant was the first-ever workshop on the topic of msm and HIV/AIDS in Africa primarily sponsored by the US-based Population Council. Held in Nairobi in May 2008, that meeting brought together dozens of activists and public health officials from ten African nations. Its report urged African governments for pragmatic reasons to recognize the existence of msm and to promote their right to health, with all that that implies for prevention, treatment, care and the need for 'an overall high quality of life'. But the report also endorsed avoiding the term msm in protocols and ethics applications, emphasized the need to 'manage' the media so as to avoid negative publicity as programmes unfold, and advocated designing studies to include injecting drug users and the disabled, notwithstanding that the principal subjects of the studies (msm) will likely object to being so included (NACC 2009).

It may be exaggerating to describe this as a 'covert' strategy – 'discreet' or 'two-stage' are probably more appropriate (that is, use implicit, euphemistic or vague language and acronyms to win over sceptical allies, and to allow politicians and public officials to dodge difficult decisions or to plausibly deny knowledge if confronted by homophobic criticism). Explicit discussions about rights will follow when circumstances are favourable, and as required to maximize the impact of the health interventions.

A preference for discreet language is of course not new, and it is apparent to some extent even among activist groups in South Africa, where rights are not seriously in dispute. Indeed, there has been something of a shift to more neutral and inclusive naming practices in South Africa than had often been the case in the 1980s and 1990s. The intention in such a shift was quite deliberate – to discursively embed the struggle for rights for sexual minorities within wider struggles for civil rights, above all, women's emancipation from patriarchal laws and customs. Hence the Triangle Project, the Forum for the Empowerment of Women and the Joint Working Group, among others. There has also been an emergence of safer social spaces for lgbti who do not necessarily want to participate in overt political activism, notably through lesbian soccer clubs and gay-friendly faith groups such as the Hope and Unity Metropolitan Community Church.

Outside of southern Africa, reluctance to name the main intended direct beneficiaries of sexual minority rights has been a strong feature of the movement as it has developed since the late 1990s. For those without insider knowledge, it is hard to tell what issues and audiences are being addressed by Alliance Rights Nigeria, Freedom and Roam Uganda, Matrix (Lesotho), the Egyptian Initiative for Personal Rights, Andiligueey (Senegal, meaning 'men working together to help other men' in Wolof), Friends of RAINKA (Zambia), the Horizon Community Association (Rwanda), Ishtar MSM or Minority Women in Action (Kenya).

Even beyond such ambiguous names, it often requires a close look at their websites to discern what the associations' priorities are. The Centre for the Development of People in Malawi, for example, introduces itself as working for the health of the country's 'most neglected minority groups', of which msm appear down the list from prisoners and (implicitly female) sex workers. Yet farther along on the website its programmes, including men's sexual health, peer education, voluntary counselling and testing, advocacy and research, indicate an overwhelming focus on msm.

The strategic embrace of health discourses is one 'cloaking' mechanism to slip sexual minority rights on to the local agenda. Nigeria's INCRESE (the International Centre for Reproductive Health and Sexual Rights), for example, lists diversity among its four core values, with msm as just one of its target populations among presumably more numerous widows and youth, and presumably female commercial sex workers and survivors of sexual violence. Yet it has emerged as one of the key actors facilitating research and lobbying against proposed homophobic laws and practices in Nigeria. The Uganda Health and Science Press Association (UHSPA) is another recent creation whose name does little to alert the opposition to sexual rights. In an important public intervention in 2010, the UHSPA was upfront that it is in fact a registered lgbtiq organization. Nor did it shy away from attacking the proposed Anti-Homosexuality Bill and calling for the compete decriminalization of same-sex sexuality between consenting adults. The bulk of its memorandum, however, focused on HIV. Aligning itself with a wide range of civil society groups, UHSPA methodically presented a harm reduction argument against the government's proposed punitive approach to HIV infection. It stressed the public health argument behind the 2009 ruling by the Delhi High Court that struck down the Indian law against 'carnal knowledge ... against the order of nature' (the exact same law imported by the British to Uganda), i.e. the law did not merely affront the privacy and dignity of same-sex-practising people but 'contributes to pushing the infliction [sic] underground, make risky sexual practices go unnoticed and unaddressed'. The UHSPA concluded with an appeal to the heterosexual majority's spirit of 'self-preservation' by emphasizing the extent of hidden bisexuality (its language) in Ugandan society.

A significant amount of sexual minority rights activism has also simply melded into mainstream HIV/AIDS lobby groups. The Treatment Action Campaign is the most famous and strikingly successful of these. TAC was founded in 1998 by Zackie Achmat and several other of the driving activists behind the sexual orientation clause in South Africa's constitution. The immediate motivation to form TAC, according to Achmat, had been the death of pioneering black gay activist Simon Nkoli (Power 2003). Nkoli had not been able to access the anti-retroviral drugs that were saving the lives of better-insured citizens, including Achmat himself. TAC today makes virtually no reference to these origins and only minimally to homophobia as a stigma that impacts HIV/AIDS. Other mainstream HIV/AIDS NGOs have meanwhile similarly begun to incorporate msm in their vocabulary, learning in the process to be discreet. As one such worker reported from Mali, an initial lack of discretion had sparked protests against a planned workshop on HIV/AIDS and homosexuality. 'They made such a fuss about this, accusing the organizers of trying to lure teenagers into homosexuality; as a result we had to cancel the workshop. Today we try to run our activities more discreetly, *we are flying under the radar* [my emphasis]. Recently we were invited to join Afrigay, a network of lgbti organizations that fight against HIV and AIDS, but we had to decline this opportunity for fear of protests by people.'

None of this is to suggest disingenuousness. On the contrary, health clearly played a significant role in motivating same-sex-practising people into political activism. As PEMA (Persons Marginalized and Aggrieved, a Mombasa-based lgbti association) puts it, the group owes its existence to the lonely death of a member of the community who was ostracized by his family. In the soul-searching that followed, friends in mourning determined to do something to address the issues that contributed to the tragedy. But if health starts as a pragmatic focus, it also provides a lens that leads to a wider political consciousness and engagement. By its own account, PEMA quickly transformed from a male-only association to one that includes lesbians and transgender women. Many of the other groups noted above similarly first coalesced around the health threat, then broadened their focus as the research revealed the complexity of issues. A pattern has emerged in that regard. The initial threat is anecdotally evident in high death rates in tight-knit communities. It is then documented along with the unsafe practices that led to the high mortality among msm. The research method – msm respondent-driven sampling – itself helps to conscientize or empower the subjects (knowledge, self-confidence, sense of professionalism). Once in place these groups quite quickly began to invoke the right to privacy, to freedom of association, to freedom of speech, and to equality of access to healthcare and health information as necessary parts of the pragmatics of addressing disease, not just among msm but the population as a whole (see Niang et al. 2003 as a pioneering example of such work; and Nguyen 2010 for a healthcare professional's reflections on the process from West Africa).

The network mentioned above (Afrigay) had its origins in France and currently connects associations in eight francophone countries in North and West Africa. An even broader network is the African Men for Sexual Health and Rights (AMSHeR), a Johannesburg-based NGO established in 2009 with a mandate 'to address the vulnerability of gay and bisexual men, male-to-female transgender women and other MSM, to HIV'. Here too we can see the delicate balancing of language and claims. According to its website, AMSHeR was the brainchild of both HIV and human rights advocates, and indeed, its first executive director was a former employee of IGLHRC who holds a graduate degree in international human rights law (Joel Gustave Nana). AMSHeR clearly indicates that it uses 'a rights-based approach which recognizes the need to protect our members – who often work in repressive environments'. Yet one can sense a gentle pulling of punches. The main stated goal is to fulfil the right *to health* for men who have sex with men. The rights to freedom of speech or association or privacy remain implicit. The list of its institutional objectives also suggests an element of caution. The cultivation of self-esteem, self-consciousness, political self-confidence, community and identity are all more or less claimed in the profiles of the individual board members. The ordering of institutional objectives, however, suggests a hierarchy that places directly addressing human rights violations dead last:

1 Strengthen capacity of national agencies and individuals working to improve policy, legislation and programming related to MSM sexual & reproductive health.
2 Increase the visibility of MSM issues across various levels such as policy, legislation, communities and service delivery.
3 Identify, advocate and increase access for greater resources, including technical and financial, for better access to prevention, treatment and care services.
4 Facilitate the creation and dissemination of an evidence base for a better public health response on MSM issues.
5 Advocate for the protection of gay men and other men who have sex with men from human rights violations.

This is not a criticism of AMSHeR, which is in fact quite bold in its reference to gay men and lgbt. Indeed, even msm, invented precisely to get around those identity politics by categorizing people according to activity rather than sexual orientation, remains inflammatory in some contexts. AMSHeR found itself the focus of hostile attention in that regard at the 2011 International Conference on AIDS and STIs in Africa in Addis Ababa. A coalition of Christian churches threatened to close down its proposed workshop on msm with a massive public protest. The crisis was averted only through the direct intervention of the Ethiopian minister of health.

The NACC report on msm also noted that the term msm has been met with 'obstructionism' by health officials in Zambia and Kenya. For that reason, it advocates deploying a new acronym as a preferred way to ease the concept past suspicious eyes –

MARP, or Most At-Risk Population. MARPs refer primarily to msm, intravenous drug users and female sex workers, but also include presumably heterosexual long-distance truck drivers, street children, fishing and beach communities, widows, lesbians who may be subject to so-called curative rape, and any other groups whose life circumstances structurally undermine their ability to make or to negotiate safer sex choices. The NACC report explicitly advises groups seeking local ethical approval to use the term MARPs 'in lieu of "MSM"' in their applications.

Other language the NACC employs in its strategy recommendations to get rights for sexual minorities on to the national agenda is also instructive. Rather than demand, challenge, speak up, mobilize and protest, it suggests consult, share, advocate, manage, include, encourage, non-confrontational, peer approach, engage, integrate, share and sensitize. Also interesting are the recurrent terms 'circumvent' and 'avoid'. The latter is explicitly urged in the case of stigmatizing language, including such phrases as 'hard to reach' or 'high-risk group'. But it is also implicitly suggested in the recommendation for activists and mid-level bureaucrats to direct their lobbying efforts away from potentially prickly national governments and political appointees: 'Advocate at the donor level of MSM in National Strategic Plans (NSPs), as most NSPs are externally funded.' Similarly, NSP language should be couched in generic terms so as to circumvent national laws that criminalize same-sex practices – for example, using phrases such as 'people-centred' in Zambia's NSP. Since msm are people, as are sex workers, drug users, lesbians and other disapproved-of populations, this allows programming to be developed for them without the dreaded requirement of naming of them. NACC further suggests avoiding any appeals to human rights documents in favour of 'epidemic modelling as a tool of persuasion'.

Does this strategy work? Sometimes, clearly not. Senegal's Andiligueey was one of the first active msm health support groups in West Africa, with terrifying numbers to support its arguments (up to 29 per cent seroprevalence among msm versus 1 per cent of adults in the general population). It did not survive the negative publicity it garnered. An msm drop-in centre in Malindi, for another example, was closed down by public protest shortly after opening, while healthcare professionals have been implicated in the ongoing abuse of msm in Mombasa. The public health approach also remains deeply controversial within the lgbti movement. How will women who have sex with women be included in an approach that necessarily emphasizes the high-risk nature of many current msm practices? How can a stigmatized population avoid further stigmatization if publicity focuses on the health dangers they pose to the general population? How are the goals of self-esteem and political confidence nurtured among young lgbti when the main associations representing them prioritize disease and practise deception? Might short-term success (such as access to medicine) lead to long-term failure (depoliticization of the issue)? Do the risks of a mostly male-centred, health-focused, externally funded strategy outweigh the benefits of more radical approaches, such as the trans activism of groups like South Africa's Gender DynamiX, or feminist-identified associations like the Coalition of African Lesbians?

On the face of it, again, perhaps not. In 2010 CAL became the first lgbti association to apply for observer status with the African Commission on Human and Peoples' Rights, which was flatly denied. By contrast, several groups that work with 'at-risk' populations were granted observer status. Alternatives-Cameroon is a noteworthy case in point as it is primarily focused on seeking justice for msm (Ndashe 2011). Its major distinction from CAL appears not to be in the nature of its work or comprehension of the issues but the fact that it lacks an 'offensive' word in its name.

The differential response of the Cameroonian state to rival sexual minority associations in that country is also revealing. Alternatives-Cameroon was founded and led by a medical doctor (Steave Nemande), who was motivated by the growing numbers of unhealthy msm he was encountering in his private practice. The association from the beginning benefited from foreign funding, primarily from the US-based Foundation for AIDS Research or amfAR, without incurring the wrath of the state. Indeed, despite its deserved reputation for homophobic persecution of gay men in particular, the Cameroonian state itself has accepted foreign money with an explicit commitment to fund msm projects. Yet when Alice Nkom, the head of the rival rights-oriented association ADEFHO, was successful in her application for funding from the European Union, she was immediately threatened with arrest and a fatwa by pro-government youth groups.

Hints of evidence elsewhere similarly suggest that the health track can work even in countries where the political rhetoric has been most discouraging. Several African countries have officially sanctioned such an approach in their National Strategic Plan, including the country that kickstarted the political homophobia in the mid-1990s (Zimbabwe). While the political leadership is unlikely to trumpet this move in public, and funding may not be forthcoming as required, it is nonetheless a vindication of the argument that public health pragmatism can potentially trump even the noisiest homophobic rhetoric. We might infer as much from many of the leaked US embassy cables gathering information on the issue in 2009/10. One in particular suggests that Rwanda's dramatic change in policy at the United Nations and in facilitating the creation of sexual minority support groups domestically owes much to the role of 'Minister of Health Sezibera, one of the more influential figures in government'. The turnaround in Kenya since the late 1990s may be another such case. Kenya's then president, Daniel arap Moi, was following in Robert Mugabe's footsteps with demagogic attacks on gays and lesbians. There were ongoing attacks on lgbti associations, even those predominantly focused on health issues. Today the situation has changed dramatically. The World Bank study goes so far as to say that 'support from the Kenyan government, or at least lack of forceful opposition to the development of effective health care and advocacy organization for MSM in the country, can serve as a model for its neighboring countries and the continent as a whole' (Beyrer et al. 2011: 89).

We do not yet have any close studies of institutional decision-making processes and policy formulation on the 'health versus rights' approaches to sexual minorities, nor comprehensive fieldwork to assess the views of health and rights advocates. In their absence, it is impossible to say for certain whether an emphasis on public health is more effective in promoting attitudinal and policy changes than one that focuses more directly on the achievement of sexual minority rights. But ultimately it may be a moot question. The two in practice complement each other – indeed, necessitate each other. As the NACC report puts it: 'When you walk over hot coals, you need both of your shoes' (NACC 2009: 7). Significantly, as an empirical demonstration of this, the public health approach that the World Bank praised in Kenya coincided closely with the emergence of a public profile of gay-identified people and their allies who are seeking equal rights. GayKenya, PEMA, GALCK and other secular associations, Other Sheep East Africa (Christian outreach), the Kenyan Human Rights Commission report (calling for decriminalization of sodomy among other reforms) and an openly gay man running for a seat in Senate (David Kuria, unsuccessfully) all indicate that change can happen relatively quickly when the mix of approaches is attuned to the local circumstances.

Struggles and strategies

6 | Conclusion

Stigma, discrimination and violence against sexual minorities in Africa impose much bigger costs upon the whole of society than has previously been realized or acknowledged. Homophobia, and to a lesser extent heterosexism or blindness and apathy to the issues, is thus not an 'elitist' concern but affects the lives of people from all walks of life: poor, married, Muslim women in Bamako, out black lesbians in Kampala, men in prison in Nigeria, boy victims of rape in Addis Ababa, transwomen and lesbians, traditional healers, development planners, diplomats, families, friends, lovers ... it is indeed about the whole landscape of human relations. The costs can be measured by economists in dollars and Disability Adjusted Life Years, and by epidemiologists in lives lost. The costs are also movingly attested in the currency of emotional anguish and social conflict as revealed by African artists, scholars and by ever more vocal lgbti communities themselves.

The second point I hope to have established in this book is that there are significant differences in the ways in which discrimination, anxiety or hatred is expressed towards non-normative sexualities. In other words, homophobias (plural) are complicated. Moreover, they are historical, and a great diversity of factors has contributed over a long period of time to the abusive speech, discrimination and violence against sexual minorities in Africa witnessed in recent years. These include fractures and fictions within traditional patriarchal cultures, colonial legacies, economic stress, popular anger at the West, the rise of new fundamentalist, nostalgic, evangelical, literalist and/or retribution-oriented expressions of faith, and calculated political opportunism. Cast of millions! Sisters, fathers, ancestors, healers, truck drivers, bureaucrats, missionaries (both Christian and Muslim), hairdressers, kings, bishops, mothers, gods, anthropologists ... many people and institutions have added their voices to the growing culture of intolerance towards sexual difference. Ironically, in light of my point above about anger at the West, the export of homophobic ideologies from the West under the guise of pseudo-science, healing and Christian compassion is one of the most alarming external influences upon the debates both historically and in recent years.

Given this complexity, responses to homophobias will need to be sensitive to the different factors and nuanced enough to consider the specific issues at play in each country, city or culture. My third argument is that Africans do not need to look exclusively or even primarily to the West for ideas on how to do this. They have their own resources to tap into to develop effective responses. Admittedly, we hear a lot about harmful traditional practices, dogmatic and hateful interpretations of scripture and shari'a, and hand-me-down 'humour' about Adam and Steve. However, there is another side to African discourses about gender and sexuality. Traditional religions or *Ubuntu* provide a strong ethic of community, family and respect. An element of sex positivity and of respect for individuals' relationships with Allah remain part of the dominant practice of Sufi Islam in Africa. And while it is more difficult to find sex positivity in Christian practice in Africa, the legacy of anti-colonialism and anti-racism on the part of African Christian leaders offers a promise of resistance to dogmatic ideologies being imported into Africa by foreign evangelists. As I believe should be evident from the many African names among the authors I have drawn upon to make my arguments, there is cause to celebrate in the fact that Africans are increasingly taking the lead in thinking about African culture as a source, and not just an obstacle, for the development of humane and pragmatic ways that can mitigate the harms of intolerance of sexual diversity and gender variance.

My fourth major point is directed principally to those who fail to recognize the ambivalent record of the West in this struggle. Individual rights, whether sexual or any other, are widely perceived in much of Africa as a Western concept that has been forced upon

Africa against its historically non-individualistic values. This is not paranoia. Going back to the days of the slave trade and colonialism, Europeans' rights to private property were taken to justify horrific crimes against African people. Soaring rhetoric about the 'rights of man' meanwhile provided bare cover for the squalid theft of Africans' land, the forcible break-up of African families, and the sneering ridicule of African history and cultures. The inalienable right to self-determination proclaimed in the aftermath of the First World War apparently applied to Europeans only, while speeches about freedom and liberty during the Cold War did little to hide Western support for racialist regimes in southern Africa and brutal dictatorships elsewhere. More recent demonstrations of Western evasiveness or hypocrisy regarding regime-change wars and intellectual property (notably, multinational corporate profits from life-saving medicines), plus cynicism towards African leaders who cosy up to the West or who sign human rights documents for international audiences while pillaging the national treasury and torturing their local critics, add to the sorry history.

Activists in the West who mock African leaders and homophobic prejudice in generalized terms do a disservice to their cause when they forget this history. Hence, while solidarity and support from the West have often been very helpful to Africans and are often gratefully acknowledged as such, blunt, uncritical or chauvinistic appeals to human rights – only recently accepted in Western countries (and still not consistently applied!) – are unlikely to have the desired outcomes. Activists in the West should consider devoting part of their energies and critical self-reflection to the current practices and structures that shore up Western power and exacerbate socio-economic inequalities in Africa (as indeed in the West as well), providing fertile ground for homophobic ideologies to grow. A fifth point, however, is that legitimate anger at Western bossiness and hypocrisies need not allow us to be blinded by those who cry 'human rights imperialism' or 'gay international'. A fair accounting of the 'gay international' will certainly find clumsiness, some arrogance and perhaps some cultural racism applied to African activists and scholars. It will also, however, reveal a more prevalent ethic of solidarity and some very impressive, concrete achievements. The ideals of human rights and protections are meanwhile not in fact narrowly Western but are increasingly articulated as universal aspirations by intellectuals and activists from the global South. One of the key proponents of mainstreaming human rights into development practice was the Indian economist Amartya Sen, a strong critic of the West through the Cold War years. The African Charter on Human and Peoples' Rights is also crystal clear on the desirability and the universality of human rights, including the attainment of gender equality. Thousands of Africans in civil society groups across the continent meanwhile stake their reputations, if not their members' lives, upon those goals in their struggles over land, environmental protection, governance, media and much more. African jurists and statesmen/women have been important contributors to the key documents defining sexual minority rights at the global level.

Support for sexual minority rights is thus not a marker of Westernization. How, though, to get that message out when so many politicians and moral entrepreneurs actively conspire against it? I have argued that moving to a language of justice rather than rights offers a way ahead. Justice sends a clear signal about who can participate – anyone with the heart to do so. Justice is also something that can be found and fought for on many different fronts and as our diverse individual skills and circumstances allow: in the courts, in the schools, in clinics, out in the streets, in the media, and through the dogged pursuit of research. Research, after all, is really just a fancy way to say 'provide accurate witness'. It is to seek to understand the gaps between what is happening and what people *believe is* or *should be* happening. On the topic of sexuality in general those gaps between what is and what should be (according to the cultural ideal) can be enormous. Same-sex sexuality is especially difficult to know about given how laden it is with moral judgements, denial and euphemism. Countless secrets intrude, including secrets people keep from themselves by playing with words or finessing silences. From that difficulty, and from the invisibility of same-sex relationships in most of Africa,

179

arise all kinds of dangerous practices, misplaced aid money and misconceived policies.

To do research with ethics front and centre – that is, to bear accurate witness – thus has the potential to contribute to ending dangerous practices, to directing aid to where it can be effective, and to reformulating policies so that no citizens are left out of the attainment of Africans' democratic aspirations. It is to empower with accurate information those activists who place their primary focus on the struggle for legal rights and protections. The fact that the claim 'homosexuality is un-African' can be demonstrated to be untrue (not just asserted) is an example of how research can undermine one of the pillars of homophobic rhetoric. Evidence can also empower those who prefer to take a less overtly combative route to the same ends through the development of programmes that more effectively target dangers to public health.

My final point is that among the many mutually enriching forms of activism that people are currently undertaking, and with important successes on the transnational or global scale, there are also triumphs happening at the local or even more intimate scale. Indeed, social justice can be conceived in our beds or wherever else we manage to express erotic desire and to forge intimate relationships based on mutual respect for human dignity. Is this going to help the boy or girl who sells sex in Dakar or Mombasa in order to feed his or her family or pay for school? Will it help the man who hides his affairs with men behind a façade of marriage to a woman? Will it protect lesbians and transwomen at heightened risk of rape? Not right away. But if we think of erotic justice as a framework to begin with, and that necessarily, intrinsically, the erotic connects to gender justice, and social and economic justice more conventionally understood, then it is to strike a blow (yes, I am being optimistic) against the injustices that allow or compel exploitative, transactional sex and rape, and the compulsory performance of heterosexuality. It is to strike a blow that can make sexual rights and sexual health a possibility for everyone. Royalties from this book, modest as they are, go to support initiatives that support the attainment of that dream.

Notes

Chapter 1: Introduction

Journalistic accounts of the persecution of lgbti in Africa abound, as do, albeit less commonly, stories that acknowledge triumphs in the struggle for human rights for sexual minorities. These are most easily accessed through various website digests devoted to the topics. *Behind the Mask* was the first of these sites (www.mask.org.za), with the added benefit of providing quick links to local activist sites such as *GayKenya* (one of the stronger ones, in my view). I have used it extensively over the years, although those references are now unaccessible as the site was closed down in 2012. *African Activist* (www.africanactivist.org), the *Coalition of African Lesbians* (www.cal.org.za/), *Iranti.org: queer vernaculars visual narratives* (www.iranti-org.co.za/), *African Men for Sexual Heath and Rights* (amsher.net), *Afrigay: contre le sida* (www.africagay.org/), the *International Gay and Lesbian Human Rights Commission* (www.iglhrc.org) and the *International Lesbian and Gay Association* (www.ilga.com) fill the gap. ILGA produces an annual report on the state of sexual minority rights globally (Bruce-Jones and Itaborahy 2011), which the US Department of State now also tracks (USA 2010). The historic UN resolution introduced by South Africa and Brazil resulted in UN 2011a, while the Gay and Lesbian Memory in Action archives ('Without queer history there is no queer pride') can be found at www.gala.co.za/.

The Bahati Bill as originally framed is readily available online (look for The Anti Homosexuality Bill 2009 – for example, nationalpress.typepad.com/files/bill-no-18-anti-homosexuality-bill-2009.pdf) (accessed 31 October 2011). The original motion was withdrawn. However, at the time of writing Bahati has reintroduced it with the provision for the death penalty obscured. See

Wright and Zouhali-Worrall (2012) for a sympathetic perspective on opponents of the bill.

The debate over whether homosexuality is un-African and whether homosexuals deserve human rights is dramatically captured by a remarkable BBC talk show on the topic featuring none other than David Bahati and the former president of Botswana (Festus Mogae, in support of sexual minority rights), among others, staged before a live audience in Johannesburg on 12 and 13 March 2011 (www.africanactivist.org/2011/02/bbc-debate-on-is-homosexuality-un.html). Scholarly analysis of these events and debates also abound, and indeed their number is growing rapidly. I refer to many of these through the course of the book. For now, let me just note the belated 'discovery' of msm by the influential medical journal *The Lancet* (Smith et al. 2009), Niang et al. (2003) and Kajubi et al. (2008) as examples of African-led scientific investigations, plus a brilliant dissection of the Semenya kerfuffle by Dworkin, Swarr and Cooky (forthcoming). Ekine and Abbas (2013) arrived too late for me to incorporate its passion and insights but will surely become a key text. The point about Western missionary activity is made by Kaoma (2009, 2012). Tsvangirai's 'coming out' in favour of gay rights (on the BBC while visiting London) was widely reported – for example, 'MPs tackle Tsvangirai over gays' (www.newzimbabwe.com/news-6362-Tsvangirai%20tackled%20by%20MPs%20over%20gays/news.aspx, accessed 26 October 2011).

The case for 'mainstreaming' sexuality into development practice and studies is most persuasively made in the vast scholarship on the sociology and history of HIV/AIDS, including, for example, Becker et al. (1999), Jolly (2000), Kalipeni et al. (2004), Abdool Karim and Abdool Karim (2005) and Adams and Pigg (2005). See also the eloquent statement by Burundian anti-AIDS activist Jeanne Gapiya (2012). Significant overlap exists between this literature and the scholarship on African feminisms. Among the most important of many powerful contributions are McFadden (1992), Arnfred (2004) and Gaza (2007). Much of this material is unaware of or uninterested in the possibility of female–female sexuality, but see Potgeiter (2005), Salo and Gqola (2006), Morgan and Wieringa (2005) and Tamale (2011) for pioneering exceptions to that tendency. Morgan, Marais and Wellbeloved (2009) and Swarr (2009 and 2012) push the analysis yet farther into theorization of trans experiences. The anti-nudity bill in Nigeria is the focus of Bakare-Yusuf (2011).

The Scott Lively interview in which he makes these and other startling claims can be accessed through Van Zeller (2010). The points about the role of Europeans in constructing the 'un-African' stereotype are the main thesis of my *Heterosexual Africa?* (Epprecht 2008), but see also Epprecht (2007) for a translation and exegesis of that strangely compelling novel by De Sade, a large section of which is set in an imagined Africa.

The concept of 'erotic justice' was, to my knowledge, first coined by Ellison (1996), and then elaborated from a feminist, global South perspective by Kapur (2005). I also appreciate the arguments of one of the pioneers of the field of sexuality studies in the West, Weeks (2010), and a global overview of the potential and pitfalls of a rights-based approach to gender equity in Mukhopadhyay and Meer (2008). Teunis and Herdt (2007) elaborate the links between sexual (and gender) inequalities and other social inequalities, with case studies mostly from ethnic minority communities in the USA that demonstrate the seamlessness of erotic and social justice movements. Jakobsen and Pellegrini (2004) provide an overview of the tensions between justice and tolerance.

The debate about 'pink imperialism' can perhaps be traced back to Achmat's (1993) robust critique of Western scholars' interpretation of male–male erotic relationships in the prisons and industrial compounds of South Africa. See also Massad (2007) and Hoad (2007), plus press releases from a network of African activists warning against donor coercion (African LGBTQ Human Rights Defenders 2007 and AMSHeR 2011). The debates became quite heated following allegations of homonationalism and Islamophobia made against UK activist Peter Tatchell in Kuntsman and Miyake (2008). Without necessarily taking sides, I would have to say that the end result seems strongly to corroborate the critique (that is, critics of whites' claims to global leadership are forced to apologize and driven out of print). A special issue of *Feminist Legal Studies* ably reviews the issues at stake (Douglas et al. 2011). The concept of 'pinkwashing' is best explained by its leading proponents, www.pinkwatchingisrael.com/.

The following discussion of terminology draws on the rich literature already mentioned above, but I would like further to acknowledge the generous interpretation of the meanings of Africa and African in Bennett (2011), and thoughtful reflection on racial identifiers in Mkhize et al. (2010). The word queer is dispensed with quite nicely by Morgan and Wieringa (2005) in their discussion of woman–woman relationships in southern and eastern Africa, but more vigorous challenges to it from one of the pioneers of global homosexualities research can be found in Murray (2009). On the use of lower case for lgbti, see Steyn and Van Zyl (2005), while Murray (2009) very helpfully explores the plurality of homophobias.

Animals cannot, of course, be compared with humans, and I am not suggesting that same-sex sex acts between animals are in any way equivalent to homosexual orientation. It is nonetheless an important point to make given how often homophobes compare humans unfavourably to animals on account of how the latter are supposedly more natural. Bagemihl (1999) was the breakthrough study on this issue, while the Wikipedia entry (at the time of writing) offers a balanced overview of the topic, with links to both the scientific articles on instances of same-sex behaviour, and to critics of those who would co-opt animals to a human political agenda (en.wikipedia.org/wiki/Homosexual_behavior_in_animals (accessed 14 October 2012). The translation of *inkhonkhoni* comes from Nkabinde (2008).

The international context is revealed in another large literature, including a thoughtful reflection by Australian activist Dan Altman on the tensions between his own understanding of coming out as a gay white man and what he observed in Asia (1997, elaborated in 2001). Matthew Roberts (1995) offers what is in retrospect a somewhat optimistic essay on the steady if not inexorable progression around the world of consciousness and sense of identity linked to gay men's HIV activism. See also Cruz-Malavé and Manalansan (2002), Aggleton et al. (2012) and Manalansan (2009), the latter for an astute critique of anti-homophobia as a marker of white privilege. Of particular interest on the global scene, because of both its chosen strategy and noteworthy successes, is the Naz Foundation (India) Trust, (www.nazindia. org/program.htm, accessed 28 December 2011). Gay white South Africans also mobilized around HIV issues in the 1980s, when they were believed to be the primary population at risk (Isaacs and McKendrick 1992).

The application of rights discourses and instruments in African contexts is the focus of a great deal of literature, including Gevisser and Cameron (1994), Stychin (1998), Hoad et al. (2005) on the history of the movement to attain the sexual orientation clause in the South African constitution, which Currier (2012) helpfully extends to current struggles there and in Namibia. Phillips (2010) applies this history to a learning context for future legal professionals. Ndashe (2010, 2011), Msibi (2012) and Mutua (2011) give pithy analyses of the prospects (and risks) of a litigation route to sexual minority rights, while Letsike (2011) provides a moving claim to human rights as an African lesbian. The African Charter on Human and Peoples' Rights can be accessed directly online at www.africa-union.org/official_documents/treaties_%20 conventions_%20protocols/banjul%20charter.pdf, while I discuss the Zimbabwean constitutional wrangling in Epprecht (2012c).

My points about the USA are implicit in Ellison (1996) among a truly vast body of critical studies that range right across the philosophical and political spectrum. See also Herzog (2008), which has the added interest of connecting the crisis in the USA to the Uganda shenanigans I discuss in Chapter 4.

The ACHPR Protocol on the Rights of Women can be found at www.achpr.org/english/_info/women_en.html. The limitations of this approach to gender equality are abundantly discussed, sometimes with a heavy dose of cynicism towards the African state.

See Jolly and Jeeves (2010) for a case study of the contradictions between rights on paper and patriarchy in practice in relation to HIV and gender violence in rural South Africa.

Chapter 2: Demystifying sexuality studies in Africa

My understanding of gender equality, women's empowerment and sexuality in development is grounded in works cited in the previous chapter, and supported by the demographic facts provided by the World Bank (2012), the CIA World Factbook and the CEDAW. Maticka-Tyndale, Tiemoko and Makinwa-Adebusoye (2007) provide an important, if uneven, intervention from the African Regional Sexuality Resource Centre in Lagos.

Claims about 'African sexuality' before the European conquest need to be taken with a large pinch of salt. However, let me mention three of the most influential African scholars: Diop (1960), Amadiume (1987) and Oyéwùmí (1997), who imagine non- or alternatively gendered pre-colonial pasts. Bleys (1995) gives a panoramic overview of the early ethnography in global perspective, while the relative invisibility of same-sex sexuality in the scholarship by European and American authors is the focus of Epprecht (2008). The African authors and artists who began to chip away at the un-African stereotype are analysed in Dunton (1989), Azuah (2005), Eke (2007), Migraine-George (2003), Ellerson (2005), Muholi (2011) and Munro (2012), among others.

The full Ruling of the Constitutional Court in the case of the National Coalition for Gay and Lesbian Equality, unopposed, 9 October 1998, can be found through the South African Legal Information Institute (www.saflii.org/za/cases/ZACC/1998/15.html, accessed 12 June 2012). The unnamed Rwandan ambassador is quoted in the UN press release about the discussion (www.un.org/News/Press/docs/2010/ga11041.doc.htm, accessed 20 April 2012). See also 'Positive change of attitude towards homosexuality in Rwanda', reported on www.mask.org.za/positive-change-of-attitude-towards-homosexuality-in-rwanda/, accessed 20 April 2012.

The question of where homosexuality comes from is the subject of yet another truly vast, often highly technical and contested scholarship. I am not going to bore people with that beyond recommending several encyclopaedic overviews that contain significant discussions of African evidence: Greenberg (1988), Murray (2000), Aldrich (2006) and Gerstner (2006). Similarly, the history of the 'invention' of the homosexual in European and North American discourse, with critical assessments of Freud, Gramsci, Foucault, Butler, Sedgwick et al., would require a thick book on its own. I would simply point people to a series of very tight essays discussing the historiographic traditions in diverse regions of the world introduced by Canaday (2009). Statistics on sexual practices, orientation, identity and more are closely followed by the Kinsey Institute for Research on Sex, Gender and Reproduction, upon which I have relied – www.kinseyinstitute.org/. Kurt Falk speaks for himself in Murray and Roscoe (1998), while the case of Marie Bonaparte is the topic of Frederiksen (2008).

Chapter 3: Faiths

You could open a good-sized library just with books and journals on the subject of religion in Africa. For a comprehensive overview of the big issues (*Ubuntu*, patriarchy, sorcery, fundamentalism, and so on) you can hardly go wrong between Murove (2009) and Bongmba (2012). See also Appiah (2006) for a thoughtful meditation on the meanings of African philosophy in the globalizing present. I would also draw specific attention to first-hand accounts from female *sangomas* married to women in Njinje and Alberton (2002) and Nkabinde (2008), as well as Khaxas and Wieringa (2005) on woman–woman marriages among the Damara of Namibia. An insightful documentary that features both a traditional healer and a deeply Christian, trans-identified man is Alberton and Reid (2000).

Ritual same-sex practices among the Yoruba that may have crossed the Atlantic during the slave trade are considered by Matory (2005), also of interest for his pointed critique of that strand of African scholarship that denies or minimizes pre-colonial gender oppression. Izugbara (2011) provides a wide-

Notes

ranging overview of occult beliefs around sexuality in Africa, while the bulk of the research specifically on same-sex relations and gender variance in pre-Christian, pre-Islamic Africa derives from my own earlier work, Epprecht (2006) in particular.

Christian homophobia is introduced here with a quotation taken from Didymus (2011), and other examples gleaned from the reportage of *Behind the Mask*. Critics of Christianity in general terms among African sexual rights activists include Leo Igwe, formerly president of the Humanist Institute (see John 2011), and Audrey Mbugua (2011), the latter movingly counterpoised by Kaggwa's (2011) profession of faith. On Christian theology and translation issues, but also offering numerous moving testimonials from gay Christians including priests and ministers, Germond and De Gruchy (1997) set a very high standard. The quotation from Tutu appears in his foreword to this volume. See also Alexander and Preston (1996), and Haddad (2011). Most churches now offer some form of gay-friendly interpretation of scripture or social and spiritual support, whether officially, as in the Lutheran and Episcopal churches, or through websites maintained by members of the congregation who wish to remain faithful in spite of their churches' hostility – Axios, for example, out of the USA, caters to Orthodox lgbti (www.axios.org/doku. php). The contentious debate within the Anglican Church is analysed in Ward (2002) and Hoad (2007).

The early history of Christian thought about sexuality includes, influentially, Boswell (1994), who has been criticized since for overstating the level of tolerance (or admiration!) that pre-modern theologians in Europe had for same-sex relationships. The pickings on this topic in Africa are exceedingly thin. I am relying significantly upon Greenberg (1988), and extrapolating from more general discussions of Coptic and Ethiopian history in Armanios (2011), Bryon (2009) and Zaborowski (2012). The latter is especially interesting for reproducing a text from over a thousand years ago which explicitly makes the point about Coptic sexual mores being more righteous than those of the Muslim invaders. Thornton (1998) narrates the story of Dona Beatriz.

On the role of Protestant missionaries, Swiss missionary Henri Junod deserves special mention for bringing the issue of 'mine marriages' to the fore of public discussion in southern Africa (Junod 1962 [1916]). The most substantive treatment of 'fictive' marriages among schoolgirls remains that of American anthropologist Judith Gay on the Basotho (Gay 1985).

Eshete (2009) is helpful for understanding the charismatic and evangelical movements, while Hackman (2013) examines the ex-gay ministry in Cape Town. As one might expect with any movement that prioritizes evangelism (spreading the word, proselytizing), there is an abundance of websites that explain the particulars of the faith. I will simply mention the extremely influential Rick Warren on account of his strong connection to Africa, and Rwanda in particular, through his church's HIV/AIDS iniative (www.rwandahealthcare.com/pages/). See also Defend the Family International, an arm of Abiding Truth Ministries (www.defendthefamily.com), whose president Scott Lively is at the cutting edge of the export to Africa of US-style homophobia.

Edward Said (2003 [1978]) remains the classic study of how stereotypes about Islam emerged in Western culture, which Massad picks up with specific reference to same-sex sexuality and some combative words about Western activists (2007). Chapters in the eclectic collection by Murray and Roscoe (1997) range widely through Islamic history, art and the Muslim world, including several chapters dealing with Egypt. For the theological side of things I have based my discussion on the Alan Jones translation of the Qur'an (2007). Duran (1993), Sulayman X (1999), Malik (n.d.), Hendricks (2008), Taleb (2007), Habib (2010) and Kugle (2010) discuss ways of reading Islamic texts that could be amenable to sexual minority rights, while Imam (2001), Ali (2006) and Badran (2011) are my main sources for understanding feminist analysis of the potential for women's rights and gender justice within Islam.

Shepperd (1988) and Jeay (1991) seem to be the first empirical studies primarily focused on how same-sex sexuality is conceived and practised by Muslims in Africa south of the Sahara (Kenya and Mali, respectively), followed soon afterwards by Neil Teunis's study from Senegal (1996). Moroccan psychologist Abdelhak Serhane (2000) may be too sweeping in his bolder assertions but they seem to fit with other claims made about the Maghreb as a sex tourism destination, and as a place where anti-colonial politics included a marked element of homonormativity (Hayes 2000). The finest ethnolinguistic study of gay-identified Muslims I have seen from anywhere is Rudoph Gaudio's (2009) on the *'yan daudu* in Kano, Nigeria, while Mohammed (2005) and Baraka (Baraka and Morgan 2005) offer personal accounts from lesbian-identified women in Tanzania and Kenya, respectively. Broqua's study of men who have sex with men in Bamako, Mali (2013), takes on poignancy in light of the Tuareg secessionist movement and the excesses of shari'a law in the north, 2012–13.

The reformist vision of Mahmud Muhammed Taha is discussed in An'Naim (1988), Duran (1993) and Thomas (2011), which, I acknowledge, may be guilty of overstating his progressive credentials (Taha is not cited by any of the feminist authors in Badran 2011, tellingly). Larsen (2008) and Arnfred (2011) assess the phenomena of spirit possession, women's sexual autonomies and *zina* in Swahili/Makhuwa Sufism.

Chapter 4: Sex and the state

The early history of sexuality in state formation in southern Africa is one of the main topics in Epprecht (2006), from which much of the following is adapted. Readers will find reference there to a broad range of studies, but I will highlight Musisi (1991) for her account of grand polygyny in Buganda, Achebe (2011), with judicious points for those who would impose lesbian desire on the African past, and Donham (1990) on the *ashtime* (but also containing some thoughtful reflections on research methods). The place of sexuality in the highly politicized historiography of Shaka and the formation of the Zulu kingdom is reviewed in Epprecht (2008). Let me draw attention to just one author, influential African nationalist intellectual Ali Mazrui (1975), who makes a direct link between Shaka's assumed homosexuality and his erratic leadership.

My discussion of the Mamelukes is heavily indebted to Murray and Roscoe (1997), while the masculinity of the Egyptian elites during its colonial adventure in Sudan is discussed in Jacob (2005). The Buganda controversy is reviewed in Hoad (2007), to which I would add the 'spun' version on the official website of the Kingdom of Buganda (www.buganda.com/martyrs.htm, accessed 24 April 2012).

Much of the scholarship mentioned so far is predominantly focused on the colonial period, including critiques of the role of anthropology and other earlier forms of academic writing about Africans. See Lyons and Lyons (2004), as well as Moodie with Ndatshe (1994) and Harries (1994) for their seminal studies on 'mine marriage'. The connection to India through governance structures and law is the topic of Human Rights Watch (2008). A close study of the system of indirect rule under the Belgians, including the allegations against Musinga, is to be found in Des Forges (2011). The 'renegade' whom Newell (2006) discusses was a self-described Uranist who lived in Onitsha in the 1910s–1930s – that is, he claimed to love young African men platonically. What makes him especially interesting is that he was outspokenly critical of British rule and was accorded a hero's funeral by the Igbo whom he defended.

The reference to Sierra Leone's law (and to the Anglican row in Sudan, below) comes from that fascinating window into the operations and thinking of the US State Department, the trove of leaked and wonderfully searchable documents posted on Wikileaks in 2010. Simply enter 'homosexuality' or whatever term you prefer to search, then specify the country, and *voila*! (www. cablegatesearch.net/search.php?q=homosexuality&qo=39936&qc =0&qto=2010-02-28).

To my knowledge, no history of gender and sexuality in Ethiopia exists, but I have extrapolated from the overview of Christianity there in Eshete (2009) and, to a lesser extent, Tadele's (2012) groundbreaking study of msm in Addis Ababa. The South African history is best accessed through Gevisser and Cameron (1994), Hoad et al. (2005), among many others. The aVersion project is the specific focus of Van Zyl et al. (1999). Zimbabwe has generated a relatively rich trove of memoirs and scholarship, including GALZ (1995, 2008), Phillips (1997) and Goddard (2004).

The role of the USA in creating the conditions for the rise of political homophobia is alluded to in Human Rights Watch (2005) and Thornton (2009), referencing the ideological nature of PEPFAR. So far, we owe much of our knowledge of the connections between the Christian right and Africa to the investigative journalism of Kapya Kaoma (2009, 2012) and Jeff Sharlet (2010). Rachel Maddow has also had a series of hard-hitting television interviews and documentaries beginning in December 2009 and still ongoing (Maddow 2009). Many of the key players in the controversy have appeared on the show to defend or deny their actions, including David Bahati, Jeff Sharlet, Bob Hunter, Richard Cohen and Republican senator James Inhofe. See also Clarkson (2006) and Sullivan-Blum (2009) for background on the battle for mainline churches in the USA. Of course, one can also go directly to the websites of the pastors themselves, including the Institute for Religion and Development (www.theird.org/) and the East African Centre for Law and Justice for a sample of the packaging of 'African values' by an American-funded institute (eaclj.org/features/religion.html, accessed 16 October 2012). Rigollo (2009) makes an important contribution to understanding the Christian right's fight against condoms, including the selective and manipulative use of science, while De Waal (2006) illustrates the political benefits of an HIV/AIDS crisis when skilfully managed by such leaders as Museveni.

Chapter 5: Struggles and strategies

This chapter derives in part from my article in *African Affairs* (Epprecht 2012a). In addition to the official documents cited in the text, I would point to important contributions by African scholars, including Gueboguo's case study of Alternative-Cameroun (2009), various lgbti activists' accounts of their experiences at the African Commission on Human and Peoples' Rights in a special issue of *Pambzuka News* (for example, Vilakazi and Ndashe 2010), the stirring manifesto on lgbti rights and erotic justice in Tamale (2011), and overviews of the issues by Ahlberg and Kulane (2011). Robert Lowray offers close, nuanced ethnographic studies of how these tensions and aspirations play out in contemporary Namibia (2006 and 2008, for example).

Much of the discussion of the public health approach is gleaned from the websites of key actors in the debates, including CEDEP: the Centre for the Development of People (www. cedepmalawi.org/, accessed 20 May 2011). To be fair, CEDEP also collaborated in an important 'outing' of lgbti in Malawi (Watson 2010), and it is acquiring a profile in the mainstream Malawian media as an advocate of gay rights. Other sources include 'Welcome to INCRESE', the International Centre for Reproductive Health and Sexual Rights (www.increse-increse. org/, accesssed 31 May 2011); 'Contact AMSHeR', African Men for Sexual Health and Rights (amsher.net/AboutAMSHeR/tabid/56/ Default.aspx, accessed 28 May 2011); 'Ugandan LGBTI Community Petition Parliament over the Right to Health and HIV/AIDS Control Bill 2010', Uganda Health and Science Press Association (uhspauganda.blogspot.com/2011/04/ugandan-lgbti-community-petition.html, accessed 22 May 2011); Persons Marginalized and Aggrieved (PEMA Kenya), Gay and Lesbian Coalition of Kenya (galck.org/index.php?option=com_content&view=article&id=76: persons-marginalized-and-aggrieved-pema-kenya&catid=3:galck-members&Itemid=3, accessed 25 May 2011); 'The Women's Inheritance Case Gives Hope to Gay Rights' (www.bonela.org/ index.php?option=com_k2&view=item&Itemid=223&id=103:17-october-2012; www.genderdynamix.co.za/ and www.cal.org.za/, accessed 12 January 2012).

My discussion of TAC is based primarily upon Power (2003), Friedman and Mottiar (2006), the TAC website (www.tac.org. za/about_us, accessed 17 October 2012), and personal communications. The Mali quote (italics added) comes from the now defunct *Behind the Mask* website, Jerina Chendze Messie, 'Homophobia Drives Malian MSM Underground' (www.mask.org. za/homophobia-drives-malian-msm-underground/#more-4313, accessed 22 May 2011). An account of the Addis Ababa controversy can be found in 'The Homophobic Disruption of AMSHeR's Pre-ICASA Meeting: What really happened' (www.mask.org.za/the-homphobic-disruption-of-amsher%E2%80%99s-pre-icasa-meeting-%E2%80%93-what-really-happened-2/, accessed 5 January 2012). The threats against Cameroon's ADEFHO and Alice Nkom continue, described in a joint press release with the Spanish group Fondación Triángulo (www.fundaciontriangulo.org/adefho/index-en.html, accessed 12 January 2012); see also Awondo (2010).

On Rwanda's change of tack, see the Wikileaks file – 'Ministry of Health Lobbies against Anti-Homosexuality Legislation', 09KIGALI860 (www.cablegatesearch.net/cable.php?id=09KIGALI860&q=homosexuality, accessed 12 January 2012). A Rwandan government spokesperson recently almost acknowledged as much by claiming that its Health Development Initiative since 2009 is behind a more 'positive attitude' towards sexual minorities – Dr Aflodis Kagaba, cited in www.mask.org.za/positive-change-of-attitude-towards-homosexuality-in-rwanda/, accessed 12 January 2012. One of the most articulate defenders of the African-ness of lgbti rights in the BBC debate noted earlier was Rwandan Paula Akugizibwe (BBC 2011).

Works cited

Abdool Karim, S. S. and Q. Abdool Karim (eds) (2005) *HIV/AIDS in South Africa*, Cambridge: Cambridge University Press.

Achebe, Nwando (2011) *The Female King of Colonial Nigeria: Ahebi Ugbabe*, Bloomington and Indianapolis: Indiana University Press.

Achmat, Zackie (1993) '"Apostles of civilised vice": "immoral practices" and "unnatural vice" in South African prisons and compounds, 1890–1920', *Social Dynamics*, 19(2): 92–111.

Adams, Vincanne and Stacy Leigh Pigg (eds) (2005) *Sex in Development: Science, Sexuality and Morality in Global Perspective*, Durham, NC: Duke University Press.

African LGBTQ Human Rights Defenders (2007) Public statement of warning, mrzine. monthlyreview.org/2007/increse310107.html, accessed 7 February 2012.

Afrigay (2012) *Afrigay: un combat africain*, www.africagay. org/wp-content/themes/ag/pdf/120705_AfGay_FR.pdf, accessed 18 October 2012.

Afrika, Tatamkhulu (1996) *Tightrope*, Cape Town: Majibuye Books.

Aggleton, Peter, Paul Boyce, Henrietta L. Moore and Richard Parker (eds) (2012) *Understanding Global Sexualities – new frontiers*, New York and London: Routledge.

Ahlberg, Beth Aina and Asli Kulane (2011) 'Sexual and reproductive health and rights', in S. Tamale (ed.), *African Sexualities: A Reader*, Dakar: Pambazuka Press, pp. 313–39.

Alberton, Paulo and Graeme Reid (dirs) (2000) *Dark and Lovely, Soft and Free*, Johannesburg: Gay and Lesbian Archives.

Aldrich, Robert (2006) *Gay Life and Cultures: A World History*, New York: Universe.

Alexander, Marilyn B. and James Preston (1996) *We were Baptized Too. Claiming God's Grace for Lesbians and Gays*, Louisville, KY: Westminster John Knox Press.

Ali, Kecia (2006) *Sexual Ethics and Islam: Feminist Reflections on Qur'an, Hadith and Jurisprudence*, Oxford: Oneworld.

Altman, Dennis (1997) 'Global gaze/global gays', *GLQ*, 3: 417–36.

— (2001) *Global Sex*, Chicago, IL: University of Chicago Press.

Amadiume, Ifi (1987) *Male*

Daughters, Female Husbands: Gender and Sex in an African Society, London: Zed Books.

AMSHeR (2011) Statement of African social justice activists on the threats of the British government to 'cut aid' to African countries that violate the rights of LGBTI people in Africa, www.amsher.net/news/ViewArticle.aspx?id=1200, 27 October, accessed 28 October 2011.

An'Naim, Abdullahi Ahmed (1988) 'Mahmud Muhammed Taha and the crisis of Islamic reform: implications for interreligious relations', Journal of Ecumenical Studies, 25(1): 1–21.

Antonio, Eduardo (1997) 'Homosexuality and African culture', in Paul Germond and Steve de Gruchy (eds), Aliens in the Household of God, Cape Town: David Philip, pp. 295–315.

Appiah, Anthony Kwame (2006) Cosmopolitanism: Ethics in a World of Strangers, New York: W. W. Norton.

Arac de Nyeko, Monica (2007) 'Jambula tree', in Ama Ata Aidoo (ed.), African Love Stories, Banbury: Ayebia Clarke Publishing.

Armah, Ayi Kwei (1979) Two Thousand Seasons, London: Heinemann.

Armanios, Febe (2011) Coptic Christianity in Ottoman Egypt, Oxford and New York: Oxford University Press.

Arnfred, S. (ed.) (2004) Re-thinking Sexualities in Africa, Uppsala: Nordiska Afrikainstitutet.

— (2011) Sexuality and Gender Politics in Mozambique: Rethinking Gender in Africa, London and Uppsala: James Currey and Nordiska Afrikainstitutet.

Awondo, Patrick (2010) 'The politicisation of sexuality and the rise of homosexual mobilisation in postcolonial Cameroon', Review of African Political Economy, 37(125): 315–28.

— (2011) 'Identifications homosexuelles, construction identitaire, et tensions postcoloniales entre le Cameroun et la France', espace et société, 13(1), espacepolitique.revues.org/index1818.html, accessed 14 October 2011.

Ayuba, J. M. (2011) 'Politics and sexuality in northern Nigeria in the second half of the twentieth century', in Toyin Falola and Bessie House Soremekun (eds), Gender, Sexuality and Mothering in Africa, Trenton, NJ, and Asmara: Africa World Press.

Azuah, Unoma N. (2005) 'The emerging lesbian voice in Nigerian feminist literature', in Flora Veit-Wild and Dirk Naguschewski (eds), Versions and Subversions in African Literatures I: Body, Sexuality and Gender, Amsterdam: Rodopi, pp. 129–41.

Badran, Margot (ed.) (2011) Gender and Islam in Africa: Rights, Sexuality, and Law, Washington, DC, and Stanford, CA: Woodrow Wilson Center Press and Stanford University Press.

Badri, Malik (1997) The AIDS

Crisis: An Islamic Socio-cultural Perspective, Kuala Lumpur: Institute of Islamic Thought and Civilization.

Bagemihl, Bruce (1999) *Biological Exuberance: Animal homosexuality and natural diversity*, New York: St Martin's Press.

Bagnol, Brigitte and Esmeralda Mariano (2011) 'Politics of naming sexual practices', in S. Tamale (ed.), *African Sexualities: A Reader*, Dakar: Pambazuka Press, pp. 271–87.

Bakare-Yusuf, Bibi (2011) 'Nudity and morality: legislating women's bodies and dress in Nigeria', in Sylvia Tamale (ed.), *African Sexualities: A Reader*, Dakar: Pambazuka Press, pp. 116–29.

Baraka, Nancy with Ruth Morgan (2005) '"I want to marry the woman of my choice without fear of being stoned": female marriages and bisexual women in Kenya', in Ruth Morgan and Saskia Wieringa (eds), *Tommy Boys, Lesbian Men and Ancestral Wives: Female Same-Sex Practices in Africa*, Johannesburg: Jacana, pp. 25–53.

BBC (2011) 'The world debate: is homosexuality un-African?', British Broadcasting Corporation World Service.

Becker, Charles, Jean-Pierre Dozon, Christine Obbo and Moriba Touré (eds) (1999) *Vivre et Penser le Sida en Afrique. Experiencing and Understanding AIDS in Africa*, Dakar/Paris: CODESRIA/IRD.

Bennett, Jane (2011) 'Subversion and resistance: activist initiatives', in Sylvia Tamale (ed.), *African Sexualities: A Reader*, Cape Town: Pambazuka Press, pp. 77–100.

Beyrer, Chris, Andrea Wirtz, Damian Walker, Benjamin Johns, Frangiscos Sifakis and Stephan D. Baral (2011) *The Global HIV Epidemics among Men Who Have Sex with Men*, Washington, DC: World Bank, siteresources.worldbank.org/ INTHIVAIDS/Resources /375798-1103037153392/MSMReport.pdf, accessed 2 February 2012.

Bleys, Rudi C. (1995) *The Geography of Perversion: Male–Male Sexual Behaviour outside the West and the Ethnographic Imagination*, New York: New York University Press.

Bongmba, Elias K. (ed.) (2012) *A Companion to African Religion*, Oxford: Blackwell.

Boswell, John (1994) *Same-Sex Unions in Premodern Europe*, New York: Villard Books.

Broqua, Christophe (2013) 'Male homosexuality in Bamako: a cross cultural and cross historical comparative perspective', in S. N. Nyeck and M. Epprecht (eds), *Sexual Diversity in Africa: Politics, Theory and Citizenship*, Montreal: McGill-Queen's University Press.

Bruce-Jones, Eddie and Lucas Paoli Itaborahy (2011) *State-sponsored Homophobia: A world survey of laws criminalising same-sex sexual acts*

Works cited

between consenting adults, New York: ILGA.

Bryk, Felix (1964 [1925]) *Voodoo-Eros: Ethnological Studies in the Sex-Life of the African Aborigines*, New York: United Book Guild.

Bryon, Gay L. (2009) 'Expanding the field. Ancient Ethiopia and the New Testament: ethnic (con)texts and racialized (sub)texts', in Randall C. Bailey, Tat-siong Benny Liew and Fernando F. Segovia (eds), *They were all together in one place?: toward minority biblical criticism*, Atlanta, GA: Society of Biblical Literature.

Camara, Mohammed (dir). (1997) *Dakan*, Conakry: ArtMattan.

Canaday, Margaret (2009) 'Thinking sex in the transnational turn: an introduction', Forum on Sexuality, *American Historical Review*, 116.

Chigweshe, Rudo (1996) 'Homosexuality: A Zimbabwean religious perspective', BA dissertation, University of Zimbabwe.

Clarkson, Frederick (2006) 'The battle for the mainline churches', *Public Eye Magazine*, 20(1), www.publiceye.org/magazine/v20n1/clarkson_battle.html, accessed 10 April 2012.

Colman, Robert (dir.) (1998) *After Nines!*, Unpublished play transcript and oral history research, Gay and Lesbian Memory in Action, AM 2894.

Cruz-Malavé, Arnaldo and

Martin F. Manalansan IV (eds) (2002) *Queer Globalizations: Citizenship and the Afterlife of Colonialism*, New York: New York University Press.

Currier, Ashley (2012) *Out in Africa: LGBT Organizing in Namibia and South Africa*, Minneapolis: University of Minnesota Press.

De Waal, Alex (2006) *AIDS and Power: Why There is No Political Crisis – Yet*, London: Zed Books.

Des Forges, Alison Liebhafsky (2011) *Defeat is the Only Bad News: Rwanda under Musinga, 1896–1931*, Madison: University of Wisconsin Press.

Dibia, Jude (2005) *Walking with Shadows*, Lagos: BlackSands Books.

Didymus, John Thomas (2011) 'Muslims, Christians and gays in Nigeria's ring of hatred', *Digital Journal*, 9 December, www.digitaljournal.com/article/315852, accessed 20 April 2012.

Diop, Cheikh Anta (1960) *L'Afrique Noire Précoloniale*, Paris: Présence Africaine.

Donham, Donald L. (1990) *History, Power, Ideology: Central Issues in Marxism and Anthropology*, Cambridge: Cambridge University Press.

Douglas, Stacey, Suhraiya Jivraj and Sarah Lamble (2011) 'Liabilities of queer anti-racist critique', *Feminist Legal Studies*, 19(2): 107–18.

Duiker, Sello (2001) *The Quiet Violence of Dreams*, Cape Town: Kwela Books.

Dunton, Chris (1989) '"Wheyting be Dat?" The treatment of homosexuality in African literature', *Research in African Literatures*, 20(3): 422–48.

Duran, Khalid (1993) 'Homosexuality and Islam', in Arlene Swindler (ed.), *Homosexuality and World Religions*, Valley Forge, PA: Trinity Press International.

Dworkin, Shari, Amanda Lock Swarr and Cheryl Cooky (2013) 'Sex and gender (in)justice in sport: the treatment of South African track star Caster Semenya', in S. N. Nyeck and M. Epprecht (eds), *Sexual Diversity in Africa: Politics, Theory and Citizenship*, Montreal: McGill-Queen's University Press.

Eboussi Boulaga, Fabien (ed.) (2007) 'Dossier: l'homosexualité est bonne à penser', Special issue of *Terroirs, Revue Africaine des Sciences Sociales et de Philosophie*, 1/2.

Eke, Maureen Ngozi (2007) '*Woubi Chéri*: negotiating subjectivity, gender, and power', in Ada Uzoamaka Azodo and Maureen Ngozi Eke (eds), *Gender and Sexuality in African Literature and Film*, Trenton, NJ, and Asmara: Africa World Press.

Ekine, Sokari and Hakima Abbas (eds) (2013) *Queer African Reader*, Dakar, Nairobi, Oxford: Pambazuka Press.

Ellerson, Beti (2005) 'Visualizing homosexualities in Africa-*Dakan*: an interview with filmmaker Mohamed Camara', in Lahoucine Ouzgane and Robert Morrell (eds), *African Masculinities: Men in Africa from the Late Nineteenth Century to the Present*, London: Palgrave, pp. 61–73.

Ellison, Marvin M. (1996) *Erotic Justice: A Liberating Ethic of Sexuality*, Louisville, KY: Westminster John Knox Press.

Epprecht, Marc (2006) *Hungochani: The History of a Dissident Sexuality in Southern Africa*, Montreal: McGill-Queen's University Press.

— (2007) 'The Marquis de Sade's Zimbabwe adventure: a contribution to the critique of African AIDS', *Sexualities*, 10(2): 241–58.

— (2008) *Heterosexual Africa?: The History of an Idea from the Age of Exploration to the Age of AIDS*, Athens and Scottsville: Ohio University Press and University of KwaZulu-Natal Press.

— (2012a) 'Advancing the right to sexual orientation and "erotic justice" in Africa through public health strategies', *African Affairs*, 111(443): 223–43.

— (2012b) 'Transnationalism in sexuality studies: an "Africanist" perspective', in Peter Aggleton et al., *Understanding Global Sexualities – new frontiers*, New York and London: Routledge, pp. 186–202.

— (2012c) *The Constitution Process and Sexual Minority Rights in Zimbabwe*, 21 June, Solidarity Peace Trust, www.

solidaritypeacetrust.org/1226/ the-constitution-process-and-sexual-minority-rights-in-zimbabwe, accessed 30 June 2012.

Eshete, Tibebe (2009) *The Evangelical Movement in Ethiopia: Resistance and resilience*, Waco, TX: Baylor University Press.

Evans-Pritchard, E. E. (1970) 'Sexual inversion among the Azande', *American Anthropologist*, 72: 1428–34.

Fanon, Frantz (1967 [1952]) *Black Skin, White Masks*, New York: Grove Press.

Frederiksen, Bodil Folke (2008) 'A 1930s controversy over African and European female sexuality: Jomo Kenyatta, Marie Bonaparte and Bronislaw Malinowski on clitoridectomy', *History Workshop Journal*, 65: 23–48.

Friedman, Steven and Shauna Mottiar (2006) 'Seeking the high ground: the Treatment Action Campaign and the politics of morality', in Richard Ballard, Adam Habib and Imraan Valodia (eds), *Voices of Protest: Social movements in post-apartheid South Africa*, Scottsville: University of Kwa-Zulu-Natal Press, pp. 23–44.

GALZ (1995) *Sahwira*, Harare: Gays and Lesbians of Zimbabwe.

— (2008) *Unspoken Facts: A History of Homosexualities in Africa*, Harare: Gays and Lesbians of Zimbabwe.

Gapiya, Jeanne (2012) 'Pourquoi s'investir auprès de gays quand on est une femme séropositive?', *Afrigay*, 36/37.

Gasa, Nomboniso (ed.) (2007) *Women in South African History*, Cape Town: HSRC Press.

Gaudio, Rudolph Pell (2009) *Allah Made Us: Sexual Outlaws in an Islamic African City*, Hoboken, NJ: Wiley-Blackwell.

Gay, Judith (1985) '"Mummies and babies" and friends and lovers in Lesotho', *Journal of Homosexuality*, 11(3/4): 93–116.

Germond, Paul and Steve de Gruchy (eds) (1997) *Aliens in the Household of God*, Cape Town: David Philip.

Gerstner, David A. (2006) *Routledge International Encyclopedia of Queer Culture*, London and New York: Routledge.

Gevisser, Mark and Edwin Cameron (eds) (1994) *Defiant Desire: Gay and Lesbian Lives in South Africa*, Johannesburg: Ravan.

Global Commission on HIV and the Law (2012) *HIV and the Law: Risks, Rights and Health*, New York: United Nations Development Programme.

Goddard, Keith (2004) 'A fair representation: the history of GALZ and the gay movement in Zimbabwe', *Journal of Gay and Lesbian Social Services*, 16(1): 75–98.

Greenberg, David F. (1988) *The Construction of Homosexuality*, Chicago, IL, and London: University of Chicago Press.

Gueboguo, Charles (2009) 'Penser les « droits » des homosexual/les en Afrique: due sens et de la pouissance de l'action associative militante au Cameroun', *Canadian Journal of African Studies/Revue Canadienne des Études Africaines*, 43(1): 129–50.

Habib, Shamir (ed.) (2010) *Islam and Homosexuality*, Santa Barbara, CA: Praeger.

Hackman, Melissa (2013) '"Ex-gay" subjectivities: tracking cultural convergences in post-apartheid South Africa', in S. N. Nyeck and M. Epprecht (eds), *Sexual Diversity in Africa: Politics, Theory and Citizenship*, Montreal: McGill-Queen's University Press.

Haddad, Beverly (ed.) (2011) *Religion and HIV and AIDS: Charting the Terrain*, Scottsville: University of KwaZulu-Natal Press.

Harries, Patrick (1994) *Work, Culture and Identity: Migrant Laborers in Mozambique and South Africa, c. 1860–1910*, Portsmouth, NH: Heinemann.

Hayes, Jarrod (2000) *Queer Nations: Marginal Sexualities in the Maghreb*, Chicago, IL: University of Chicago Press.

Hendricks M. (2008) 'A way forward through ijtihad: a Muslim perspective on same-sex marriage', in M. Judge, A. Manion and S. de Waal (eds), *To Have and to Hold: The making of same-sex marriage in South Africa*, Auckland Park: Fanele, pp. 219–27.

Herzog, Dagmar (2008) *Sex in Crisis: The new sexual revolu-tion and the future of American politics*, New York: Basic Books.

Hoad, Neville (2007) *African Intimacies: Race, Homosexuality and Globalization*, Minneapolis: University of Minnesota Press.

Hoad, Neville, Karen Martin and Graeme Reid (eds) (2005) *Sex and Politics in South Africa*, Cape Town: Double Story.

Huchu, Tendai (2010) *The Hairdresser of Harare*, Harare: Weaver Press.

Human Rights Watch (2005) *The Less They Know, the Better: Abstinence-Only HIV/AIDS Programs in Uganda*, hrw.org/reports/2005/uganda0305/1.htm#_Toc98378357, accessed 20 November 2006.

— (2008) *This Alien Legacy: The Origins of 'Sodomy' Laws in British Colonialism*, New York: Human Rights Watch.

Igwe, Leo (2006) 'On the proposed Bill to ban same sex marriages in Nigeria', *Sexuality in Africa*, 3(1): 13–15.

Iliffe, John (1997) *Africans: The History of a Continent*, Cambridge: Cambridge University Press.

Imam, Ayesha (2001) 'The Muslim religious right ("fundamentalists") and sexuality', in Patricia Beattie Jung, Mary E. Hunt and Radhika Balakrishnan (eds), *Good Sex: Feminist Perspectives from the World's Religions*, New Brunswick, NJ: Rutgers University Press, pp. 15–30.

Isaack, Wendy (2010) 'The fallacy

of human rights at the African Commission', *Pambazuka News*, 506: Special Issue: 'African Commission blocks LBGTI human rights', www.pambazuka.org/en/issue/506, accessed 25 September 2012.

Isaacs, Gordon and Brian McKendrick (1992) *Male Homosexuality in South Africa: Identity Formation, Culture and Crisis*, Cape Town: Oxford University Press.

Izugbara, Chimaraoke O. (2011) 'Sexuality and the supernatural in Africa', in Sylvia Tamale (ed.), *African Sexualities: A Reader*, Dakar: Pambazuka Press, pp. 533–58.

Jacob, Wilson Chacko (2005) 'The masculine subject of colonialism: the Egyptian loss of the Sudan', in Lahoucine Ouzgane and Robert Morrell (eds), *African Masculinities: Men in Africa from the Late Nineteenth Century to the Present*, London: Palgrave, pp. 153–69.

Jakobsen, Janet R. and Ann Pellegrini (2004) *Love the Sin: Sexual Regulation and the Limits of Religious Tolerance*, Boston, MA: Beacon Books.

Jeay, Anne-Marie (1991) 'Homosexualité et Sida au Mali, variations sur l'étrange et l'étranger', in Michael Pollack, Rommel Mendes-Leite and Jacques van dem Borghe (eds), *Homosexualités et Sida: Actes du Colloque International*, Lille: Cahiers Gai-Kitsch-Camp, pp. 60–8.

John, Andrew (2011) 'Campaigner: religion is behind homophobic persecution in Africa', www.digitaljournal.com/article/316138#ixzz1gnmJd3vk, accessed 15 December 2011.

Johnson, Cary Alan (2007) *Off the Map: How HIV/AIDS Programming is Failing Same-Sex Practicing People in Africa*, New York: International Gay and Lesbian Human Rights Commission.

Jolly, Rosemary and Alan Jeeves (2010) '"Yes, there are rights but sometimes they don't work": gender, equity, HIV and democracy in rural South Africa since 1994', *Canadian Journal of African Studies/ Revue Canadienne des Études Africaines*, 44(3): 524–51.

Jolly, Susie (2000) '"Queering" development: exploring the links between same-sex sexualities, gender and development', *Gender and Development*, 8(1): 78–88.

Jones, Alan (trans.) (2007) *The Qur'an*, Exeter: Gibb Memorial Trust.

Junod, Henri (1962 [1916]) 'Unnatural vice in the Johannesburg compounds', in *The Life of a South African Tribe*, vol. 1, New York: University Books.

Kaggwa, Julius (2011) 'Intersex: the forgotten community', in Sylvia Tamale (ed.), *African Sexualities: A Reader*, Cape Town: Pambazuka Press, pp. 231–4.

Kajubi, P. et al. (2008) 'Gay and

bisexual men in Kampala, Uganda', *AIDS and Behavior*, 12(3): 492–504.

Kalende, Val (2012) 'Gay Ugandans: loud and proud', *Huffington Post*, 15 August, www.huffingtonpost.com/val-kalende/gay-ugandans-loud-and-proud_b_1785222.html, accessed 27 September 2012.

Kalipeni, E., S. Craddock, J. R. Oppong and J. Ghosh (eds) (2004) *HIV/AIDS in Africa: Beyond Epidemiology*, Oxford: Blackwell.

Kaoma, Kapya (2009) *Globalizing the Culture Wars: U.S. Conservatives, African Churches, and Homophobia*, Somerville, MA: Political Research Associates.

— (2012) *Colonizing African Values: How the U.S. Christian Right is Transforming Sexual Politics in Africa*, Somerville, MA: Political Research Associates.

Kapur, Ratna (2005) *Erotic Justice: Law and the New Politics of Postcolonialism*, London: Glasshouse Press.

Kenya Human Rights Commission (2011) *The Outlawed amongst Us: A Study of the LGBTI Community's Search for Equality and Non-Discrimination in Kenya*, Nairobi: KHRC.

Kenyatta, Jomo (1961 [1938]) *Facing Mount Kenya*, London: Mercury Books.

Khaxas, Elizabeth and Saskia Wieringa (2005) '"I am a pet goat, I will not be slaughtered": female masculinity and femme strength amongst the Damara

in Namibia', in Ruth Morgan and Saskia Wieringa (eds), *Tommy Boys, Lesbian Men and Ancestral Wives: Female Same-Sex Practices in Africa*, Johannesburg: Jacana, pp. 123–98.

Kugle, Scott (2010) *Homosexuality in Islam: Critical Reflection on Gay, Lesbian and Transgender Muslims*, Oxford: Oneworld Publications.

Kuntsman, Adi and Esperanza Miyake (eds) (2008) *Out of Place: Interrogating Silences in Queerness/Raciality*, London: Raw Nerve Books.

Larsen, Kjertsi (2008) *Where Humans and Spirits Meet: The Politics of Rituals and Identified Spirits in Zanzibar*, New York and Oxford: Berghahn Books.

Le Pape, Marc and Claudine Vidal (1984) 'Libéralisme et vécus sexuels à Abidjan', *Cahiers Internationaux de Sociologie*, LXXVI: 111–18.

Letsike, Mmapaseka 'Steve' (2011) 'The "Steve" in me has a right', in Alleyn Diesel (ed.), *Reclaiming the L-Word: Sappho's Daughters Out in Africa*, Athlone, SA: Modjaji Books, pp. 145–60.

Lowray, Robert (2006) 'Dispelling "heterosexual African AIDS" in Namibia: same-sex sexuality in the township of Katatura', *Culture, Health and Sexuality*, 8(5): 435–49.

— (2008) '"Where can I be deported?" Thinking through the "foreigner fetish" in Namibia', *Medical Anthropology*, 27(1): 70–97.

Works cited

Lyons, Andrew P. and Harriet D. Lyons (2004) *Irregular Connections: A History of Anthropology and Sexuality*, Lincoln and London: University of Nebraska Press.

Mack, Beverly (2011) 'Muslim women's knowledge production in the Great Maghreb: the example of Nana Asma'u of northern Nigeria', in Margot Badran (ed.), *Gender and Islam in Africa: Rights, Sexuality, and Law*, Washington, DC, and Stanford, CA: Woodrow Wilson Center Press and Stanford University Press, pp. 17–40.

Maddow, Rachel (2009) 'Uganda be kidding me', www.msnbc. msn.com/id/26315908/ns/msnbc_tv-rachel_maddow_show/, accessed 2 February 2012.

Maddy, Yulisa Amadu (1973) *No Past, No Present, No Future*, London: Heinemann.

Malik, Faris (n.d.) *Queer Sexuality and Identity in the Qur'an and Hadith*, www.well.com/user/aquarius/Qurannotes.htm, accessed 25 June 2012.

Manalansan IV, Martin F. (2009) 'Homophobia at New York's Gay Central', in David A. B. Murray, *Homphobias*, Durham, NC: Duke University Press, pp. 34–47.

Massad, J. (2007) *Desiring Arabs*, Chicago, IL: University of Chicago Press.

Maticka-Tyndale, Eleanor, Richmond Tiemoko and Paulina Makinwa-Adebusoye (2007) *Human Sexuality in Africa: Beyond Reproduction*, Auckland Park, SA: Fanele.

Matory, J. Lorand (2005) *Black Atlantic Religion: Tradition, Transnationalism, and Matriarchy in the Afro-Brazilian Candomblé*, Princeton, NJ, and Oxford: Princeton University Press.

Matyschak, Derek (2011) 'Dealing with blackmail – notes from a Zimbabwean lawyer', in R. Thoreson and S. Cook (eds), *Nowhere to Turn: Blackmail and Extortion of LGBT People in Sub-Saharan Africa*, New York: IGLHRC, pp. 111–29.

Mazrui, Ali (1975) 'The resurrection of the warrior tradition in African political culture', *Journal of Modern African Studies*, 13(1): 67–84.

Mbugua, Audrey (2011) 'Gender dynamics: a transsexual overview', in Sylvia Tamale (ed.), *African Sexualities: A Reader*, Cape Town: Pambazuka Press, pp. 238–46.

McFadden, Patricia (1992) 'Sex, sexuality, and the problem of AIDS in Africa', in Ruth Meena (ed.), *Gender in Southern Africa*, Harare: SAPES, pp. 157–95.

Migraine-George, Thérèse (2003) 'Beyond the "internalist" vs. "externalist" debate: the local-global identities of African Homosexuals in two films, *Woubi Chéri* and *Dakan*', *Journal of African Cultural Studies*, 16(1): 45–56.

Mkhize, Nonhlanhla, Jane Bennett, Vasu Reddy and Relebohile Moletsane (2010)

The Country We Want to Live In: Hate Crimes and Homophobia in the Lives of Black Lesbian South Africans, Cape Town: HSRC Press.

Mohammed, Sophia Musa (2005) '"Immoral and satanic": loving secretly in Dar es Salaam', in Ruth Morgan and Saskia Wieringa (eds), *Tommy Boys, Lesbian Men and Ancestral Wives: Female Same-Sex Practices in Africa*, Johannesburg: Jacana, pp. 53–64.

Moodie, T. Dunbar with Vivienne Ndatshe (1994) *Going for Gold: Men's Lives on the Mines*, Berkeley: University of California Press.

Morgan, Ruth and Saskia Wieringa (eds) (2005) *Tommy Boys, Lesbian Men and Ancestral Wives: Female Same-Sex Practices in Africa*, Johannesburg: Jacana.

Morgan, Ruth, Charl Marais and Joy Rosemary Wellbeloved (eds) (2009) *Trans: Transgender Life Stories from South Africa*, Auckland Park, SA: Fanele.

Msibi, Thabo (2012) '"I'm used to it now": experiences of homophobia among queer youth in South African township schools', *Gender and Education*, 24(5): 515–34.

Muholi, Zanele (2011) *African Women Photographers #1*, Casa Africa and La Fábrica.

Mukhopadhyay, Maitrayee and Shamim Meer (2008) *Gender, Society and Development: A global sourcebook*, Amsterdam: Royal Tropical Institute.

Munro, Brenna M. (2012) *South Africa and the Dream of Love to Come: Queer Sexuality and the Struggle for Freedom*, Minneapolis and London: University of Minnesota Press.

Murove, Munyaradzi Felix (ed.) (2009) *African Ethics: An Anthology of Comparative and Applied Ethics*, Scottsville: UKZN Press.

Murray, David. A. B. (ed.) (2009) *Homophobias: lust and loathing across time and space*, Durham, NC: Duke University Press.

Murray, Stephen O. (2000) *Homosexualities*, Chicago, IL: University of Chicago Press.

— (2009) 'Southern African homosexualities and denials', *Canadian Journal of African Studies/Revue Canadienne des Études Africaines*, 43(1): 168–73.

Murray, Stephen O. and Will Roscoe (eds) (1997) *Islamic Homosexualities: Culture, History and Literature*, New York: New York University Press.

— (1998) *Boy-Wives and Female Husbands: Studies in African Homosexualities*, New York: St Martin's Press.

Musisi, Nyakanyiki (1991) 'Women, "elite polygyny", and Buganda state formation', *Signs*, 16(4): 757–86.

Mutongi, Kenda (2000) 'Dear Dolly's advice: representations of youth, courtship, and sexualities in Africa, 1960–1980', *International Journal of African Historical Studies*, 33(1): 1–23.

Mutua, Makau (2011) 'Sexual orientation and human rights:

putting homophobia on trial', in Sylvia Tamale (ed.), *African Sexualities: A Reader*, Cape Town: Pambazuka Press, pp. 452–63.

NACC (National AIDS Control Council of Kenya) and Population Council (2009) *The Overlooked Epidemic: Addressing HIV prevention and treatment among men who have sex with men in sub-Saharan Africa, report of a consultation, Nairobi, Kenya, 14–15 May 2008*, Nairobi: Population Council, www.popcouncil.org/pdfs/HIV_KenyaMSMMeetingReport.pdf, accessed 2 January 2012.

Ncgobo, 'Ponie' Nozipho (2011) 'Discovering my identity', in Alleyn Diesel (ed.), *Reclaiming the L-Word: Sappho's Daughters Out in Africa*, Athlone, SA: Modjaji Books, pp. 171–6.

Ndashe, Sibongile (2010) 'The battle for the recognition of LGBTI human rights', *Perspectives: Political Analysis and Commentary from Africa*, 4(10): 4–9.

— (2011) 'Seeking the protection of LGBTI rights at the African Commission for Human and Peoples' Rights', *Feminist Africa*, 15: 17–37.

Newell, Stephanie (2006) *The Forger's Tale: The Search for Odeziaku*, Athens: Ohio University Press.

Nguyen, Vinh-Kim (2005) 'Uses and pleasures: sexual modernity, HIV/AIDS and confessional technologies in a West African metropolis', in Vincanne Adams and Stacy Leigh Pigg (eds), *Sex in Development: Science, Sexuality and Morality in Global Perspective*, Durham, NC: Duke University Press.

— (2010) *The Republic of Therapy: Triage and Sovereignty in West Africa's Time of AIDS*, Durham, NC: Duke University Press.

Niang, Cheikh Ibrahim, Moustapha Diagne, Youssoupha Niang and Amadou Mody Moreau (2003) '"It's raining stones": stigma, violence, and HIV vulnerability among men who have sex with men in Dakar, Senegal', *Culture, Health, and Sexuality*, 5(6): 499–512.

Niehaus, Isak (2002) 'Renegotiating masculinity in the South African Lowveld: narratives of male–male sex in labour compounds and in prisons', *AIDS in Context*, Special Issue of African Studies, 61(1): 77–97.

Njinje, Mpumi and Paolo Alberton (dirs) (2002) *Everything Must Come to Light*, Johannesburg: Out of Africa Films.

Nkabinde, Nkunzi Zandile (2008) *Black Bull, Ancestors and Me: My life as a lesbian sangoma*, Auckland Park, SA: Fanele.

Nkoli, Simon (1994) 'Wardrobes: coming out as a black gay activist in South Africa', in Mark Gevisser and Edwin Cameron (eds), *Defiant Desire: Gay and Lesbian Lives in South Africa*, Johannesburg: Ravan, pp. 249–57.

Nyeck, S. N. (2013) 'Mobilizing

against the invisible: erotic nationalism, mass media and the "paranoid style" in Cameroon', in S. N. Nyeck and M. Epprecht, *Sexual Diversity in Africa: Politics, Theory and Citizenship*, Montreal: McGill-Queen's University Press.

Nyeck, S. N. and M. Epprecht (eds) (2013) *Sexual Diversity in Africa: Politics, Theory and Citizenship*, Montreal: McGill-Queen's University Press.

O'Flaherty, Michael and John Fisher (2008) 'Sexual orientation, gender identity and human rights law: contextualizing the Yogakarta Principles', *Human Rights Law Review*, 8(2): 207–48.

Ouologuem, Yambo (1971) *Bound to Violence*, London: Heinemann.

Oyéwùmí, Oyèrónké (1997) *The Invention of Women: Making an African Sense of Western Gender Discourses*, Minneapolis: University of Minnesota Press.

Palitza, Kristin (2011) *Conference Report: Struggle for equality: Sexual orientation, gender identity and human rights in Africa*, www.boell.de/democracy/ promotion/promotion-of-democracy-conference-report-struggle-equality-sexual-orientation-gender-identity-human-rights-africa-11680.html, accessed 29 October 2012.

Phillips, Oliver (1997) 'Zimbabwean law and the production of a white man's disease', in

L. Moran (ed.), *'Legal Perversions': Social and Legal Studies*, 6(4): 471–92.

— (2010) 'Teaching sexuality and law in southern Africa: locating historical narratives and adopting appropriate conceptual frameworks', in P. Kameri-Mbote, J. Stewart, S. Tamale and A. Tsanga (eds), *Breaking the Mould: Innovative Regional Approaches to Teaching, Researching and Analysing Women and Law*, Harare: Weaver Press.

Potgeiter, Cheryl (2005) 'Sexualities? hey, this is what Black, South African Lesbians have to say about relationships with men, the family, heterosexual women and culture', in M. Steyn and M. van Zyl, *Performing Queer: Shaping Sexualities, 1994–2004*, Cape Town: HSRC Press, pp. 177–92.

Power, Samantha (2003) 'Letter from South Africa, "The AIDS Rebel"', *New Yorker*, 19 May, pp. 54–67.

Pruzen, Julie E. (2011) 'Islam, gender and democracy in Morocco: the making of Mudawana Reform', in Margot Bardan (ed.), *Gender and Islam in Africa: Rights, Sexuality, and Law*, Washington, DC, and Stanford, CA: Woodrow Wilson Center Press and Stanford University Press, pp. 233–61.

Puar, Jasbir K. (2007) *Terrorist Assemblages: Homonationalism in queer times*, Durham, NC: Duke University Press.

Raw Nerves (2009) 'Peter Tatchell:

apology and correction', www.rawnervebooks.co.uk/ Peter_Tatchell.pdf, accessed 10 February 2012.

Reid, Graeme (2013) *How to be a Real Gay: Gay Identities in Small-Town South Africa*, Scottsville: UKZN Press.

Rigollo, Nicole (2009) 'Faith in God but not in condoms: churches and competing visions of HIV prevention in Namibia', *Canadian Journal of African Studies/Revue Canadienne des Études Africaines*, 43(1): 34–59.

Roberts, Matthew (1995) 'Emergence of gay identity and gay social movements in developing countries. The AIDS crisis as a catalyst', *Alternatives*, 20: 243–64.

Said, Edward (2003 [1978]) *Orientalism*, 25th anniversary edn, New York: Pantheon.

Salo, Elaine and Pumla Dineo Gqola (2006) 'Editorial: subaltern sexualities', *Feminist Africa 6: Subaltern Sexualities*, September, pp. 1–7.

Semugoma, Paul, Steave Nemande and Stefan D. Baral (2012) 'The irony of homophobia in Africa', *The Lancet*, 380(9839): 312–14.

Serhane, Abdelhak (2000 [1996]) *L'Amour circoncis*, Paris: Editions EDDIF.

Sharlet, Jeff (2010) 'Straight man's burden: the American Roots of Uganda's anti-gay persecution', *Harper's*, September, pp. 36–48.

Sheppherd, Gill (1988) 'Rank, gender and homosexuality: Mombasa as a key to understanding sexual options', in Pat Caplan (ed.), *The Cultural Construction of Sexuality*, London: Tavistock, pp. 240–70.

Shilts, Randy (1987) *And the Band Played On: Politics, People and the AIDS Epidemic*, New York: St Martin's Press.

Smith, Adrian, Placide Tapsoba, Norbert Peshu, Edward J. Sanders and Harold W. Jaffe (2009) 'Men who have sex with men and HIV/AIDS in sub-Saharan Africa', *The Lancet*, 20 July, doi: 10.1016/S0140-6736(09)61118-1.

Steyn, M. and M. van Zyl (2005) *Performing Queer: Shaping Sexualities, 1994–2004*, Cape Town: HSRC Press.

Stychin, Carl Franklin (1998) *A Nation by Rights: National Cultures, Sexual Identity Politics, and the Discourse of Rights*, Philadelphia, PA: Temple University Press.

Sulayman X (1999) *Confessions of Sulayman X*, www.well.com/ user/queerjhd/confessions. htm, accessed 10 June 2012.

Sullivan-Blum, Constance R. (2009) '"It's Adam and Eve, not Adam and Steve": what's at stake in the constitution of contemporary American Christian homophobia', in D. A. B. Murray, *Homophobias*, Durham, NC: Duke University Press, pp. 48–63.

Swarr, Amanda Lock (2009) 'Stabane, intersexuality, and same-sex relationships in Soweto', *Feminist Studies*, 35(3): 524–48.

— (2012) *Sex in Transition: Remaking Gender and Race in South Africa*, Buffalo, NY: SUNY Press.

Tadele, Getnet (2012) 'Sexuality and rights: men who have sex with men in Addis Ababa, Ethiopia', in Segun Ige and Tim Quinlan (eds), *African Responses to HIV/AIDS: Between Speech and Action*, Scottsville: UKZN Press, pp. 177–208.

Taleb, Hamid Abou (2007) 'Sexual education from an Islamic perspective', in Eleanor Maticka-Tyndale, Richmond Tiemoko and Paulina Makinwa-Adebusoye (eds), *Human Sexuality in Africa: Beyond Reproduction*, Auckland Park, SA: Fanele, pp. 29–51.

Tamale, Sylvia (2003) 'Out of the closet: unveiling sexuality discourses in Uganda', *Feminist Africa*, 2, October/November, pp. 42–9.

— (ed.) (2011) *African Sexualities: A Reader*, Dakar: Pambazuka Press.

Tessmann, G. (1998 [1921]) 'Homosexuality among the Negroes of Cameroon and a Pangwe tale', trans. B. Rose, in S. O. Murray and W. Roscoe (eds), *Boy Wives and Female Husbands*, New York: St Martin's Press, 149–61.

Teunis, Niels (1996) 'Homosexuality in Dakar: is the bed the heart of a sexual subculture?', *Journal of Gay, Lesbian, and Bisexual Identity*, 1(2): 153–69.

Teunis, Niels and Gilbert Herdt (eds) (2007) *Sexual Inequalities and Social Justice*, Berkeley: University of California Press.

Thomas, Edward (2011) *Islam's Perfect Stranger: The Life of Mahmud Muhammad Taha, Muslim Reformer of Sudan*, London: Tauris Academic Studies.

Thornton, John (1998) *The Kongolese Saint Anthony: Dopna Beatriz Kimpa Vita and the Antonian Movement, 1684–1706*, Cambridge: Cambridge University Press.

Thornton, Robert (2009) *Unimagined Communities: Sex, Networks, and AIDS in Uganda and South Africa*, Berkeley: University of California Press.

Tutu, Desmond (1996) 'Foreword', in Marilyn B. Alexander and James Preston, *We were Baptized Too. Claiming God's Grace for Lesbians and Gays*, Louisville, KY: Westminster John Knox Press.

— (1997) 'Foreword', in Paul Germond and Steve de Gruchy (eds), *Aliens in the Household of God*, Cape Town: David Philip.

UN (2011a) *Discriminatory laws and practices and acts of violence against individuals based on their sexual orientation and gender identity: Report of the United Nations High Commissioner for Human Rights*, New York: United Nations, November, www2.ohchr.org/english/bodies/hrcouncil/docs/19session/A.HRC.19.41_English.pdf, accessed 3 January 2012.

— (2011b) *Commentary to the Declaration of the Right and Responsibility of Individuals, Groups and Organs of Soceity to Promote and Protect Universally Recognized Human Rights and Fundamental Freedoms. UN Special Rapporteur on the Situation of Human Rights Defenders*, www.ohchr.org/Documents/Issues/Defenders/CommentarytoDeclaration-ondefendersJuly2011.pdf, accessed 18 October 2012.

USA (2010) 'United States Department of State Human Rights Reports for 2009', *Global Equality*, 11 March, www.global equality.org/storage/documents /pdf/2009%20hr%20report%20sogi%20refer-ences.pdf, accessed 20 May 2011.

Van Zeller, Mariana (2010) 'Scott Lively, father of Uganda's "Pro-Family" Movement', *Vanguard*, www.youtube.com/watch?v=o8HpzqZAQ_g.

Van Zyl, Mikki, Jeanelle de Gruchy, Sheila Lapinsky, Simon Lewin and Graham Reid (1999) *The Aversion Project: human rights abuses of gays and lesbians in the South African Defence Force by health workers during the apartheid era*, Cape Town: Simply Said and Done.

Vilakazi, Fikile and Sibongile Ndashe (2010) 'The day the African Commission disavowed humanity', *Pamba-zuka News*, 506, Special Issue: African Commission blocks LBGTI human rights, www.pambazuka.org/en/issue/506, accessed 25 September 2012.

Wade, A. S. et al. (2005) 'HIV infec-tion and sexually transmitted infections among men who have sex with men in Senegal', *AIDS*, 19(18): 2133–40.

Ward, Kevin (2002) 'Same-sex rela-tions in Africa and the debate on homosexuality in East African Anglicanism', *Anglican Theological Review*, LXXXIII(1): 81–112.

Watson, Patricia (2010) *Queer Malawi: Untold Stories*, Johan-nesburg: Gay and Lesbian Memory in Action and CEDEP.

Weeks, Jeffrey (2010) 'Making the human gesture: history, sexu-ality and social justice', *History Workshop Journal*, 70: 5–20.

Willemse, Karin and Ruth Mor-gan with John Meletse (2009) 'Deaf, gay, HIV positive and proud: narrating an alternative identity in post-apartheid South Africa', *Canadian Journal of African Studies/Revue Can-adienne des Études Africaines*, 43(1): 84–105.

World Bank (2012) *Gender Equality*, Washington, DC: IBRD.

Wright, Katherine Fairfax and Malika Zouhali-Worrall (dirs) (2012) *Call Me Kuchu*, New York: Lindyhop Pictures LLC.

Zaborowski, Jason R. (2012) 'Coptic Christianity', in Elias K. Bongmba (ed.), *A Companion to African Religion*, Oxford: Blackwell, pp. 220–33.

Index

President's Emergency Program for AIDS Relief (PEPFAR), 141–2
Primates Council, 78
primitivity of Africa, perceived, 42
prisoners, sexuality of, 50
prisons: homosexuality in, 161; provision of condoms in, 162
privacy, right to, 150, 153
prostitution: in Temple, 80; same-sex, 80
Protestant evangelical movements, 87–9; hostile to African customs, 88
public health approach, 149, 165–75
public health threats deriving from sexuality, 161
punishments: for homosexuality, 75 (death penalty, 2, 3, 84–5, 97); for sexual behaviour, 72, 73, 78, 80, 84, 88 (in Islam, 96–7); for *zina*, 102

Qaeda, al-, 140
queer, use of term, 23–4
Queer Jihad organization, 103
queer theory, 23, 45
Qur'an, 18, 96; literal interpretation of, 103; translations of, 99–100

'Rain Queen', 111
Rainbow Church of God, 79
raising of seed, 71
rape, 33, 38, 47, 59, 80, 123, 154, 164; as strategy of humiliation, 83; conjugal, 161; corrective, 52, 161, 172; in Islamic religious schools, 99, 105
Reid, Graeme, 9
religion, 66–108; fluidity of belief systems, 66; fundamentalism, 18; syncretic, 66; traditional,

63–4, 66, 68–77, 177; used to negate rights, 32
Renault, Mary, 151
reporting of homosexual activity, 2
research: barriers to, 44; on same-sex sexuality, 41–3; reliability of, 17
respectability, colonial ideology of, 124–5
rights: conjugal, 29; emerging from local struggles, 160; for sexual minorities *see* sexual minority rights; not to have sex, 161; of assembly and protest, 162; of men, to sex, 29; of motherhood, 38; rhetoric of, 178; sexual, 26–35, 94 (focused on heterosexual women, 32–3; inseparable from gender equality, 40; of children, 33); seen as un-African, 26; to access advocacy funding, 163; to accountability, 164; to choose forms of dress, 31; to develop new ideas, 163; to equality before the law, 163–4; to family life, 164; to freedom of expression, 162–3; to freedom of movement and asylum, 164; to health, 161–2; to information about sexuality, 163; to privacy, 1, 150, 161; to protection, 161; to remain anonymous, 161; viewed as Western concept, 177 *see also* gay rights *and* sexual minority rights
rights approach, 149, 150
ritual homosexuality, 83
ritual sex acts, 80
Robertson, Pat, 146
Robinson, Gene, 147

CPSIA information can be obtained
at www.ICGtesting.com
Printed in the USA
LVHW051126090321
680971LV00003B/270